The Criminology of Place

The Criminology of Place

STREET SEGMENTS AND OUR UNDERSTANDING OF THE CRIME PROBLEM

David Weisburd, Elizabeth R. Groff,
and Sue-Ming Yang

OXFORD

UNIVERSITY PRESS

OXFORD
UNIVERSITY PRESS

Oxford University Press is a department of the University of Oxford.
It furthers the University's objective of excellence in research,
scholarship, and education by publishing worldwide.

Oxford   New York

Auckland   Cape Town   Dar es Salaam   Hong Kong   Karachi
Kuala Lumpur   Madrid   Melbourne   Mexico City   Nairobi
New Delhi   Shanghai   Taipei   Toronto

With offices in

Argentina   Austria   Brazil   Chile   Czech Republic   France   Greece
Guatemala   Hungary   Italy   Japan   Poland   Portugal   Singapore
South Korea   Switzerland   Thailand   Turkey   Ukraine   Vietnam

Oxford is a registered trade mark of Oxford University Press
in the UK and certain other countries
Published in the United States of America by
Oxford University Press
198 Madison Avenue, New York, NY 10016

© Oxford University Press 2012

Library of Congress Cataloging-in-Publication Data
Weisburd, David.
The criminology of place : street segments and our understanding
of the crime problem / David Weisburd, Elizabeth R. Groff, and Sue-Ming Yang.
p.   cm.
Includes bibliographical references.
ISBN 978-0-19-992863-7 (alk. paper)
ISBN 978-0-19-536908-3 (alk. hardback)
1. Crime—Environmental aspects.   2. Geographical offender profiling.
3. Criminal behavior, Prediction of.   4. Crime scenes.   5. Crime analysis.
6. Crime prevention.   I. Groff, Elizabeth (Elizabeth R.)
II. Yang, Sue-Ming.   III. Title.
HV6150.W45 2012
364.9—dc23   2011049713

1 3 5 7 9 8 6 4 2

Printed in China
on acid-free paper

David Weisburd:
For Noam—Who has led in war, and is committed to peace.
With admiration and love for the man he has become.

Elizabeth R. Groff:
For Jo Fraley—With love and gratitude for her faith in me
and her support while I pursued my dreams.

Sue-Ming Yang:
For Chuen-Ying Liu and Shang-Shyng Yang—Who have
raised me and set wonderful role models for my life. It is you
I have always looked up to.

{TABLE OF CONTENTS}

{LIST OF TABLES}

{LIST OF FIGURES}

{ACKNOWLEDGMENTS}

There are many people that we need to thank who have helped us in the development of this research and in the preparation of the manuscript. We are especially indebted to the National Institute of Justice for recognizing the potential of our research and for providing funding for the project (#2005-IJ-CX-0006). We also want to thank our grant monitor, Carrie Mulford, for keeping us on track and reminding us of the importance of getting our work completed. Of course the points of view in this book are those of the authors and do not necessarily represent those of the U.S. Department of Justice. We thank the ever-efficient Kimberly Schmidt of the University of Maryland for her help and support in managing the NIJ grant. We are also grateful to Dean Jack Censor of George Mason University, for his creation of a general fund for the Center for Evidence-Based Crime Policy that was used to support research assistance, travel, and other costs to complete this book.

We owe a significant debt to then Chief Gil Kerlikowske of Seattle, who supported our research from the outset and facilitated our collection of official crime data as well as other data sources in Seattle. Chief Kerlikowske's willingness to support basic research on crime was a key reason why we were able to carry out this ambitious project. While there were a number of members of the Seattle PD who helped our research effort, special mention needs to be made regarding Lt. Ron Rasmussen, who was our main contact regarding data drawn from the police department. We cannot name them all here, but we are very much indebted to many Seattle and King County government agencies and their employees who assisted us in identifying potential data sources and obtaining data. Their cooperation speaks well of the support of city government more generally for research endeavors.

A number of research assistants helped us in identifying, collecting and preparing data for this project. Kristen Miggans, then a graduate student at the University of Maryland, was particularly important in getting data collection off the ground and collected quite a bit of it. Rachel Philofsky, Chien-min Lin, Nancy Morris, Amy J. Steen, and Janet Hagelgens, also of the University of Maryland, provided important assistance in the early stages of the project. Breanne Cave, Julie Hibdon, and Cody Telep, all assistants at George Mason University, played key roles in helping us complete the study. We are grateful to all of these younger scholars for their commitment and interest in our work. Julie Hibdon deserves special recognition for the many hours she spent on map production. Cody Telep deserves special mention because of his efforts in the rewrites, development of tables and figures, and editing of the report. Cody added tremendously to the quality of this work and kept the authors sane over the long journey to its completion.

Several scholars provided valuable advice along the way. Cynthia Lum, of George Mason University, was particularly important in the design of this study. We draw heavily from her work on crime data in Seattle from an earlier project on crime trends that was published with David Weisburd and other colleagues in 2004. She was also a generous advisor in helping us work with Seattle data. We also thank Dan Nagin for his assistance with trajectory models and more general quantitative analyses, Wayne Osgood for his review of the multinomial logistic modeling, Ned Levine for his comments on spatial point pattern statistics and Richard Heiberger for his assistance with R programming related to the cross-K analysis. Finally we want to thank Shai Amram, Gerben Bruinsma, Frank Cullen, John Eck, Marcus Felson, Badi Hasisi, Emily Owens, Robert Sampson, Tal Yonaton, Pamela Wilcox, and James Willis, as well as the anonymous reviewers for reading our work in draft and providing insightful comments. Our work is much enriched because of their efforts.

The Criminology of Place

{ 1 }

Introduction

Neighbors next door are more important than relatives far away.
遠親不如近鄰

—Chinese Folk Saying

When we think about crime, we usually think about criminals. The crime problem in this sense is about people and why they commit crime. What causes them to become involved in crime? What can society do to prevent ordinary people from becoming criminals? How must we deal with criminals on the streets, and what kinds of punishments should society bring to those who commit crimes? These are the questions that scholars, practitioners, and lay people have generally asked about the crime problem. They are questions that assume that the key component of crime is the individual and that our research about crime and our efforts to do something about crime are best focused on those individuals who commit crimes.

In this book, we take a very different approach to the crime problem. We do not begin with the people that commit crime, but rather with the places where crime occurs. This is a radical reconceptualization of the crime problem, but one that we will show is warranted by the reality of crime in the city. The focus on criminals is a policy choice, not an inevitable outcome of what is necessary to do something about the crime problem. Scholars, policy makers, and practitioners have assumed that if we want to understand and prevent crime, we by necessity need to focus on criminality. Crimes are committed by criminals, and in this sense an approach to the crime problem that begins with the criminal seems natural.

Why is it necessary to reconsider the "person-focused" crime and justice model of the last century? One reason is simply that the yield of this approach has been questioned for more than three decades. A core assumption of a crime and justice policy that focuses primarily on offenders is that we are able to predict with some certainty those who are likely to become serious offenders or the timing and types of future offenses that repeat offenders are likely to commit. Studies of criminals have suggested that this is a very difficult effort (e.g., Albrecht and Moitra, 1988; Auerhahn, 1999; Barnett and Lofaso, 1985; Bersani, Nieuwbeerta, and Laub, 2009; Blumstein and Cohen, 1979; Elliott, Dunford, and Huizinga, 1987; Estrict et al., 1983; Ezell and Cohen, 2005; Gottfredson and Gottfredson, 1992; Laub and Sampson, 2003; Sampson and Laub, 2003, 2005). Moreover, a recent review of the ability of criminological theory to explain criminality suggests that not much has changed over the last few decades (Weisburd and Piquero, 2008). Prediction levels remain very low. Given the difficulty of predicting criminality, it is perhaps not surprising that applied research in offender-centered crime prevention has more often than not illustrated the significant barriers that are faced in the development of successful interventions. Beginning with Robert Martinson's critique of rehabilitation programs in 1974 (see also Lipton, Martinson, and Wilks, 1975), a series of studies have documented the failures of traditional crime prevention initiatives (e.g., Sechrest, White, and Brown, 1979; Whitehead and Lab, 1989). Recent reviews of correctional programs are more positive, pointing to a number of rehabilitation efforts that do provide benefit in terms of reducing future offending (e.g., Andrews et al., 1990; MacKenzie, 2006; Mitchell, Wilson, and MacKenzie, 2007). Nonetheless, even where research is more positive, the overall story of offender-based interventions provides reason for serious concern. Nagin, Cullen, and Jonson (2009: 178), for example, in a careful review of what we have gained from the increased rates of incarceration over the last three decades, conclude that "the great majority of studies point to a null or criminogenic effect of the prison experience on subsequent offending."

Summarizing the push in the 1980s to find new approaches for addressing the crime problem, the noted Canadian criminologists Patricia and Paul Brantingham (1990: 19) wrote: "If traditional approaches worked well, of course, there would be little pressure to find new forms of crime prevention." In this book, we explore one of these new directions that we believe has particular importance for improving crime control and adding new knowledge to criminology. It can be subsumed broadly under what Lawrence Sherman, Patrick Gartin, and Michael Buerger (1989) coined as the "criminology of place." It pushes us to examine very small geographic areas within cities, often as small as addresses or street segments, for their contribution to the crime problem. It focuses our attention on "hot spots of crime," or crime concentrations in such micro geographic areas. This is a radical new conception for how we should understand and prevent crime, but as we detail in this chapter, its roots lie in the innovations in criminology of the last three decades.

Our book will illustrate that this focus on the criminology of place yields significant new criminological insights that both advance theory and practical crime prevention. Our research, as we describe in the following chapters, leads us to five main conclusions:

1) Crime is tightly concentrated at "crime hot spots," suggesting that we can identify and deal with a large proportion of crime problems by focusing on a very small number of places.[1]
2) These crime hot spots evidence very strong stability over time, and thus present a particularly promising focus for crime prevention efforts.
3) Crime at places evidences strong variability at micro levels of geography, suggesting that an exclusive focus on higher geographic units, like communities or neighborhoods, will lead to a loss of important information about crime and the inefficient focus of crime prevention resources.
4) It is not only crime that varies across very small units of geography, but also the social and contextual characteristics of places. The criminology of place in this context identifies and emphasizes the importance of micro units of geography as social systems relevant to the crime problem.
5) Crime at place is very predictable, and therefore it is possible to not only understand why crime is concentrated at place, but also to develop effective crime prevention strategies to ameliorate crime problems at places.

In the following chapters, we report on a large longitudinal study that provides solid empirical justification for a policy approach that positions "places" at the center of the crime equation. Linking 16 years of official crime data on street segments (both block faces between two intersections; see our later discussion) in Seattle, Washington, to a series of data sets examining the social and physical characteristics of places over time, we are able to extend present knowledge and explore areas that have not been the subject of systematic research to date. Our purpose in this book is not to "debunk" traditional concern with criminals, but rather to raise the possibilities of what we can achieve by reorienting our approach to the crime problem so that place takes a central role. Criminals, of course, play a key role in the criminology of place. But taking this approach, the criminal is one component of the crime problem, and the place becomes the point at which we begin our inquiries.

In this introductory chapter, we wanted to provide a context for our approach to the criminology of place and our identification of data relevant to understanding and explaining crime concentrations and developmental patterns of crime. Accordingly, we turn next to the theoretical perspectives that led to interest in the criminology of place, and the empirical data that have reinforced interest in this area. We then turn to the key questions that form the primary focus of our work. The next section of the chapter describes the site for our research, and the units of analysis that we use to examine the criminology of place. Finally, we describe the chapters that follow.

For the last century, criminologists have focused on describing the nature and causes of individual offending. In this book, we turn our attention to a different problem that has only recently drawn criminological attention, but has the potential to improve our predictions of crime and also our ability to develop practical crime prevention strategies. Our focus is on how crime distributes across very small units of geography. A Chinese proverb suggests that "neighbors next door are more important than relatives far away." Criminologists have often neglected the importance of neighbors next door, and more generally the role of the immediate geographic context to crime. The chapters that follow will argue that the action of crime research and practice should be focused much more on the "criminology of place."

The Emergence of the Criminology of Place

The primary focus of research in criminology has been on individuals and why they become involved in crime (Eck and Eck, 2012; Sherman, 1995; Nettler, 1978).[2] For example, criminologists have sought to understand why certain people as opposed to others become criminals (e.g., see Akers, 1973; Gottfredson and Hirschi, 1990; Hirschi, 1969; Raine, 1993), or to explain why certain offenders become involved in criminal activity at different stages of the life course or cease involvement at other stages (e.g., see Laub and Sampson, 2003; Moffitt, 1993; Sampson and Laub, 1993). But criminologists have also been interested in places, often studying states (e.g., see Loftin and Hill, 1974), cities (e.g., see Baumer et al., 1998), and neighborhoods (e.g., see Bursik and Grasmick, 1993; Sampson, 1985; Wilson, 1987). For example, criminologists have often tried to explain why certain types of crime or different levels of criminality are found in some communities as contrasted with others (e.g., see Agnew, 1999; Bursik and Grasmick, 1993; Sampson and Groves, 1989; Sampson and Wilson, 1995; Shaw, 1929), or how community-level variables, such as relative deprivation, low socioeconomic status, or lack of economic opportunity may affect individual criminality (e.g., see Agnew, 1992; Cloward and Ohlin, 1960; Merton, 1968; Wolfgang and Ferracuti, 1967).

While the individual and "macro" units of place, such as the community, have long been a focus of crime research and theory, only recently have criminologists begun to explore crime at very small "micro" units of geography. The roots of such approaches can be found in the efforts of scholars to identify the relationship between specific aspects of urban design (Jeffery, 1971) or urban architecture (Newman, 1972) and crime, but broadened to take into account a much larger set of characteristics of physical space and criminal opportunity (e.g., Brantingham and Brantingham, 1975, 1977, 1981; Duffala, 1976; Hunter, 1988; LeBeau, 1987; Mayhew et al., 1976; Rengert, 1980, 1981; Stoks, 1981). These studies drew important distinctions between the site in question and the larger geographical area (such as the neighborhood, community, police beat, or city) that surrounds it.

But the key to the origins of the criminology of place is a group of emerging theoretical perspectives that developed as a reaction to the limitations identified in offender-based criminology in the 1970s that we described earlier. In a ground-breaking article on routine activities and crime, for example, Cohen and Felson (1979) suggested that a fuller understanding of crime must include a recognition that the availability of suitable crime targets and the presence or absence of capable guardians influence crime events. Cohen and Felson were to turn traditional conceptions of the crime problem on their head by suggesting that crime could be prevented without changing the supply or motivation of offenders in society.

In the routine activities model, victims, offenders, and guardians were all essential parts of the crime equation. While traditional conceptions had focused on offenders, using data on crime rates in the United States in the post–World War II period, Cohen and Felson (1979) illustrated that changes in other parts of the crime equation could impact the level of crime in society. For example, they found that changes in the value of property or the ease of which it could be stolen affected burglary rates. Decreasing size and weight of electronic devices (e.g., televisions) and the increasing value of goods found in homes were found to be related to increases in victimization. They also found that changes in the presence of "capable guardians" influenced crime. In this case, the entrance of women into the work force and the resulting lack of "guardian-ship" at homes led to significant increases in house burglaries. The routine activities perspective was a radical one in American criminology at the time, because it pushed criminologists to extend their vision beyond the traditional concern with the causes of criminality and their focus on offenders.

Having introduced other elements of the crime equation, Cohen and Felson's (1979) work naturally led to a focus on crime opportunities, an issue we will examine in more detail in chapter 2. Victims, offenders, and guardians are likely to intersect in physical space. The spatial component of crime thus became a key component of this perspective:

> Unlike many criminological inquiries, we do not examine why individuals or groups are inclined criminally, but rather we take criminal inclination as given and examine the manner in which the spatio-temporal organization of social activities helps people to translate their criminal inclinations into action. Criminal violations are treated here as routine activities which share many attributes of, and are interdependent with, other routine activities. This interdependence between the structure of illegal activities and the organization of everyday sustenance activities leads us to consider certain concepts from human ecological literature. (Cohen and Felson, 1979: 589)

Researchers at the British Home Office, in a series of studies examining "sit-uational crime prevention," also challenged the traditional focus on offenders and communities (Clarke, 1983). Situational crime prevention moved the focus of the crime equation away from the people who commit crime and instead considered the context of criminal events to be critical. At the core of situational prevention is the concept of rational choice (Clarke, 1995; Cornish, 1993). In contrast to offender-based approaches to crime prevention, which usually focus on the dispositions of criminals, situational crime prevention begins with the opportunity structure of the crime situation (Felson and Clarke, 1998). Such opportunities affect whether potential offenders will choose to commit crime. Importantly, such choices are seen to be the result of a decision employing "bounded rationality" (Clarke and Cornish, 1985, 2001). That is, potential offenders use the limited knowledge about victims or guardians in specific situations that is easily available to consider relative costs and benefits (Johnson and Payne, 1986).

Situational crime prevention is concerned with the "opportunity structures" of specific contexts and places. By opportunity structure, advocates of this perspective are not referring to the broad societal structure of opportunities that underlie individual motivations for crime (e.g., see Merton, 1938), but to the immediate situational components of the context of crime. In this context, crime prevention may involve efforts as simple and straightforward as target hardening (e.g., Poyner et al., 1988; Webb and Laycock, 1992) or access control (e.g., Matthews, 1990; Poyner and Webb, 1987), and often follows a straightforward and commonsense notion of how to deal with crime problems that has long been accepted by citizens and practitioners who deal with crime prevention at the everyday level of protecting property or reducing victimization (Tonry and Farrington, 1995). Importantly, place at a "micro" level is key to situational crime prevention theory since it focuses on the immediate opportunities for crime, which are generally structured within very small geographic areas.

Around the same time as routine activities theory and situational crime prevention developed, Paul and Patricia Brantingham published their seminal book *Patterns in Crime*, which emphasized the role of place characteristics and human activity in shaping the type and frequency of human interaction (Brantingham and Brantingham, 1984). Environmental criminology, also known as crime pattern theory, explores the distribution and interaction of targets, offenders, and opportunities across time and space (Brantingham and Brantingham, 1981). Both rational choice and situational opportunities play a key role in crime pattern theory. The concept of place, in turn, is essential to crime pattern theory. Not only are places logically required (an offender must be in a place when an offense is committed), but also their characteristics are seen to influence the likelihood of a crime and the likelihood that particular places will become crime hot spots. Crime pattern theory links places with desirable targets and the context within which they are found by focusing on how places come to the attention of potential offenders.

One implication of these emerging perspectives was that places at a "micro" geographic level should be an important focus of criminological inquiry. While concern with the relationship between crime and place is not new and indeed goes back to the founding generations of modern criminology (see chapter 2), the "micro" approach to places suggested by recent theories had just begun to be examined by criminologists.[3] Places in this "micro" context are specific locations within the larger social environments of communities and neighborhoods (Eck and Weisburd, 1995). They are sometimes defined as buildings or addresses (e.g., see Green, 1996; Sherman, Gartin, and Buerger, 1989); sometimes as block faces, "hundred blocks," or street segments (e.g., see Taylor, 1997; Weisburd et al., 2004); and sometimes as clusters of addresses, block faces, or street segments (e.g., see Block, Dabdoub, and Fregly, 1995; Sherman and Weisburd, 1995; Weisburd and Green, 1995).

The Tight Coupling of Crime at Place

Recent studies point to the potential theoretical and practical benefits of focusing research on crime places. A number of studies, for example, suggest that there is a very significant clustering of crime at places, irrespective of the specific unit of analysis that is defined (Brantingham and Brantingham, 1999; Crow and Bull, 1975; Pierce, Spaar, and Briggs, 1988; Roncek, 2000; Sherman, Gartin, and Buerger, 1989; Weisburd and Green, 1994; Weisburd, Maher, and Sherman, 1992; Weisburd et al., 2004). The extent of the concentration of crime at place is dramatic. In one of the pioneering studies in this area, Sherman, Gartin, and Buerger (1989) found that only about 3 percent of the addresses in Minneapolis, Minnesota, produced 50 percent of all calls to the police. Fifteen years later in a study in Seattle, Washington, Weisburd and colleagues (2004) reported that between 4 and 5 percent of street segments in the city accounted for 50 percent of crime incidents for each year over 14 years. These studies and others (Brantingham and Brantingham, 1984; Clarke, 1983; Curtis, 1974; Maltz, Gordon, and Friedman, 1990 [2000]; Pyle, 1976; Rengert, 1980; Skogan, 1990) have challenged a prevailing view among criminologists that has prevented micro conceptions of place from becoming an important part of the criminological lexicon.

Criminologists have assumed that crime is "loosely coupled" to place. The idea of loose and tight "coupling" has been used in many disciplines to identify the extent to which parts of systems are linked or dependent one to another (e.g., see Orton and Weick, 1990). In criminal justice, the terms "tight coupling" and "loose coupling" are used frequently in organizational studies of the criminal justice system (e.g., Hagan, Hewitt, and Alwin, 1979; Maguire and Katz, 2002; Manning, 1982; Thomas, 1984). What we mean here by "loose coupling" of crime at places is that criminologists have traditionally not seen the bonds that tie crime to place as very strong, even though it has been clear from the outset that crime occurs in specific settings. Sutherland (1947), for example,

recognized the importance of place in the crime equation even as he presented
his theory of differential social learning among individuals. He noted in his
classic introductory criminology text that "a thief may steal from a fruit stand
when the owner is not in sight but refrain when the owner is in sight; a bank
burglar may attack a bank which is poorly protected but refrain from attacking
a bank protected by watchmen and burglar alarms" (1947: 5). Nonetheless, like
other early criminologists (e.g., Hirschi, 1969; Merton, 1938; Sykes and Matza,
1957), Sutherland did not see such places as a relevant focus of criminological
study. This was the case, in part, because crime opportunities provided by places
were assumed to be so numerous as to make crime prevention strategies targeting specific places of little utility for theory or policy. In turn, criminologists
traditionally assumed that situational factors played a relatively minor role in
explaining crime as compared with the "driving force of criminal dispositions"
(Clarke and Felson, 1993: 4; Trasler, 1993).

The findings of tremendous concentrations of crime at place suggest a "tight
coupling" of crime with the places where crime occurs.[4] Research demon-
strating that crime is not only concentrated at a small number of places, but
also that these concentrations remain stable over time reinforces this idea of
tight coupling. Spelman (1995), for example, examined calls for service at
schools, public housing projects, subway stations, and parks and playgrounds
in Boston. He found evidence of a very high degree of stability of crime at the
"worst" of these places over a four-year period. Taylor (1999) also reported
evidence of a high degree of stability of crime at place over time examining
crime and fear of crime at 90 street blocks in Baltimore, Maryland, using a
panel design with data collected in 1981 and 1994 (see also Taylor, 2001).
Weisburd and colleagues (2004) reported long-term stability of crime hot spots
in their longitudinal study of street segments in Seattle.[5]

If crime is strongly concentrated at place, and such concentrations are
stable over long periods, then it is possible to assume that a focus on crime
hot spots can have important crime prevention benefits. In the first case, the
concentration of crime suggests that police or other crime prevention agents
can focus on a very small number of targets and have a large impact on crime
problems overall. This is a particularly important idea when we consider that
traditional policing often emphasized the spreading of police resources over
large areas, for example, through random preventive patrol (Weisburd and
Eck, 2004). The fact that crime hot spots are stable across long periods reinforces the potential utility of such approaches, because it implies that if crime
prevention agents did not intervene the problem would persist. These are the
implications of the tight coupling of crime and place that have been observed
in prior studies.

But the potential for the criminology of place in crime prevention is not
just theoretical. These basic research findings have been reinforced by evaluations of practical crime prevention efforts. A series of randomized field trials

demonstrate that police efforts focused on hot spots can result in meaningful reductions in crime and disorder (see e.g., Braga and Bond, 2008; Braga et al., 1999; Sherman and Weisburd, 1995; Weisburd and Green, 1995). Braga, Papachristos, and Hureau (forthcoming; see also Braga, 2001, 2005, 2007) report in this regard in a Campbell Collaboration systematic review that 20 of 25 tests from 19 experimental or quasi-experimental evaluations of hot spots policing reported noteworthy crime or disorder reductions. This strong body of rigorous evaluations led the National Research Council Committee to Review Research on Police Policy and Practices (2004: 35; see also Weisburd and Eck, 2004) to conclude: "There has been increasing interest over the past two decades in police practices that target very specific types of crimes, criminals, and crime places. In particular, policing crime hot spots has become a common police strategy for reducing crime and disorder problems. While there is only preliminary evidence suggesting the effectiveness of targeting specific types of offenders, a strong body of evidence suggests that taking a focused geographic approach to crime problems can increase the effectiveness of policing." In addition, a variety of other crime prevention measures focused on micro places have demonstrated success (Guerette and Bowers, 2009; Lab, 2007; Schneider and Kitchen, 2007; Tilley, 2009).

Importantly, and again reinforcing the importance of the tight coupling of crime at place, there is little evidence in these studies of displacement of crime to areas nearby targeted hot spots. Displacement has long been seen as a threat to practical crime prevention programs that focus on specific places (e.g., see Reppetto, 1976). If the application of crime prevention strategies at a specific place will simply displace crime to areas nearby, it would be difficult to capitalize on the concentration of crime in hot spots that has been observed in basic research. Crime in this sense would simply "move around the corner" as a response to targeted policing at hot spots. However, recent reviews of place-based crime prevention suggest that crime displacement is not common (Braga, 2001, 2005, 2007; Braga, Papachristos, and Hureau, (forthcoming; Bowers et al., 2011; Guerette and Bowers, 2009). Indeed, these reviews conclude generally that the more likely outcome of focused prevention efforts at places is a "diffusion of crime control benefits" (Clarke and Weisburd, 1994; Weisburd et al., 2006)—meaning that areas nearby also improve as a result of crime prevention interventions at hot spots.

We think that the tight coupling of crime and place provides a straightforward explanation for why displacement is not a common outcome of place-based crime prevention. Simply put, crime does not move easily to other places because crime and offenders are "tightly coupled" to place. The displacement hypothesis, like other traditional objections to the criminology of place, is based on an assumption that people and crime are loosely coupled to place and will move easily to other places. The empirical literature on crime places suggests just the opposite. What is surprising in this context is displacement and

not its absence, a theme we will return to later when discussing the policy implications of our work in chapter 8.

Key Questions in the Criminology of Place

The data that we describe in this book allow us to extend existing knowledge
about the concentration and stability of crime at place. Looking at the longest
time series yet available for criminologists studying the criminology of place,
our data confirm the strong concentration of crime at micro units of geography,
as well as the stability of crime concentrations over time (see chapter 3). Indeed,
we raise the question in later chapters as to whether there is a "law of crime
concentrations" at places applicable not only across time but across cities.

Our study also raises a number of key questions that have not yet been
addressed in prior research. One of these relates to the extent to which the
"action" of crime is at these small area hot spots, or whether alternatively the
hot spots of crime merely reflect larger community-wide influences.[6] This
question is particularly important because traditional research on crime places
has often assumed that the primary generator of crime is the neighborhood or
community (e.g., see Hawley, 1950; Reiss, 1986; Sampson, Raudenbush, and
Earls, 1997; Shaw and McKay, 1942 [1969]). In this context, we might question
whether examining hot spots of crime at a micro geographic level simply dis-
guises the workings of social forces operating at higher levels. The criminology
of place provides a very different portrait of the crime problem that focuses
attention on variability of crime patterns within communities. And in doing so,
it allows us to explore the question of whether micro level patterns have
something unique to add to our understanding of crime.

In the work that follows, we provide the most detailed and systematic
assessment of the distribution of crime at place at a micro geographic level that
has been developed so far. Our research leads to a portrait of crime that reinforces the criminology of place. First, it shows that there is tremendous variability of crime patterns street by street in the city, and that this variability
indicates that social forces are not simply pushing down on crime places, but
rather that forces at a very micro geographic level are exerting pressures upward
in developing what we normally think of as the crime problem. Indeed, we will
use the example of overall crime trends to show that perspectives focusing only
on larger areas to understand and interpret crime miss very important local
trends. Specifically, our analyses show that it is misleading to speak of "crime
declines" across cities as had become common in discussions of what many
have called the crime drop of the 1990s (Blumstein and Wallman, 2000). In
fact, our data show that most streets in Seattle had stable crime trends during a
period of a strong overall crime decline in the city, and that many streets experienced crime waves during that time.

A second area where our work stakes out important new ground is in identifying and describing the geographic and temporal patterns of characteristics that have been theoretically linked to crime at place. While scholars have posited that specific characteristics of places can explain variability in crime at place, to date we know little about how those characteristics vary across the urban landscape. Do crime opportunities vary in significant ways across a city? Are there "hot spots" for potential offenders, for victimization, and for guardianship? Do these characteristics vary across time or are they relatively stable? Importantly, we not only examine the distribution of measures commonly associated with micro geographic processes, but also social aspects of places that are often seen as primarily related to larger area or community trends in crime. This application of social disorganization theories (see chapter 2) to the criminology of place allows us to examine to what extent such characteristics vary across place and later to link them to our understanding of crime at place.

Our findings, detailed in later chapters, are not uniform, but they illustrate overall that just as crime is concentrated and relatively stable at hot spots, so are the characteristics of places that we identify and measure. This of course suggests intriguing questions examined later in our work. Are hot spots of crime correlated with hot spots of opportunity or social disorganization at places? What factors provide the strongest explanations for crime at place, and how do different theoretical approaches fare when they are compared in an overall model for predicting crime at place?

Ours is one of a very small number of emerging studies that allow us to link social and opportunity characteristics of places to crime at place.[7] Among the key questions we will ask are: What characteristics of places are associated with crime hot spots, and how do the characteristics of hot spots differ from places that are relatively crime free? What accounts for different developmental crime trends that have been identified at micro units of place over time? For example, what leads some micro places to experience a large decline in crime trends over time, while others in the same city experience crime waves?

Our findings, detailed later, are intriguing and provide an understanding as to why crime is coupled so strongly to place. We noted earlier the importance of opportunity theories in the development of the criminology of place. Our work provides strong confirmation of the importance of routine activities, and crime opportunities more generally, to the generation of crime. But we also find that social and structural factors that are more often associated with community-based theories of crime are also important factors in understanding crime trends at micro places. This finding is important because it necessarily leads us to broaden and expand the theoretical foundations of the criminology of place, an effort we return to in our conclusions.

Our work here not only reinforces and expands existing theoretical grounding of the criminology of place, but it also suggests the tremendous opportunities that this approach has for developing theories about crime. We will illustrate later that the variation in crime at place is highly predictable. Indeed, though our work is one of the first to systematically model crime at micro units of geography, our models explain a very large proportion of the variability we observe. This means that the factors that explain the tight coupling of crime at place appear at this early stage of development of this field more robust in predicting crime than those ordinarily identified in person- and community-based studies. This, as we discuss in our conclusions, has important implications for policy and practice as well.

The Focus of Our Research: Seattle, Washington

While our study draws from a large array of data over a 16-year period, it is in some sense a case study of the criminology of place because our inferences are drawn from a single jurisdiction. Most studies of crime are limited in this way, for example identifying a specific site for drawing their cases and samples. Our interest in the geographic distribution of crime at a very small geographic level naturally leads us to follow this approach. As we describe below, we include more than 24,000 crime places in our analyses. A study in one jurisdiction thus offers a very large sample from which to draw inferences about the criminology of place. However, this means that our choice of which city to study is particularly important. We turn now to how we identified Seattle as a research site and provide some detail about the historical, physical, and social characteristics of the city.

Seattle makes a good choice for a longitudinal study of places for several reasons. As a large city, it has enough geography, population, and crime to undertake a micro level study. Having enough crime is a particularly important issue as we progress down the geographic cone of resolution to the micro place level of analysis. Only larger cities are likely to have enough intensity of crime at small levels of geography to make it possible for us to identify and explain crime patterns across place.

Given the importance of official police data in identifying crime in a city, it was also critical at the outset that we identify a jurisdiction for study where the chief of police would be fully supportive of the importance of our research. Anyone that has worked with police agencies knows how difficult it can be to acquire data, even when there seems to be legal access to information. Especially in our case, where we sought archival and historical records, the burdens on the police agency were not insignificant. It was also the case that we intended to ask many other city agencies for computerized data and the full support of the chief executive of the police agency in a city was in our experience also a key factor in gaining cooperation and support for a study of this type. In this case as well, Seattle made an appropriate site. The department was led at the time of our study by a chief of police, Gil Kerlikowske, who recognized the importance of basic research on crime for advancing crime prevention. The chief and his staff turned out, as we had hoped, to be an important part of the success of our work, facilitating our efforts and helping us to overcome many significant barriers to the research along the way.

These factors were important in our choice of Seattle. However, there were a number of cities large enough and with innovative and progressive police chiefs during the time that we set out to collect these data. The distinguishing feature of Seattle was the length of the time for which they had crime data available. In identifying Seattle, a national search was carried out that sought to identify larger cities that had maintained records on crime events linked to specific places over a long period. We were surprised at how few cities kept historical crime data in ways that could be analyzed geographically. Indeed, only a handful of larger cities could provide longitudinal crime data for our study, and Seattle was not only among those with the longest historical records, but also agreed to cooperate fully with us from the outset.[8]

SEATTLE IN HISTORICAL PERSPECTIVE

While the focus of our study is the 16-year period between 1989 and 2004 for which we were able to collect historical records on crime, the city of Seattle's history stretches back more than 150 years.[9] We think it important at the outset to provide a brief history of Seattle to give context to our study.

Seattle was incorporated in 1869 after initial settlement in the early 1850s led by Arthur Armstrong Denny. The city was named for Chief Sealth (sometimes spelled as Si'ahl), leader of the Duwamish and Suquamish tribes, which had villages in the area when settlers arrived. In its early days, the city's economy was dominated by the lumber and coal industries. In 1883, the city was connected to the Northern Pacific Railway Company's transcontinental railroad western terminus in Tacoma, leading to a rise in the city's population throughout the 1880s and a rapid increase in building construction. Because of the major lumber industry in the area, nearly all buildings were constructed from wood. This reliance on wood had major negative consequences, however, during the great Seattle fire in June 1889. The initial fire caused by glue being left over a gasoline fire for too long spread quickly, destroying the majority of 29 downtown blocks (nearly the entire business district) and creating millions of dollars in property damage (Lange, 1999). Almost immediately after the fire, the city council passed regulations requiring all new buildings to be fireproof and built of brick and stone.

Additionally, the rebuilding process after the fire gave Seattle an opportunity to address another constant problem in the early years of the city, flooding from the Puget Sound as a result of the city's location at sea level. High tide was a constant source of trouble for the young city; the excitement of newly available indoor plumbing, for example, was greatly reduced by frequent geysers of sewage that erupted from toilets when the tide came in. (Bagley, 1916). During the rebuilding process, city officials decided to reconstruct the streets above the floodplain. Thus, the streets were essentially raised a floor above sea level. While at first this created a difficult situation for pedestrians because the sidewalks remained at sea level, eventually the sidewalks were raised as well, creating a situation in the downtown area where the second level of most buildings was actually at ground level. Some of the original first levels salvageable after the fire were still used, but many were left abandoned for decades (Crowley, 2001).

In 1897, the discovery of gold in Alaska and the Yukon Territory in Canada led to an economic boom as gold miners flocked to the Seattle area. This, along with additional railroad connections at the end of the nineteenth century, led to a prosperous economy in the early years of the twentieth century. In 1907, the Pike Place Market on the Seattle waterfront began operation. The market continues today as one of the nation's oldest public farmers' markets and includes the famous Pike Place Fish Market (Crowley, 1999). Seattle celebrated its growth in the new century with the 1909 Alaska-Yukon-Pacific Exposition, an international fair showcasing economic and cultural achievements in the region. In 1914, the 38-storey Smith Building was completed in Pioneer Square; it was the tallest building west of the Mississippi until 1934 and the tallest building on the West Coast until the Seattle Space Needle was built in 1962.

As a major port, Seattle remained prosperous during World War I; the city was a major producer of ships for the war effort. After the war, however, Pioneer Square and the original downtown area of the city began to decline as the economy slowed with the end of the war and business moved northward and into suburban areas. One of the early connections of crime to place came out of this urban decline. The current usage of the term "skid road" or "skid row" came into being through the preaching of Reverend Mark A. Matthews. He spoke out against the problems in Pioneer Square, which had "become a place where out-of-work loggers, alcoholics, and pensioners congregated in cheap hotels and were sustained by missions" (Turner, 1986: A20). He argued in his sermons that "Yesler Way was once a skid road down which logs were pushed to Henry Yesler's sawmill on the waterfront. Today it is a skid road down which human souls go sliding to hell!" (Newell, 1956: 114).

The revitalization of Pioneer Square was a slow process. It was not until the 1950s that local publicist Bill Speidel spearheaded efforts to restore some of the underground city that existed in Pioneer Square and had been largely abandoned after the great fire. He began the Underground Tour in 1954, (see http:// www.undergroundtour.com) which continues to this day and allows visitors to explore several blocks of this once largely forgotten part of Seattle. In the 1960s, Speidel promoted efforts to obtain recognition of the 30 acres of Pioneer Square as a historic district. Pioneer Square today has a vibrant arts scene and is the home of many of the city's architecture and design firms (Crowley, 2001).

Outside of Pioneer Square, the city's economy was revitalized in World War II with the massive growth of the Boeing Corporation. William Boeing started the company in 1916, but the need for a large number of bombers in the World War II made the company a major force in the Seattle economy. By March of 1944, Boeing was producing 350 B-17 and B-29 bombers a month. During the war, Boeing increased the size of its work force by more than 1200 percent and annual sales jumped from less than $10 million to more than $600 million (Boeing Corporation, n.d.). After the war, most of the bomber orders were cancelled, and 70,000 employees lost their jobs. The decline of the company was short-lived, however. Beginning in the 1950s, Boeing became a major producer of commercial airplanes, creating the United States' first commercial plane, the 707, in 1958. Seattle celebrated the city's economic rise by hosting the 1962 World's Fair, which led to the construction of the Seattle Center, home of the Pacific Science Center, a monorail system, and the Space Needle. The Boeing Corporation again faced a slump in the early 1970s, halving its Seattle workforce as a result of decreased federal government financial support for the development of the supersonic 2707, a competitor to the Concorde.

The late 1970s and 1980s saw a rise in production in Boeing along with a diversification in the Seattle economy, driven largely by the arrival of the Microsoft Corporation. Bill Gates and Paul Allen moved the computer company from Albuquerque, New Mexico, to the Seattle suburbs in 1979. Annual sales exceeded $140 million by 1985 and $1.18 billion by 1990. By 1995, the company was the most profitable in the world. The initial public stock offering in 1986 created an estimated four billionaires and 12,000 millionaires among company employees (Bick, 2005). By 2005, the company's Redmond, Washington, headquarters in the Seattle suburbs had more than 28,000 employees and over 8 million square feet of space (*Seattle Post-Intelligencer*, 2005).

Microsoft Corporation was not the only Seattle company to expand rapidly in the 1980s and 1990s. The department store Nordstrom's, for example, went from a regional store to a national chain, adding a number of locations in the 1980s. The company's flagship store remains in downtown Seattle. The city is also the home of the world's largest coffee shop chain. Starbucks opened its first location in Seattle in 1971 and the company began a rapid expansion in the 1980s. In the 1990s, the chain was averaging a new store opening every business day (Wilma, 2000). Today, Starbucks has over 17,000 locations in nearly 50 countries. Internet retailer Amazon.com is also headquartered in the city. The company attracts nearly 65 million shoppers to its website each month and did over $24.5 billion in sales in 2009 (Amazon.com, 2010).

In the time period immediately preceding and during our study, Seattle experienced three major economic boom and bust cycles followed by growth periods. These occurred in the early 1980s, early 1990s, and between 2001 and 2004 (Crowley, 2006). During the early 1990s, Boeing Aircraft Corporation, one of

Seattle's largest employers, went through a period of economic difficulties and downsizing. By the end of the decade, Boeing seemed to have recovered. In 2001, recession hit Seattle harder than it had in at least the previous 30 years (King County Budget Office, 2004). Contractions at Boeing led to massive lay-offs. The company moved its corporate headquarters to Chicago in 2001, but still has the largest share of its employees in the Seattle area (Boeing Corporation, n.d.). These problems were compounded by the attacks of 9/11/2001 and the dot com bust in 2002. Despite an overall negative economic climate, Seattle continued to add population and in 2004 had an estimated population of 572,600 (Office of Financial Management, 2008). The more diversified economy in the past 30 years helped Seattle withstand ups and downs at the Boeing Corporation.

The city is home to the Seattle Mariners in major league baseball, the Seattle Seahawks in the National Football League, and was home to the Seattle Super-sonics in the National Basketball Association until 2008. The city also has a vibrant music scene. The Seattle Symphony Orchestra was founded in 1903 and is one of the world's most recorded orchestras (see http://www.seattlesymphony. org). The grunge-music era of the early 1990s largely got its start in the city, which was the home of a number of popular grunge bands including Nirvana, Pearl Jam, and Soundgarden.

Seattle is also home to the University of Washington, the largest employer in the region (Office of Intergovernmental Relations, 2008). The university, founded in 1861, has over 40,000 students, making it the largest in the north-western United States. The school also has more than $1 billion in research funding a year and has received more federal research funding than any other public university every year since 1974 (Roseth, 2007).

THE GEOGRAPHY OF THE CITY

Seattle is located on the West Coast of the United States, and is geographically long and narrow, giving it a noticeable north-south orientation (see figure 1.1). The city is about 100 miles south of the Canadian border. It is bounded on the west by the Puget Sound and on the east by Lake Washington. This unusual geography has significant ramifications for the criminology of place. The west-ern border of the city is permeable only to water traffic (via a ferry system). Automobile and bus traffic can enter Seattle from the east using one of two bridges. It is only on the two shortest borders (on the north and the south) that Seattle shares a land border with other jurisdictions. This attribute of Seattle is very useful for our study because it reduces the likelihood that we will miss important elements of the geography of crime trends because we are cutting the boundaries of geography artificially. In formal terms, this means that the geography of Seattle reduces the possibilities for spatial edge effects (see Bailey and Gatrell, 1995; Rengert and Lockwood, 2009).

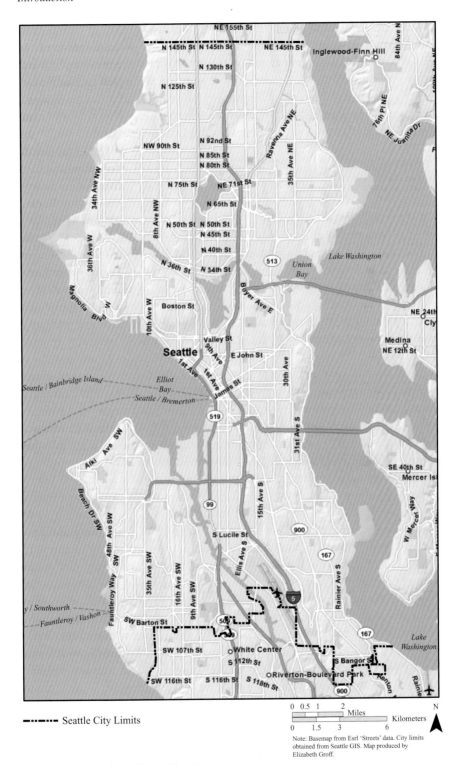

FIGURE 1.1 *Map of the City of Seattle*

Once inside Seattle, there are additional natural barriers in the form of waterways. The southern section of the city is split northwest to southeast by the Duwamish Waterway (three roads cross it). The northern section of the city is split from the central by a waterway consisting of Salmon Bay, Lake Union, Portage Bay, and Union Bay. There are six roads that cross the northern waterway. Altogether Seattle is 91.57 square miles in area. About 3.07 square miles is water and the rest is land (Seattle City Government, 2009).

KEY DEMOGRAPHIC CHARACTERISTICS OF
THE SEATTLE POPULATION

The study period we are using is 1989–2004, since this is the period for which data on crime were available for analysis. According to the U.S. Census, near the outset of our study the size of the population in the city had begun to rebound for the first time after decades of decline. In 1990, the population of Seattle was 516,259. The upward trend continued over the next decade, and by the 2000 census there were 563,374 people living in Seattle (U.S. Census Bureau, 1990, 2000). In 2000 (and continuing today), Seattle was the largest city in Washington and the Pacific Northwest, and the center of the Seattle-Tacoma-Bellevue metropolitan area, which was the 15th largest in the United States. (U.S. Census Bureau, 2000).

In addition to an increasing population, the city of Seattle had a very diverse population in terms of racial makeup (see table 1.1). In 1990, the residents of Seattle were 75.3 percent (388,858) white, 10.1 percent (51,948) African American, and 11.8 percent (60,819) Asian or Pacific Islander (U.S. Census Bureau, 1990). Seattle's African American population was smaller than the average of large U.S. cities (over 100,000 population), and its Asian population was relatively larger. Seattle is listed by the census as having the 10th largest Asian population of American cities. This diverse racial distribution of Seattle persisted in 2000 when 70.1 percent of residents (394,889) were white, 8.4 percent (47,541) were African American, and 13.6 percent (76,714) were Asian or Pacific Islander (U.S. Census Bureau, 2000).

In both 1990 and 2000, about 46 percent of homes in the city were owner occupied, which was similar to the national average for larger cities (see table 1.2). Seattle's 5.0 percent vacant housing rate in 1990 and 4.5 percent in 2000 was lower than the national average. Seattle is a fairly well-educated city, with just under a quarter of residents (at least 25 years old) having received a bachelor's degree in 1990 and nearly 30 percent in 2000. Nationally, cities over 100,000 had much lower percentages of college graduates on average (14.1 percent in 1990, 16.6 percent in 2000). Finally, Seattle enjoyed a lower poverty and unemployment rate in both 1990 and 2000 than the national average. The poverty rate in Seattle declined slightly between 1990 and 2000 from 12 to 11.8 percent, while the unemployment rate increased slightly from 3.3 to 3.6 percent (U.S. Census Bureau, 1990, 2000).

TABLE 1.1 Racial Composition of Seattle Compared to Other Cities with Populations Greater Than 100,000 (1990, 2000)

Race	1990				2000			
	Cities 100,000 +	Seattle		Cities 100,000 +	Seattle			
	Avg. Percent	Number	Percent	Avg. Percent	Number	Percent		
White	62.7	388,858	75.3	56.9	394,889	70.1		
Black/Afr.-Amer.	23.6	51,948	10.1	22.2	47,541	8.4		
Amer. Indian	0.6	7,326	1.4	0.7	5,659	1.0		
Asian	5.2	60,819	11.8	6.4	73,910	13.1		
Pacific Islander	—	—	—	0.9	2,804	0.5		
Other	7.9	7,308	1.4	1.7	13,423	2.4		
Two or more races	—	—	—	1.2	25,148	4.5		
Hispanic (any race)	9.0	18,349	3.6	12.5	29,719	5.3		
Total Population	100.0	516,259	100.0	100.0	563,374	100.0		

Notes: Asians and Pacific Islanders were combined in the 1990 Census; "Two or more races" was not an option on the 1990 Census.

TABLE 1.2 Selected Census Information on Seattle Compared to Other Cities with Populations Greater Than 100,000 (1990, 2000)

| | 1990 | | | | 2000 | | | |
| | Cities 100,000 + | Seattle | | Cities 100,000 + | | Seattle | |
	Avg. Percent	Number	Percent	Avg. Percent	Number	Percent
Owner-occ. housing	43.9	115,709	46.5	46.8	125,165	46.3
Renter-occ. housing	47.5	120,993	48.6	46.2	133,334	49.3
Vacant housing	8.7	12,330	5.0	7.0	12,025	4.4
College degree*	14.1	90,971	24.6	16.6	122,429	29.9
Foreign born	14.5	67,736	13.1	19.4	94,952	16.9
Poverty rate	17.2	61,681	12.0	16.7	64,068	11.8
Unemployment*	5.1	14,659	3.3	4.7	17,342	3.6

* Census data on the percentage of the population with at least a bachelor's degree include only those adults that are at least 25 years old. The unemployment rate includes only those who are at least 16 years old.

The Street Segment as a Unit of Analysis

A recent volume entitled *Putting Crime in its Place* (Weisburd, Bernasco, and Bruinsma, 2009) has emphasized the degree to which it is important for scholars to specify more carefully the units of analysis that would define the criminology of place (see also Bursik and Grasmick, 1993; Hipp, 2010; Sampson, 1993; Tita and Radil, 2010). The problem, of course, is that there is no ideal level of geography, and no given unit of analysis that can be assumed at the outset (Hipp, 2007, 2010; Taylor, in press). This problem is not unique to the study of places. In the 1980s, scholars began to challenge the traditional focus of criminology on individual offenders, noting that much crime was committed in co-offending groups, and the study of distinct individuals often missed key organizational and social components of the crime problem (Hindelang, 1976; Reiss, 1988; Reiss and Farrington, 1991). While there is no clear rule regarding the appropriate unit for studying crime places, there is a growing consensus among scholars in this area that this unit should be very small (Brantingham et al., 2009; Groff, Weisburd, and Morris, 2009; Oberwittler and Wikström, 2009; Taylor, 1998; van Wilselm, 2009). Starting with smaller units allows the researcher to examine how such units relate one to another. Beginning with larger geographic units can lead the researcher to miss variability within those larger units that is important to understanding the development of crime.

We follow this approach by choosing as our geographic unit of analysis the street segment (sometimes referred to as a street block or face block). We define the street segment as both sides of the street between two intersections. We chose the street segment for a variety of theoretical and operational reasons. In geographic terms, it is a very small building block from which to examine the criminology of place. At the same time, it is a social unit that has been recognized as important in the rhythms of everyday living in cities.

Theoretically, scholars have long recognized the relevance of street blocks in organizing life in the city (Appleyard, 1981; Brower, 1980; Jacobs, 1961; Taylor, Gottfredson, and Brower, 1984; Unger and Wandersman, 1983). Ecological psychology in particular has attempted to understand how places function (Barker, 1968; Wicker, 1987). From his observations of places, Barker developed "behavior settings theory." Wicker (1987: 614) defines behavior settings as "small-scale social systems whose components include people and inanimate objects." He goes on to say that "within the temporal and spatial boundaries of the system, the various components interact in an orderly, established fashion to carry out the setting's essential functions" (Wicker, 1987: 614).

Taylor (1997, 1998) made the case for why street segments (his terminology was street blocks) function as behavior settings. First, people who frequent a street segment get to know one another and become familiar with each other's routines. This awareness of the standing patterns of behavior of neighbors provides a basis from which action can be taken. For example, activity at the corner store is normal during business hours but abnormal after closing. Second, residents develop certain roles they play in the life of the street segment (e.g., the busybody, the organizer). Consistency of roles increases the stability of activities at places. On many streets, for example, there is at least one neighbor who will accept packages for other residents when they are not at home. Third, norms about acceptable behavior develop and are generally shared. Shared norms develop from interactions with other residents and observations of behaviors that take place on the block without being challenged. Fourth, blocks have standing patterns of behavior that are temporally specific. The mail carrier delivers at a certain time of day, the corner resident is always home by 5 PM, another neighbor always mows the lawn on Saturday. The specific type of frequently occurring patterns of behavior varies by temporal unit of analysis (e.g., daily, weekly, and seasonally). Fifth, a street block has boundaries that contain its setting. It is bounded by the cross streets on each end. Interaction is focused inward toward the street. Sixth, street segments, like other behavior settings, are dynamic. Residents move out and new ones move in. Land use could shift as residences become stores at street level and remain residential on the upper floors. These types of changes to the social and physical environment of the street segment can alter the standing patterns of behavior.

However, street segments do not exist in a vacuum. The rhythms of the street are influenced by nonresidents who are just passing through and ones who work on the block, as well as by the conditions of the surrounding neighborhood in which the street block is situated (Taylor, 1997, 1998). In addition, the combination of residential and nonresidential land uses on a street segment (and the blocks immediately adjacent to a block) as well as the transportation network directly influence the amount and type of activity on a street segment.

Taylor's (1997, 1998) extension of behavior settings theory to street segments offers an eloquent illustration of how street segments function as key units for informal social control at a micro-ecological level of analysis. In this way, street segments, as we discuss in more detail later in this book, provide a unit of analysis that "fits" with both ecological theories and opportunity theories and that is capable of illustrating both bottom-up and top-down processes producing crime events.

Beyond the theoretical reasons for using street segments to understand crime and place, there are other advantages. Unlike neighborhood boundaries, street segments are easily recognized by residents and have well-defined boundaries (Taylor, 1988). Moreover, the small size of street segments minimizes spatial heterogeneity and makes for easier interpretation of significant effects (Rice and Smith, 2002; Smith, Frazee, and Davison, 2000), and processes of informal social control and territoriality (Taylor, Gottfredson, and Brower, 1984) are more effective in smaller settings such as street segments. Finally, significant variations in collective participation in block-level organizations have been found across street segments (Perkins et al., 1990).

Operationally, the choice of street segments over even smaller units such as addresses (see Sherman, Gartin, and Buerger, 1989) also minimizes the error likely to develop from miscoding of addresses in official data (see Klinger and Bridges, 1997; Weisburd and Green, 1994). We recognize, however, that crime events may be linked across street segments. For example, a drug market may operate across a series of blocks (Weisburd and Green, 1995; Worden, Bynum, and Frank, 1994), and a large housing project and problems associated with it may traverse street segments in multiple directions (see Skogan and Annan, 1994). Nonetheless, we thought the street segment offers a useful compromise because it allows a unit of analysis large enough to avoid unnecessary crime coding errors, but small enough to avoid aggregation that might hide specific trends.

For this study, we operationalized the definition of street segments by referring directly to the geography of streets in Seattle. Prior studies have generally relied upon what are often defined as hundred blocks to approximate the geography of street segments (e.g., Groff, Weisburd, and Morris, 2009; Weisburd et al., 2004, Weisburd, Morris, and Groff, 2009). In this approach, researchers assume that the actual streets in a city follow the overall rule that a street segment includes addresses ranging a hundred numbers, for example from 1–100, or 101–200. While this approach is common and identifies broadly the geography of street segments in the city, we wanted our study to match as much as possible the reality of the behavior settings of streets between intersections. Because of shortcomings in the addressing scheme of Seattle (as in many other cities), hundred block ranges were not always confined to a single street segment between two intersections but sometimes spanned street segments. Using a geographically-based file to create the street segments involved a great deal of additional effort, but it ensured that the unit of analysis in our study fit our theory of street segments as behavior settings.[10] We thought this particularly important given our desire to go beyond previous descriptive studies in the criminology of place to one that specified the specific relationships between characteristics of those places and crime.

Only residential and arterial streets were included in our study. The street centerline file we obtained from Seattle GIS included many different "line" types (e.g., trails, railroad and transit lines to name a few). We thought that such transportation throughways as railroad and transit lines could make for interesting study but were not relevant to our attempt to examine crime in the behavior settings of street segments. We also excluded limited-access highways because of their lack of interactive human activity. Our study included only residential streets, arterial streets, and walkways/stairs connecting streets. This left us with 24,023 street segments.

STUDYING CRIME AT STREET SEGMENTS

We used computerized records of crime incident reports to represent crime. Incident reports are generated by police officers or detectives after an initial response to a request for police service. In this sense, they represent only those events that were both reported to the police and deemed to be worthy of a crime report by the responding officer. Incident reports are more inclusive than arrest reports, which are only produced when an arrest is made, but less inclusive than emergency calls for service—which include all events reported to the police whether they are confirmed or not. We did not consider using arrest reports because they are generally seen as too restrictive a view of crime problems, drawing only a very select group of crime events (Warner and Pierce, 1993). While previous studies have sometimes argued that calls for service are less likely to selectively identify crime events than crime incidents (Black, 1970; Sherman, Gartin, and Buerger, 1989), or that crime incidents are conversely less likely to include false crime events, or to misclassify events because they are based on citizen reports with investigation (Schneider and Wiersema, 1990), our choice of incidents was driven in good part by the data available. In Seattle, as most other cities we contacted, emergency call data are generally discarded much more quickly than incident data. Seattle kept valid emergency call information for only six years, but had valid data available on crime incidents since 1989. A previous study in Seattle that compared crime incidents and crime calls found that they generally produced similar distributions of crime across place in Seattle (Lum, 2003).

We examine crime only on street segments and not on intersections in Seattle. Overall, more than 80% of crime incidents were associated with street segments. There are two main reasons for excluding intersection crime, one technical and one substantive. Technically, intersections result from the junction of two or more street segments. Thus, each intersection is "part of" multiple street segments, and there is no direct way to link intersections to a specific street segment.[11] It is also the case that incident reports at intersections differed dramatically from those at street segments. Traffic-related incidents accounted for only 4 percent of reports at street segments, but for 45 percent of reports at intersections. In this sense, the street segments represent a very different behavior setting than the intersections to which they are attached.

We also excluded two other types of records from our study.[12] When the location on the incident was given as a police precinct or police headquarters, we did not code the incident to the street segment where the police building was located. The use of a police precinct's address as a location of a crime is common, according to the Seattle police department, when no other address can be ascertained by the reporting officer. In turn, the database for the city of Seattle also initially included crimes, which when geocoded were found to be outside the city limits. This resulted from the city of Seattle including bordering areas in its crime data system. We were left with 1,697,212 crime records that were then joined to their corresponding street segments so that crime frequencies for each of the 24,023 segments for each year could be calculated.

What Follows

In the next chapter, we examine why the criminology of place focuses so strongly on small geographic units by reviewing more generally the role of crime and place in criminology since the founding of the discipline. Importantly, as we illustrate there has been a consistent trend over the last two centuries of moving the lens of criminological interest to smaller and smaller units of geography. We also examine the key theoretical perspectives that we will consider in understanding and explaining crime at place, focusing both on what we term opportunity theories and social and structural theories of crime.

In chapter 3, we turn to the key question of the concentration of crime at place. Our work here replicates that conducted in prior studies (see Weisburd et al., 2004; Weisburd, Morris, and Groff, 2009), and lays the groundwork for linking social disorganization and opportunity factors to crime trends. As in prior studies, we find evidence of strong stability of crime trends over time, while identifying a series of distinct developmental trajectories of crime at street segments over the period observed. Chapter 4 examines the geographic distribution of these trajectory patterns and then asks to what extent there is clustering of specific crime patterns in specific places. This chapter deals with the crucial "geography" of developmental patterns of crime. Most importantly, do our data suggest that a large part of the variability of crime is located at the micro place level (i.e., street segment in our study)? Or is there evidence of strong area trends in our data? Or do we find evidence of both area and local trends?

In chapter 5, we examine the distribution of routine activities and crime opportunities at street segments. How do crime opportunities in a city differ across place and time? Are places in which routine activities encourage crime likely to be spread across the city, or are such places clustered in certain areas? Are there hot spots of opportunities for crime as there are hot spots of crime?

Much is known about the distribution of social disorganization and social capital at macro levels across the urban landscape (Bursik and Grasmick, 1993; Sampson, 1985; Sampson, Raudenbush, and Earls, 1997; Sampson, Morenoff, and Gannon-Rowley, 2002; Sampson and Groves, 1989; Sampson and Morenoff, 2004; Shaw and McKay, 1942 [1969]; Shaw, 1929). However, in chapter 6 we provide the first examination of which we are aware of this distribution at a micro place level such as the street segment. Importantly, as in chapter 5, a key question here is whether there are hot spots of social disorganization at street segments, as there are hot spots of crime.

In chapter 7, we explore the basic relationships between the developmental patterns of crime described in chapter 3 and social disorganization and opportunity variables identified in chapters 5 and 6. We begin by developing an overall model of factors that influence developmental trends of crime at place. This model allows us to compare and contrast the importance of social disorganization and opportunity theories for understanding crime at place. Which theories have the most explanatory power in understanding overall trends, or in explaining specific developmental processes? We then examine specifically what characteristics of places distinguish hot spots of crime from places with little or no crime, or places that experience "crime waves" from "crime drops."

Finally, in chapter 8 we summarize our findings, and describe their implications for theory and practice in crime and justice. Criminology has been focused on people or places at macro levels of geography. Our work demonstrates the importance of the development of a "criminology of place," to complement traditional criminological perspectives. In concluding, we focus on the implications of our work for policy and practice. What are the policy prescriptions suggested by our study? How can they be implemented?

{ 2 }

Putting Crime in Its Place

Criminology has been predominantly concerned with people, and in particular with understanding why offenders come to commit crimes. But as we noted in chapter 1, there has also been a long history of interest in place in criminology. Indeed, geographic analysis of crime played a critical role in the founding generations of criminology in Europe and was also an important catalyst for criminological innovation for the founders of American criminology. In this chapter, we describe these trends, focusing in particular on the ways in which the "criminology of place" differs from traditional interests in place in criminology.

Two themes are particularly important in this regard. The first is the movement from large areas of geography, often defined by administrative units of government, to very small units fit to the geography of crime in the city. As we will argue below, studying crime at micro units of place is not only fit to the specific contexts that recent theories have suggested, but also allows us to avoid important methodological limitations of prior work. The second theme is linked to the theoretical backdrop for understanding the criminology of place. As we will describe below, the predominant themes of place in criminology have been linked to social or structural theories. The role of social disorganization as reflected in such factors as poverty, social heterogeneity, and collective efficacy has been the key concern of scholars who have studied crime at higher levels of geography. In contrast, as we noted in chapter 1, theories that emphasize the opportunity structures for crime have been the primary sources for theoretical explanation of the criminology of place. We argue in this chapter that there is strong reason for "theoretical integration" in study of the criminology of place (Bernard and Snipes, 1996), in which both opportunity perspectives and social disorganization theory are used to understand variability in crime at micro units of geography.

Putting Crime in Its Place

Perhaps the first observation of crime's link to place came with the publication
of statistics on the French population summarized in very large areas, or *départements*, by the French Home Office in the 1820s.[1] The publication of the
Comptes Générales de l'administration de la justice criminelle en France inspired
many statisticians and other scholars to explore data on crime in more detail.
In 1829, the first geographical map of crime was published. Partly based on the
Comptes Générales de l'administration de la justice criminelle en France, Michel-
André Guerry and the Venetian cartographer Adriano Balbi published on one
large sheet three maps on the distribution of crime in France in the years 1825–
1827 (see figure 2.1). It was a novelty in the new field of criminology that they
made use of a cartographic method of presenting statistical material. Their

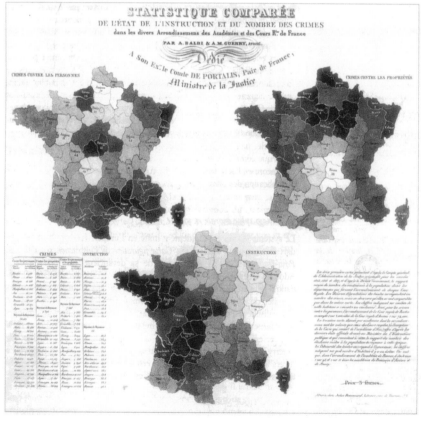

FIGURE 2.1 *Maps Comparing Crime and Social Characteristics in France*
Source: Balbi and Guerry (1829)

work was to emphasize an enduring interest of criminologists with urbanization and crime. They found that in urban areas, especially in the capital of Paris, the highest numbers of property and personal crimes could be observed.

Later, when Guerry became head of the Crime Statistics Unit of the French Ministry of Justice, he continued his work on mapping crime. In 1833, his influential *Essai sur la statistique morale de la France* was published (Guerry, 1833). Inspired by the Reform Movement[2] of the nineteenth century, Guerry examined whether poverty and density of population might lead to higher crime rates. He observed, however, an empirical complexity. The rich north *départements* were confronted with higher property crime rates than the poor *départements* in the south of France. He concluded that the level of poverty was not the direct cause of crime. Similarly, his data suggested that population density was not a cause of crime. His friend Alexandre Parent-Duchâtelet published in 1837 an empirical study containing maps on the distribution of prostitution from 1400 until 1830 in Paris (Parent-Duchâtelet, 1837). Because of the official control of brothels by the Paris authorities, systematic data were available on prostitutes, especially from the years 1817 to 1827. Even information regarding the *départements* where they came from was collected. Not surprisingly, the center of the city had the highest number of prostitutes. He used neighborhoods, as defined by administrative boundaries, as units of analyses.

The French scholar Michel-André Guerry is often bracketed together with the Belgium statistician and astronomer Adolphe Quetelet, who discovered the normal distribution in statistics with which deviations can be observed and calculated (Landau and Lazarsfeld, 1968). Quetelet (1831 [1984]) also used large areal units such as provinces and countries as units of analyses. He explained the higher rates of property crimes of the richer provinces by the unequal distribution of wealth: a great number of people possess nothing compared to the relatively few rich citizens (Quetelet, 1831 [1984]: 38). Reflecting the focus of late twentieth-century criminologists on opportunity and crime (e.g., see Cohen and Felson, 1979; Felson and Clarke, 1998), Quetelet concluded that poverty was not in itself the cause of crime, but rather that crime develops when the poor and disadvantaged "are surrounded by subjects of temptation and find themselves irritated by the continual view of luxury and of an inequality of fortune" (1831[1984]: 38).

These French and Belgian scholars were the first who scientifically analyzed crime at place. They focused on the administrative and political borders of their time in their geographical crime analyses and began to raise key issues related to poverty, urbanization, population heterogeneity, and even crime opportunities in understanding crime problems, though as we have seen they did not always come to singular conclusions. Nations, regions, counties, provinces, *départements*, and *quartiers* were the units of analyses, and they were used as a unit for systematic comparisons of crime figures. These scholars were fully dependent on official crime data and other data arranged within these larger geographic units that the government defined. While the early French and Belgian researchers concerned with the geography of crime also examined some variability of crime within cities, their overall focus was generally on larger administrative units. Importantly, these early criminologists in their focus on crime rates and official statistics also helped to encourage the more general development of a positivist empirical criminology (Beirne, 1987).

PIONEERS IN ENGLAND IN THE NINETEENTH CENTURY

France and Belgium were not the only countries where studies of crime at place were carried out in the nineteenth century. Members of the Statistical Society of London also regularly published on crime topics in their statistical journal. In 1839, an August 1835 lecture by William Greg on the spatial distribution of population density, fertility, education, and crime in the Netherlands[3] for the British Association for the Advancement of Science was published by Ridgway, Harrison, and Crosfield. He compared the crime figures on property crimes, violent crimes, and serious crimes like rape, murder, and manslaughter in the Netherlands with those of England and France. The overall crime figures showed remarkable differences (Greg, 1839: 15) reinforcing earlier findings of the importance of large geographic areas in understanding crime.

Rawson W. Rawson (1839), then secretary of the Statistical Society of London, illustrated the critical role that the unit of analysis can play in the development of our understanding of crime at place. He was the first scholar to go beyond the usual administrative and political borders (Morris, 1957: 55). Based on official data, he found that large cities had the highest crime rates and mining areas the lowest. His successor at the society, Joseph Fletcher, continued the work of Guerry and Rawson. He studied for many years the relationship between education and crime by producing maps showing the levels of crime and illiteracy of England and Wales (later published in Fletcher, 1850). He argued that not only were differences between regions important in the explanation of crime rates, but also so was the speed with which these regions changed over time economically and demographically. With these ideas Fletcher (1850) can be seen as a precursor of the French sociologist Emile Durkheim, who introduced the concept of anomie to explain the impact of societal changes on people and society (Durkheim, 1893 [1964]).

John Glyde (1856) was the first to question the validity of the research findings when large areas were chosen as units of analysis in geographic criminology. In his paper "Localities of crime in Suffolk," he showed very clearly that larger units of analysis hide underlying variations in crime. When smaller units than districts or *départements* were taken into account, significant differences in crime rates across smaller areas appeared. As Morris (1957: 58) notes: "Of the regional studies, a major criticism is that the county was the smallest territorial unit considered, but Glyde, by breaking Suffolk down into its seven-teen Poor Law Unions was able to demonstrate that the 'County Aggregate' masked considerable differences between the smaller geographical units of which it was composed."

In studies of the geography of crime in England in the nineteenth century, the work of Henry Mayhew is particularly important. He is well known in crimi-nology (and cited therefore) for his descriptive studies of the underworld of London in the middle Victorian Age (1851 [1950]). However, Mayhew also tried to uncover patterns in the distribution of crime in the city of London by combining ethnographic methods with statistical data. He interviewed prosti-tutes, criminals, and other citizens about alcoholism, poverty, housing conditions, and economic uncertainty. He was the first scholar who focused on small areas like squares, streets, and buildings as units of analysis in criminological research, predating modern interests in the criminology of place by over a century.

CHICAGO AND THE DYNAMICS OF CITIES: NEIGHBORHOODS AS UNITS OF ANALYSIS

After the turn of the century, the locus of geographic research on crime moved to the United States, and especially to the city of Chicago. At the University of Chicago, a group of sociologists undertook new research on urban problems, which centered, in part, on delinquency (Beirne and Messerschmidt, 1991; Bulmer, 1984; Faris, 1967; Harvey, 1987). They also moved the action of crime and place research from broad comparisons across large geographic areas to more careful comparisons within cities. Interestingly, the Chicago School scholars were either not aware of or ignored until 1933 the work of nineteenth-century crime and place researchers in Europe (Elmer, 1933). At this point, a group of American sociologists, among them Robert Park, William Thomas, Louis Wirth, Ernest Burgess, Clifford Shaw, and Henry McKay, took a leader-ship role in the development of geographic criminology, in contrast to the stat-isticians, criminal lawyers, or psychiatrists who dominated criminology more generally in Europe (Vold, Bernard, and Snipes, 2002).

William Thomas contributed to this work by introducing the important con-cept of "social disorganization," referring to "a decrease of the influence of existing social rules of behavior upon individual members of the group" (Thomas, 1966: 3). Though the Chicago sociologists studied many of the same variables as earlier European scholars, and especially those that focused on poverty and related social problems, they concentrated on neighborhoods or communities rather than much larger administrative areas. Robert Park, who was recruited by Thomas, was the initiator of urban social research on crime places, shifting the unit of analyses from countries and large areas to cities and their neighborhoods (Park, 1925 [1967]). The city in his opinion was more than:

a congeries of individual men and of social conveniences—streets, buildings, electric lights, tramways, and telephones, etc; something more, also,
than a mere constellation of institutions and administrative devices—
courts, hospitals, schools, police, and civil functionaries of various sorts.
The city is, rather, a state of mind, a body of costumes and traditions, and
of the organized attitudes and sentiments that inhere in these costumes
and are transmitted with this tradition. The city is not, in other words,
merely a physical mechanism and an artificial construction. It is involved
in the vital process of the people who compose it; it is a product of nature,
and particularly of human nature. (Park, 1925 [1967]: 1)

Park argued that urban life must be studied in this context in terms of "its
physical organization, its occupations, and its culture" and especially the
changes therein (Park, 1925 [1967]: 3). Neighborhoods in his view were the
elementary form of cohesion in urban life.

His younger colleague Ernest Burgess, drawing from an inventory of price
changes in housing values in Chicago areas, developed a concentric-zone
model of the distribution of social problems and crime (Burgess, 1925 [1967]).[4]
Burgess suggested that Chicago included five concentric zones (see figure 2.2),
each containing various neighborhoods, four of them situated around "The
Loop" (the business center of the city): "the typical processes of the expansion
of the city can best be illustrated, perhaps, by a series of concentric circles,
which may be numbered to designate both the successive zones of urban
extension and the types of areas differentiated in the process of expansion"
(Burgess, 1925 [1967]: 50). Burgess' unit of analysis was a series of neighborhoods within cities that share similar characteristics. He assumed that depending on the distances to the center and the special features of these zones, the
levels of crime would vary.

Clifford Shaw was one of the first Chicago sociologists to carry out exten-
sive empirical research on the geographical distribution of crime on the basis
of Burgess's zone model (Shaw, 1929). This study can be seen as a landmark in
the history of geographic studies of crime because of its detailed data collection, advanced methods, and innovative statistical tools. Based on the concentric-zone model of Burgess, he studied the distribution of truancy of young
people, juvenile delinquents, and adult offenders in Chicago. Assisted by
young researchers like Henry McKay, Frederick Zorbaugh, and Leonard
Cottrell, he defined communities as units of analyses (Abbott, 1997) but in
more detail than ever before in these kinds of studies. Shaw applied new techniques of examining spatial patterns. First, he introduced *spot maps* by plot-
ting the home address of thousands of juvenile offenders on a map of Chicago.
These were in many ways a precursor of the crime maps produced by recent
scholars concerned with the criminology of place (see figure 2.3). While Shaw
focused his theoretical interests on neighborhoods, the visual presentation of

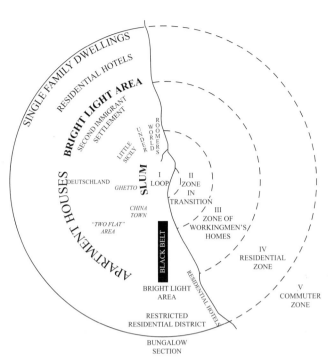

FIGURE 2.2 *Burgess's Concentric Zone Model of Chicago*
Source: Burgess (1925 [1967])

data allows the reader to consider crime at a very micro geographic level. Second, he combined the offender address data with census data to create *delinquency rate maps* of square mile areas. And finally, he constructed *radial maps* and *zone maps*, which displayed delinquency rates at regular distances from the city center (Snodgrass, 1976).

In the same year, Shaw's research assistant Harvey Zorbaugh published his dissertation in which he compared a slum neighborhood (The Lower North Side) with a wealthy area (Gold Coast) in Chicago, both situated in close proximity (Zorbaugh, 1929). In this more qualitative study, Zorbaugh presented only a few maps, all of them less detailed in information than Shaw's study. However, by examining two areas in close physical proximity his research demonstrated clearly that physical and social distances do not always coincide. Zorbaugh's work made it clear that administrative and political areas and social spaces are not identical. Depending on the size of the area, a variety of social communities with different identities can coexist. Importantly, he concluded that the smaller the unit of analysis, the greater the chance of a homogeneous community.

In 1942, Clifford Shaw and Henry McKay published their magnum opus, *Juvenile Delinquency and Urban Areas*, in which they not only presented their

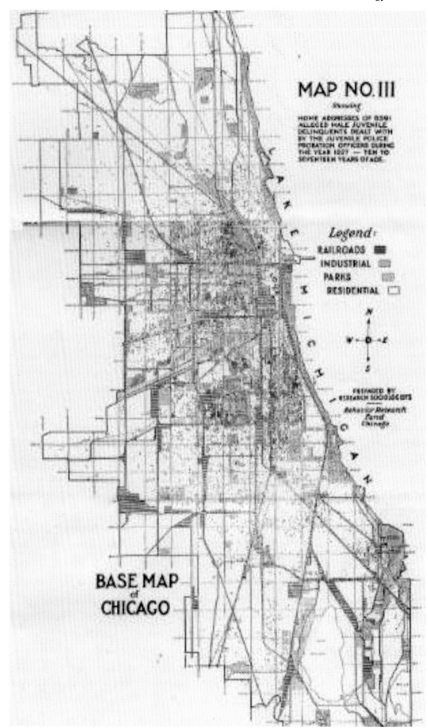

FIGURE 2.3 *Spot Maps of the Home Addresses of Juvenile Offenders Produced by Shaw*
Source: Shaw (1929)

geographical and etiological analyses of crime rates in the city of Chicago, but also those of other cities: Philadelphia, Boston, Cincinnati, Cleveland, and Richmond. In all of the studied cities, they found similar patterns in the geographical distribution of crime. The rapid changes in the city of Chicago over a long period of time enabled them also to study the effects of the dynamics of the city on crime and other phenomena. One of their findings was that "[t]he data on trends also demonstrate with equal sharpness the rapid rise in rates of delinquents in certain areas when a population with a different history and different institutions and values takes over areas in a very short period of time" (Shaw and McKay, 1942 [1969]: 382). This work established the idea of population heterogeneity as a key factor in the study of the geography of crime and criminology more generally.

The Chicago studies inspired other criminologists to carry out empirical research in other cities (e.g.,see Burgess and Bogue, 1964a, 1964b). At the same time, as the decades passed, empirical and methodological critics of the Chicago approach began to emerge (Lander, 1954). First, it was argued that Shaw (1929) and Shaw and McKay (1942 [1969]) had drawn conclusions about the distribution of crime based not on where crime occurred but where delinquents lived, neglecting the variability in the mobility of offenders (see also Boggs, 1965). Second, by relying on official crime figures, their research was seen as biased because offenders of the lower class had (and still have) a greater chance to be processed in the criminal justice system (e.g., see Beirne and Messerschmidt, 1991; Chilton, 1964; Gordon, 1967). Third, delinquency rates after 1945 in Chicago did not conform to the distribution patterns of Shaw and McKay's early assumptions (Bursik, 1984, 1986). European studies also showed contradicting results. Morris (1957) examined the offender rates of the county of Croydon, but could not confirm the zone model of Burgess. Twenty years later, Morris's findings were replicated in the city of Sheffield (Baldwin and Bottoms, 1976). In Europe, the direct and indirect consequences of the operation of housing markets produced very different geographical distributions of crime than in American cities.

Another criticism that is key to our focus on small micro units of analysis is that brought by Robinson (1950), who discussed the use of ecological correlations in large area geographical studies like that of Shaw and McKay (1942 [1969]). According to Robinson (1950: 351), the object of an ecological correlation is a group of persons, not a person: "...the individual correlation depends on the internal frequencies of the within-areas individual correlations, while the ecological correlation depends upon the marginal frequencies of the within-areas individual correlations" (Robinson, 1950: 354). Large areas may reflect similar average concentrations of data but have very different underlying structures. For example, an area classified as "middle income" may be composed of mostly middle-income residents, or it may be composed of very few middle-income residents but have many very rich residents and very poor residents.

Robinson presented the example of the relationship between immigration and literacy using U.S. state–level data. The correlation at the state level was strong and positive. But the actual correlation between immigration and literacy at the individual level was small and negative. The positive correlation at the state level came from the fact that immigrants tended to settle in states where the native population was overall better educated. He concluded more generally that ecological correlations drawn from large areas can be misleading in drawing conclusions about individual behavior.

Looking back, these empirical and methodological critiques diminished the interest of criminologists in studies of crime and place for almost 30 years.

REEMERGING INTEREST IN COMMUNITIES AND CRIME

In the 1980s, Albert J. Reiss Jr. encouraged a group of younger criminologists to return to the interests of the Chicago School where he had received his Ph.D. in 1949. Reiss (1986) saw the criminological tradition as including two major theoretical positions, one that focused on individuals and a second that focused on crimes. Communities and crime were a main focus of the latter tradition, and he sought to rekindle criminological interest in understanding variability of crime within and across communities. Editing an early volume in the *Crime and Justice* series, Reiss and Michael Tonry (1986) attempted to bring *Communities and Crime* to the forefront of criminological interests.

Reiss did not see the new interest as simply mimicking the insights of the Chicago School criminologists. Rather, he sought to raise a new set of questions about crime that had been ignored in earlier decades: "Recent work on communities and crime has turned to the observation that Shaw and McKay neglected: not only do communities change their structures over time but so often do their crime rates...a recognition that communities as well as individuals have crime careers" (Reiss 1986: 19). This volume and other work developed in this period drew upon the identification of neighborhoods and communities to expand insights about the development of crime (Bottoms, Claytor, and Wiles, 1992; Brantingham and Brantingham, 1981; Bursik and Webb, 1982; Hunter, 1988; Kobrin and Schuerman, 1981; LeBeau, 1987; Rengert, 1980, 1981; Roncek and Bell, 1981; Sampson, 1985; Sampson and Groves, 1989; Skogan, 1986; Stark, 1987).

Smith (1986), for example, identified neighborhood variation in the behavior of the police, suggesting the importance of communities in understanding not only the etiology of crime, but also the etiology of criminal justice. Skogan brought new insights not only to our understanding of the interaction of community characteristics and policing (Skogan, 1987), but also more generally to the developmental processes that led to the emergence of crime and disorder in urban communities (Skogan, 1990). More recently, scholars led by Robert Sampson have used a focus on the community to draw new insights into developmental crime patterns, arguing that social cohesion within communities, shared expectations of community members, and willingness to intervene for the common good combine to affect both crime and social disorder (Sampson and Raudenbush, 1999; Sampson, Raudenbush, and Earls, 1997). These insights are examined in our work in later chapters as they relate to small micro units of crime and place.

Consistent with Reiss's call for investigation of the criminal careers of communities, Bursik (1986; see also Bursik and Webb, 1982) revisited crime in Chicago neighborhoods over time and challenged earlier views of the stability of crime within neighborhoods and communities, arguing that stability in crime patterns was a result of long-term stability in the social characteristics of communities and that instability in such patterns would also lead to instability in crime rates. Similarly, Schuerman and Kobrin (1986) identified stability and variability in the criminal careers of communities, focusing on the residences of juvenile delinquents as had Shaw and McKay (1942 [1969]).

Interestingly, though the approach of the Chicago School called for the identification of units of geography that would be drawn not from administrative data collection, but from the social units that defined neighborhoods or communities, this new generation of scholars concerned with communities and crime have generally used officially defined units for drawing their data and conclusions. In this case, the U.S. Census definitions, most often census tracts or the smaller census block groups, have become the main source for defining the units of geography that are the focus of research in the United States. A census block group represents a cluster of census blocks that is a subdivision of a census tract; tracts typically contain one to nine block groups (U.S. Census Bureau, 1994). The average block group includes 39 square blocks (U.S. Census Bureau, 2005). Often such studies will assume that census units such as census tracts reflect actual community boundaries (Hipp, 2007), though some scholars in this area combine census units with the idea of creating boundaries of communities that are more consistent with the theoretical interests of researchers (e.g., see Sampson, Raudenbush, and Earls, 1997).

The Importance of Examining Crime at a Micro Geographic Level

The criminology of place represents a radical departure from traditional interests in place in criminology. As our short review suggests, traditionally the study of crime at place has focused on "macro" geographic units. This was certainly the case with the early nineteenth-century scholars concerned with the geography of crime and continues to be true as well for more recent inquiries into communities and crime. The criminology of place in contrast focuses on micro units of geography such as addresses, street segments, and small clusters of street segments. We have argued in chapter 1 that the street segment provides an appropriate unit for studying crime at place because it is an important "behavior setting" (Appleyard, 1981; Jacobs, 1961; Taylor, 1997) for understanding human interactions. Such units are much smaller than the census tracts or census block groups that have recently been used to define neighborhoods in studies of crime (e.g.,see Clear et al., 2003; Gorman et al., 2001; Sampson and Raudenbush, 2004).

George Rengert and Brian Lockwood (2009) note that the use of "ready-made" administrative units for the study of crime at place, irrespective of the level of analysis used, is problematic precisely because they are defined without reference to crime. What might make sense for understanding the distribution of the American population or structuring the delivery of the mail is not likely to be appropriate as a unit of analysis for understanding crime: "The problem is that most of these boundaries are constructed for administrative purposes rather than for reasons of sound research designs. For example, census boundaries are constructed for administrative purposes of the enumeration of the population, zip code boundaries for postal delivery, police districts for allocation of resources, and political boundaries for purposes of administrative responsibility" (Rengert and Lockwood, 2009: 110).

In this sense, the criminology of place has from the outset fit its units of analysis to its theoretical interests. Routine activities theory (Cohen and Felson, 1979; Felson, 2001), situational crime prevention (Clarke, 1980, 1983), and environmental criminology (Brantingham and Brantingham, 1981) naturally push the cone of geographic resolution to very low levels. The interactions of victims, offenders, and guardians occur in very specific geographic spaces. While routine activities theory can also be applied to crime trends in large geographic areas, it focuses the researcher on the specific places in which human activities are structured. Situational crime prevention also led researchers to a very low level of geography. Its interests in the specific situations of crime's occurrence focused researchers on specific places, such as bus stops, banks, or shopping centers (Clarke, 1992; Eck, 2002). Environmental criminology brought its focus to the very specific environments in which specific crimes developed and emphasized the "backcloth" that environments provide for specific crime events (Brantingham and Brantingham, 1993a, 1993b). Importantly, however, while pushing the geographic study of crime to much lower levels than traditional criminology, these theories did not specify a precise geographic unit for studying crime.

The availability of geographic data from police agencies coded at the address level meant that scholars were no longer necessarily constrained by the data available to them. In turn, the commercial availability of software for mapping crime and for spatial analysis also encouraged the exploration of crime at micro levels (Weisburd and McEwen, 1997). Of course, early innovators in this area will say that it was very difficult to map crime data when this area of research began to emerge, for example because the software was difficult to use and police departments did not collect address data accurately. Nonetheless, the difficulties facing crime and place researchers in the late 1980s and early 1990s did not begin to approach the time-consuming and tedious task that faced Shaw when he and his colleagues mapped the residences of 8,591 juvenile delinquents in Chicago 50 years earlier. And today, geographic information systems software has become relatively easy to use, and the police have come to recognize the importance of accurately linking crime data to geographic coordinates.

At what level should we study crime at place? As we have described above, there is an important trend over time toward study of crime at place at smaller units of geography. But does that trend reflect a fact about the level of geography that is important for understanding crime or is it simply a result of the specific data available and theoretical interests of scholars? Of course, we might question why the unit of geography should matter at all. Perhaps the best approach is one that is eclectic in its understanding of crime at place. In this sense, our study of street segments would simply reflect our interest in the theory of crime at these behavior settings.

While we do not discount the relevance of studying varying geographic units in coming to a more complete understanding of crime at place, it is important to recognize at the outset that studying crime at the "wrong" geographic unit may lead to a very misleading portrait of how place and crime interact. This was key to Glyde's observation more than 150 years ago that the examination of larger administrative districts hid important crime trends within those areas. In this context, examining crime patterns at larger geographic levels, even commonly used "smaller" units such as census tracts or census block groups, may mask significant lower order geographic variability.

If, for example, a census block group includes streets with very different patterns of crime, some decreasing and some increasing, the portrait gained when aggregating segments to the census block group would likely lead a researcher to conclude that there is overall a stable trend of crime over time (masking the contrasting trends at the street segment level). More generally, when there is a good deal of variability at a very local level of geography, we might in measuring higher order geographic units miss local area effects. This can be referred to as "averaging" and presents today, as in earlier decades, an important reason for studying crime at a very micro geographic level.

Such averaging can manifest itself in a number of ways that would lead to misleading interpretations of geographic data. A number of very active crime areas within a larger geographic unit might, for example, give the impression of an overall crime-prone area, when in fact most places in the larger geographic unit have low levels of crime. Similarly, when the vast majority of places have very little crime but a few very active places have very high crime counts, there can be a "washing out" effect. In some sense, a conclusion in such a case that the area overall has little crime is correct. However, such a conclusion would miss the very important fact that some places within the larger unit are "hot spots of crime."

Of course, this type of ecological fallacy may not only apply to studies that rely on larger geographic units. If the "action of crime" is at higher levels of geography, an approach that focuses only on lower-level variability can also be misleading. In this case, we might assume that there are important local effects, when they are simply reflecting higher-order influences. Take for example a study that examines street blocks and finds that a relatively small number of street blocks are responsible for a large proportion of crime. It may be that all of those street blocks are in one central area of the city. In this case, the focus on micro units of geography might obscure the importance of larger community or neighborhood effects.

Importantly, however, beginning with a micro-level approach allows the researcher to examine the influences of larger geographic units, while starting at higher levels of geography may preclude examination of local variability. This problem is similar to that presented when choosing levels of measurement. The general admonition is to collect data at the highest level of measurement (interval or ratio scales), since such data can be converted to lower levels of measurement (Weisburd and Britt, 2007). At the same time, data collected at lower levels of measurement (e.g., ordinal or nominal scales) cannot simply be disaggregated to higher levels. The same principal applies to geographic information, though the language is reversed. Collecting data at the lowest geographic level, or smallest units of analysis, allows us to examine how those trends relate to larger units of analysis at higher levels of geography. But data collection at larger units would not allow conversion to more micro units of analysis.

For this reason, our study uses a micro geographic unit—the street segment—as the basic unit of analysis. However, we recognize that the street segment is not the smallest unit of geography that can be used to study crime. Some scholars have argued for the importance of examining crime patterns across individual addresses or facilities (e.g., see Eck, Gersh, and Taylor, 2000). But as we argued in chapter 1, policing data may include significant coding errors regarding a crime's occurrence at the address level. We are much more confident in the accuracy of crime incident data at the street segment level, since getting the street of a crime's occurrence wrong is much less likely than mistaking the specific address location for a crime. Moreover, as we noted earlier, there is strong theoretical justification for the identification of street segments as key behavior settings for crime (see chapter 1).[5]

Examination of crime at the street segment level accordingly not only fits our theoretical interests but also will allow us to critically assess whether examination of crime at a very low level of geography adds important new knowledge to our understanding of the crime problem. If, for example, hot spot street segments are clustered primarily in a specific area or neighborhood, then we might argue that neighborhood or area effects are in fact the primary cause of high-activity street segments. But if crime patterns vary street by street, this would provide an important confirmation of the idea of behavior settings that we introduced in the first chapter. In chapter 4 we will examine this question directly, using spatial statistics to assess the extent to which there is variability across place in developmental crime patterns. As will be illustrated there, our findings strongly support the investigation of crime at micro levels of geography (see also Groff, Weisburd, and Yang, 2010).

Social Disorganization and Opportunity Theories: Recognizing the Importance of Theoretical Integration

A second way in which the criminology of place departs from traditional study of the geography of crime is in the predominant theoretical perspectives that have been used to explain crime variations across place. Criminology of place scholars have looked primarily to what can be termed "opportunity theories" (Cullen, 2010; Wilcox, Land, and Hunt, 2003) as an explanation for why crime trends vary at places and as a basis for constructing practical crime prevention approaches (e.g., see Eck, 1995a; Sherman, Gartin, and Buerger, 1989; Weisburd et al., 2004). Routine activities theory, situational crime prevention, and crime pattern theory all place great emphasis on the specific opportunities offered by specific places and situations. In contrast, study of crime at higher geographic levels has placed emphasis on the social characteristics of places, for example the socioeconomic levels of people who live in certain areas (Bursik and Grasmick, 1993; Sampson and Morenoff, 1997), or the degree to which there is strong population heterogeneity (Shaw and McKay, 1942 [1969]). Such perspectives may be grouped more generally as social disorganization theories (see Bursik, 1988; Kubrin and Weitzer, 2003; Sampson and Groves, 1989). As our historical review suggests, these themes are repeated again and again in traditional macro studies of place and crime.

We think it is striking that scholars who study the criminology of place have virtually ignored social disorganization theories in empirical analysis and theoretical discussion. In one sense this is understandable, since the impetus for study of micro crime places came from opportunity theories. Such theories justified examination of small geographic units because of their emphasis on the specific situations and contexts that make crime possible.

In this context, the neglect of social disorganization in the study of the criminology of place can be traced to what some scholars have called "theoretical competition" (Bernard, 2001; Bernard and Snipes, 1996). All theories cannot be right in this perspective (e.g., see Hirschi, 1979, 1989), and accordingly it is the job of criminologists to advance a single theoretical paradigm that can explain the phenomenon at hand. Advocates of this approach see the theoretical debate as one of competition, and the inclusion of multiple theories (when one perspective has particular theoretical salience) just muddies the water.

But a different perspective is interested in "theoretical integration" (e.g., see Elliott, 1985). As Bernard and Snipes write: "(w)e argue that integration is the appropriate approach because the theories primarily make different but not contradictory predictions" (1996: 302). In the context of theoretical integration, we would draw from multiple theories that can increase our overall understanding of the crime problem at micro levels of place. As Cullen (1988) notes, Cloward (1959) sought to integrate opportunity perspectives with traditional social disorganization ideas more than a half century ago. More recently, a number of criminologists have sought theoretical integration of opportunity and social disorganization theories at place, though their level of geographic analysis has been much higher than that which we propose (e.g., see Joiner and Mansourian, 2009; Wikström, et al., 2010; Wilcox, Madensen, and Tillyer, 2007).

Of course, theoretical integration of opportunity and social disorganization theories in a model for understanding crime at street segments does not make sense if social disorganization is a concept that is irrelevant to the criminology of place. This seems to be the position of many scholars in this area. Sherman, Gartin, and Buerger, for example, argued in introducing the idea of a criminology of place, that "(t)raditional collectivity theories [termed here as social disorganization theories] may be appropriate for explaining community-level variation, but they seem inappropriate for small, publicly visible places with highly transient populations" (1989: 30). Often this position is taken indirectly, simply by ignoring social disorganization theories (e.g., see Eck and Weisburd, 1995). Sometimes scholars have specifically recognized the potential relevance of social disorganization to the understanding of variations in crime at micro geographic levels (e.g., see Smith, Frazee, and Davison, 2000; Weisburd et al., 2004). However, such interest is the exception rather than the rule.

Is the concept of social disorganization "inappropriate" for understanding variability of crime at specific places? Scholars concerned with social disorganization have focused their interests on larger geographic areas, often communities, and have linked their theories to the ways in which the characteristics and dynamics of these larger social units influence crime. If indeed the only units of analysis relevant to social disorganization are large geographic units like communities or neighborhoods, then it is reasonable to say that social disorganization is irrelevant to the study of the criminology of place.

But another approach is possible, and we think relevant to the study of crime at small units of geography. Street segments, as we noted in chapter 1, do not simply represent physical entities. They are also social settings, or following Wicker (1987: 614) "behavior settings," which can be seen as "small-scale social systems." In this context, the street segments that we study in this book can be seen as examples of small-scale communities (see Taylor, 1997). As we noted in chapter 1, people who frequent a street segment get to know one another and become familiar with each other's routines. Residents develop certain roles they play in the life of the street segment (e.g., the busybody, the organizer). Norms about acceptable behavior develop and are generally shared. Blocks have standing patterns of behavior, for example people whose routines are regular like the mail carrier or the shop owner. In this context, we can see street segments as "micro communities" as well as "micro places." They have many of the traits of communities that have been seen as crucial to social disorganization theory, in that these physical units function also as social units with specific routines.

If the street segment can be seen as a type of "micro community," then social disorganization theory would seem to have direct relevance to our understanding of the criminology of place (see Rice and Smith, 2002; Smith, Frazee, and Davison, 2000; Taylor, 1997, in press). For example, street segments, like communities, are often dynamic with people moving in and out as well as shops opening and closing. Such transitions have often been seen to represent heightened social disorganization in studies of communities. In this context, it seems reasonable to ask whether high social mobility is related to crime at street segments. Similarly, poverty and social disadvantage have been identified as strongly related to crime at higher levels of geography. Is variability in wealth or social class at the street segment level also related to trends in crime? Of course, if we are to examine such relationships we have to first identify whether such characteristics vary at micro levels of geography. In chapter 6 we will turn our attention precisely to this issue. Do characteristics reflecting social disorganization vary at a street segment level of analysis, as they do across communities and neighborhoods? This is a critical empirical question, but it is one that prior studies have not systematically examined.

Conclusions

Places have been a concern in criminology for almost two centuries. But the criminology of place has brought the geographic cone of resolution for studying crime to a much lower level than traditional studies in this area. We argued in this chapter that the study of crime at street segments not only fits recent theoretical innovations in criminology, but also makes sense as a method for examining the geography of crime. A trend that has been evolving since the founding generations of geographical criminology is for studies to examine crime at smaller and smaller geographic levels. This is the case because scholars have often identified significant variation of crime within larger jurisdictional areas. We extend this idea, and argue that the study of crime at micro levels of geography is a necessary beginning to careful examination of the contributions of the criminology of place to our understanding of the crime problem.

We have also argued in this chapter for an approach that draws insights from the perspective of theoretical integration rather than theoretical competition. While the criminology of place has relied generally on opportunity theories to explain variation in crime at place, we note that the concept of "behavior settings" leads naturally to consideration of social and structural causes of crime at micro geographic units such as street segments. In this sense, social disorganization theories and opportunity theories should both be used to model variation of crime at the street segments we study. This approach, as we will see in chapter 7, leads to important new insights about the criminology of place.

Crime Concentrations and
Crime Patterns at Places

The emergence of the criminology of place is tied tightly to the idea that crime is not uniformly patterned across cities but is concentrated at specific places termed crime hot spots. In this chapter, we examine the concentration of crime at street segments in Seattle, Washington. Is crime concentrated at a relatively small number of street segments in the city? Conversely, are the great majority of street segments free of crime? Our work here replicates earlier studies in the criminology of place, though we are able to look at 16 years of data, which is the longest time series we are aware of that has been reviewed at a very small level of geography. This long time series of data also allows us to examine trends in crime concentrations over time.[1] Do crime hot spots or cool spots remain relatively stable over time? Are there specific groups of places that seem to evidence developmental trajectories over time, for example increasing or decreasing trends over the 16-year observation period?

Our data also allow us to consider crime trends in a different context than traditional studies of crime in cities. During the 1990s, most American cities, including Seattle (see below), experienced a crime drop (Blumstein and Wallman, 2000; Levitt, 2004). Ordinarily, discussions of crime trends focus on the overall crime trends across cities, and give the impression of crime changes operating similarly for most places in a city. Our work allows us to consider the crime drop in terms of trends at very small units of geography. Was there a general crime drop across street segments in Seattle? Or was the crime drop concentrated at very specific places? Or perhaps, were there "crime waves" at some street segments even during a period of an overall drop in crime in the city?

We begin the chapter by reviewing descriptively the concentration of crime at street segments in Seattle. We then turn to an examination of developmental patterns of crime, drawing from a statistical approach that allows us to place the street segments in our sample into groups with similar crime "trajectories" over time. Finally, we examine the "crime drop" in Seattle in the study period from the perspective of the criminology of place, illustrating the importance of examining crime trends at very micro units of geography.

Is Crime Concentrated at Street Segments?

As we described in chapter 1, we linked almost 1.7 million crime incidents in Seattle between 1989 and 2004 to the 24,023 street segments in the sample. Table 3.1 provides the overall distribution of incident reports in our 16 observation years. The most common was property crime (52.2 percent) followed by disorder, drug and prostitution offenses (14.4 percent), and violent person-to-person crime (10.7 percent). Another 18.9 percent of the incident reports were defined in various categories such as weapon offenses, violations, warrants, domestic disputes, missing persons, juvenile-related offenses, threats, and alarms. The remaining events were coded as traffic-related or unknown.[2]

Looking at crime incidents overall, our data at street segments suggest a "crime drop" at least since 1992 in Seattle (see figure 3.1). Between 1989 and 2004, Seattle street segments experienced a 24 percent decline in the number of incidents recorded at street segments (from 121,869 in 1989 to 93,324 in 2004). This "crime drop" in Seattle follows the pattern of crime in the nation generally during this period (Blumstein and Wallman, 2000), and is similar in magnitude to the national trend.[3]

Interestingly, a considerable number of street segments in Seattle experienced no crime incidents at all during this 16-year period. About 9.2

TABLE 3.1 Percentage of Total Incident Reports at Street Segments for Each General Type

Type of Incident Report	%
Property Crimes (any form of theft, burglary, property destruction)	52.24%
Disorder, Drugs, Prostitution	14.38%
Person Crimes (homicide, any type of assault, rape, robbery, kidnapping)	10.68%
Other Non-Traffic Crime-Related Events (e.g., weapon offenses, violations, warrants, domestic disputes, missing persons, juvenile related, threats, and alarms)	18.90%
Traffic-related (hit and run, drunk driving, accidents with injuries)	3.77%
Unknown	0.02%
Total	100%

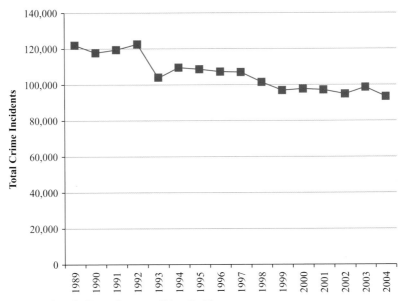

FIGURE 3.1 *Seattle Street Segment Crime Incidents*

percent of the street segments, or 2,218 streets, did not evidence a single crime incident between 1989 and 2004. The mean number of crime incidents per segment per year at street segments that had any crime was 4.42 (sd = 14.14).

Examined year by year, our data confirm findings from prior studies that indicate a strong concentration of crime in "hot spots" (see figure 3.2). Moreover, they suggest that the general concentration of crime in hot spots follows a consistent pattern over time. Between 4.7 and 6.1 percent of the street segments each year account for about 50 percent of crime incidents.[4] Eighty percent of the crime incidents each year are found on between 19 and 23 percent of the street segments, and all incidents are found on between 60 and 66 percent of the street segments each year.

A review of the crime counts at places reinforces our observation of a stability of crime concentrations over time. In figure 3.3, we report the percentage of street segments in each year with a specific number of incident reports. The overall distribution is fairly similar from year to year. The proportion of street segments with one to four incidents varies only slightly, between 38.4 percent and 41.0 percent. The proportion with more than 50 recorded crime events in a year is even more stable at approximately 1 percent across all 16 years. The proportion of street segments with no crime incidents varied somewhat more than this, between 34 percent and 41 percent, perhaps reflecting the overall crime decline since the earlier periods are likely to have on average fewer street segments with no crime incidents.

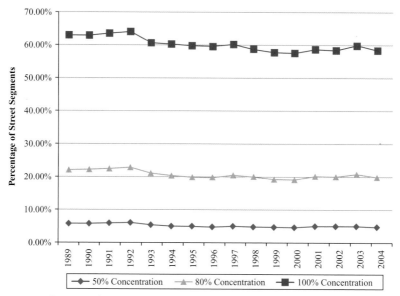

FIGURE 3.2 *Crime Incident Concentrations*

A LAW OF CRIME CONCENTRATIONS

When looking at the distribution of crime incidents year to year in Seattle, we find that crime is strongly concentrated at street segments (see also Weisburd et al., 2004). That concentration is consistent across the 16 years we examine whether we look simply at the proportion of street segments that account for 50 percent, 80 percent, or 100 percent of the crime incidents or whether we look at the average counts per year. This finding is important, suggesting a kind of "law of crime concentrations" over time. It is important to note in this regard as well that such similar levels of crime concentrations at street segments occur during a period of a substantial crime decline. While the overall number of crimes declines by more than 20 percent, the relative concentrations of crime at place, especially at the most serious crime hot spots, remain similar.

Our data are particularly intriguing considering a theory of crime advanced by Emile Durkheim more than a century ago. Durkheim suggested that crime was not indicative of a pathology or illness in society, but at certain levels was simply evidence of the normal functioning of communities (Durkheim, 1895 [1964]). For Durkheim, the idea of a normal level of crime reinforced his theoretical position that crime helped to define and solidify norms in society. But our data suggest a different story about "normal levels" of crime. While the absolute levels of crime in Seattle varied across the 16-year study period, the extent of crime concentrations remained similar. Might this imply that there is a "normal level" of crime concentrations across very micro units of geography?

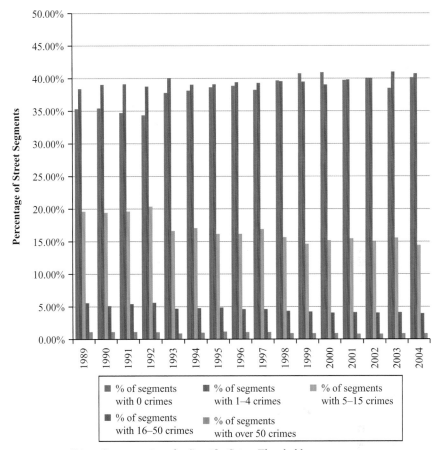

FIGURE 3.3 *Crime Concentrations for Specific Crime Thresholds*

Data from other studies appear to reinforce the idea of a constant level of concentration, at least across cities.[5] Sherman, Gartin, and Buerger (1989), in their analysis of data in Minneapolis, Minnesota in the mid-1980s, found that 3.5 percent of the addresses produced 50 percent of the crime calls. Pierce, Spaar, and Briggs (1988) found a remarkably similar concentration of crime at addresses in Boston, Massachusetts drawing data from about the same period. Also in Boston, Braga, Papachristos, and Hureau (2010) examined incidents of gun violence between 1980 and 2008. They too found incidents of gun violence were stable and concentrated at less than 3 percent of street segments and intersections. In an analysis replicating our Seattle study in Tel Aviv, Israel, Weisburd and Amram (forthcoming) find almost the same level of concentration of crime as reported here. Despite Tel Aviv being a city with very different characteristics, located more than half way across the world from Seattle, about 50 percent of the crime incidents in 2010 were also concentrated at just 5 percent of the street segments.

Accordingly, in analyses across cities we find concentrations that are very similar, and within Seattle we identify crime concentrations year to year that are almost identical. While much more research would need to be done within other cities before we can draw a very strong conclusion, we think that enough is known to speculate on a "law of crime concentrations" at places across time.

What might lead to this stability? It is important to note at the outset that the concentration of crime follows patterns of concentration in many other areas of scientific inquiry (e.g., see Bak, 1994; Eck, Clarke, and Guerette, 2007; Hill, Maucione, and Hood, 2007; Koch, 1999; Sherman, 2007). Joseph Moses Juran (1951) first noted this concentration in looking at economic activities, coining the phrase "the vital few and the trivial many." Juran sought to emphasize to managers that they should focus on the small number of events or cases that produce the majority of relevant business activities, for example the small number of defects that cause most complaints about products, or the small number of clients that are responsible for a majority of revenue.

Juran termed this phenomenon the "Pareto Principal" after Vilfredo Pareto (1909), who first brought attention to what is sometimes referred to as the 80–20 rule (see also Koch, 1999). Pareto observed that a number of distributions seem to follow this specific pattern of concentration. For example, in studying land ownership in Italy he found that 80 percent of the land was controlled by just 20 percent of the population. He also observed that 20 percent of the pea pods in his garden produced 80 percent of the peas. The 80–20 rule is generally seen only as an approximation, and indeed there are other concentration rules that have been noted—for example, the 90–10 rule as applied to computer processing (Lipovetsky, 2009). Crime follows closely Juran's observations of concentrations in business, and the 80–20 rule that is drawn from Pareto's work applies fairly well to our data in Seattle. Of course, the question remains, what leads to the tremendous concentration and stability of crime at micro geographic places over time?

We think a plausible explanation for stability within cities has to do with the stability of place characteristics over time. The physical structure of places, for example, is likely to be enduring in the sense that changes may take very long periods of time. We will return to this question in chapters 5 and 6 when we examine directly the characteristics of street segments over time. But the stability of characteristics of place would not explain the similarity in crime concentrations across cities. Perhaps this element of concentration relates to a natural concentration of "opportunities" for crime in the city. Or, perhaps, cities will naturally tolerate only a relatively small number of places that have very serious crime problems.

This again would bring us back to Durkheim, who saw the level of crime as representing a needed social form which helped to define and reinforce normative community values. By observing crime, people in society could define more clearly where the boundaries of normative behavior lie. It may be that crime hot spots have the same functions in modern societies. We will return to these questions in more detail in our conclusions in chapter 8 after we have better defined the longitudinal development of place characteristics that are associated with crime.

Developmental Patterns of Crime at Place

Though the proportion of street segments with a specific threshold of crime activity remains fairly consistent year to year, it may be that the specific segments within each of these thresholds change. For example, though a similar proportion of hot spot street segments are found to produce 50 percent of the crime each year, the specific street segments involved could be different each year. This would, for example, suggest a law of concentrations, but not stability of crime concentrations at specific places year to year. This is not an outlandish possibility as there is a well-known principal in statistics termed "regression to the mean" (Galton, 1886), which predicts that cases with extreme values are likely to return to average levels over time. Perhaps specific street segments are hot for a year or two and then cool down, while others that were cooler become hot and replace them.

This model is not consistent with the "tight coupling" of crime and place that we introduced in chapter 1. Tight coupling suggests that specific places have specific characteristics that lead them to become hot spots of crime. Unless those characteristics change rapidly, we would expect hot spots of crime to remain hot over long periods of time (e.g., over multiple annual measurements). Of course, places may change over time, and this also would lead us to expect changes in the rates of crime at those places. Accordingly, it is important to identify not only the general patterns of street segments over time, but also how each of the 24,023 street segments' crime frequencies changed. This descriptive exercise on the aggregate data leads to two key questions. First, is the stability evidenced in our simple descriptive analysis of the proportion of places with a specific threshold of crime in a specific year replicated if we examine the developmental patterns of offending of places over time? Do the hottest street segments remain hot throughout the study period? Do "cool segments" remain cool? Second, are there different patterns of crime over time for different groups of street segments? For example, are there specific groups of street segments that evidence declining trends over time or specific groups of places that evidence "crime waves"? Evidence of crime waves in Seattle would be of particular interest, because of the general description of the period of our study as a time of a "crime drop" in Seattle and other American cities.

The tracking of developmental patterns over time is not a simple statistical process. It is easy to understand the difficulties when one considers that in our data there are more than 24,000 street segments, each in some sense with its own "trajectory" or crime pattern over time. Of course, many street segments will have similar trajectories. We have already seen that about 9 percent of the street segments in Seattle have no crime at all during the study period. This is an easy-to-classify pattern, as it represents a "no crime" trajectory. Classifying the other street segments is much more difficult, especially since there are an unending number of potential developmental patterns.

In recent years, social scientists have developed a number of statistical techniques to deal with such data in the case of human development (Bryk and Raudenbush, 1987, 1992; Goldstein, 1995; McArdle and Epstein, 1987; Meredith and Tisak, 1990; Muthén, 1989; Nagin, 1999, 2005; Nagin and Land, 1993; Willet and Sayer, 1994). All of them draw from the idea that developmental patterns represent a dynamic process that must be modeled by the specific statistical analyses that are used. Previously, social scientists had often examined such developmental processes using static models, for example that predicted the final outcomes of a developmental process with specific characteristics at specific times earlier in that process. The problem of course is that this approach simply assesses one stage of development (e.g., the final outcome), failing to recognize that there may be developmental processes that operate much earlier.

For our examination of developmental patterns of crime at place, we use a statistical approach developed by Nagin (1999, 2005) and Nagin and Land (1993) called group-based trajectory analysis. This approach provides a simple descriptive portrait of the patterns of data in our study. In particular, it allows us to identify patterns at the individual street segment level over the 16 years of observation and then group those patterns into distinct developmental trajectories. In this sense, it clusters our data in such a way that we are left with a relatively small number of groups, which can then be examined and analyzed using standard statistical methods. Importantly, group-based trajectory analysis has been used in a number of studies of developmental patterns of individual criminality (e.g., Blokland, Nagin, and Nieuwbeerta, 2005; Bushway, Sweeten, and Nieuwbeerta, 2009; Nagin, 1999; Nagin and Tremblay, 1999, 2001; Nagin, Farrington, and Moffitt, 1995). More recently, it has also been applied to crime places at different levels of geography (Griffiths and Chavez, 2004; Weisburd et al., 2004; Weisburd, Morris, and Groff, 2009).

Formally, the model specifies that the population is composed of a finite number of groups of individuals or trajectories that follow distinctive developmental trajectories. Each such group is allowed to have its own offending trajectory (a map of offending rates throughout the time period) described by a distinct set of parameters that are permitted to vary freely across groups. A key component of the analysis is what is called the "posterior probability," which specifies the likelihood that any given street segment should belong to a specific trajectory. The determination of the optimal model depends on many things:

the Bayesian Information Criterion (BIC), the posterior probability, the odds of correct classification (OCC), and the substantial meaning of the groups (for more information about the decision-making process underlying the final model selection, see appendix 1). In this context, it is important to recognize that group assignments are made with error (see Nagin, 2005; Roeder, Lynch, and Nagin, 1999).[6]

While trajectory analysis is useful to reduce complicated phenomenon into some manageable patterns, some scholars have criticized its utility as a theory-testing tool to support crime typologies (Laub, 2006; Moffitt, 2006; Skardhamar, 2010). The argument centers on the issue of whether the latent groups extracted from trajectory analysis are "real and distinct." It is possible and even likely that the boundaries of such groups are not precise. Accordingly, especially when comparing groups that are similar in level of crime and pattern over time, caution should be used (see Eggleston, Laub, and Sampson, 2004; Skardhamar, 2010).[7]

In some sense, this reflects the costs associated with a statistical technique that allows us to more easily interpret and analyze the patterns of crime at place. Any grouping or clustering of cases risks arbitrary cutoffs, for example when we try to compare individuals of different ages by converting a continuous distribution such as age to an ordinal distribution such as categories of age (e.g., ages 10–15 versus ages 16–20). Making sense of our data demands that we try to categorize and simplify the distributions or patterns of crime at place. Moreover, the dangers of misclassification (see Eggleston, Laub, and Sampson, 2004; Skardhamar, 2010) become much less when we compare distributions that differ greatly. For example, in later chapters we develop models that distinguish very-high-rate trajectory groups from a "no crime" trajectory, or an increasing to a decreasing trajectory.

The trajectory approach is particularly useful when there is, as in our case, no strong theoretical basis from prior studies to make a priori assumptions regarding the basic patterns over time that may be observed (Muthén, 2001; Nagin, 1999, 2005; Raudenbush, 2001). In other words, trajectory analysis is extremely useful as a summarizing tool to extract basic patterns existing in the population, which is also the main purpose of applying this method in our study (Skardhamar, 2010).

In developing this analysis, we had to identify a distribution that would be appropriate for analyzing data like ours that reflect "counts" of crime (i.e., numbers of crimes at specific street segments). We found that the Zero Inflated Poisson (ZIP) distribution provided the best fit to our data.[8] In choosing the number of groups or trajectories, we relied upon the Bayesian Information Criteria (BIC), because conventional likelihood ratio tests are not appropriate for defining whether the addition of a group improves the explanatory power of the model (D'Unger et al., 1998).[9] In addition to the BIC, trajectory analysis also allows the researcher to consider the utility of group assignments relying

on the posterior probabilities of trajectory assignments, the odds of correct
classification, and using visual displays of the data (see later) to identify whether
meaningful groups are revealed (for a more detailed discussion, see Nagin,
2005).

In terms of the procedure used to identify the optimal model, we followed
the exhaustive approach detailed in Nagin (2005). That is, we tested for all possible combinations of numbers of groups and polynomial order of each trajectory. After reviewing the Bayesian Information Criteria and the patterns
observed in each solution, it was determined that a 22-group model was optimal
for understanding the crime data at street segments. More detail about the pro-
cedures used for this analysis can be found in appendix 1.

The validity of this solution was confirmed when we reviewed the posterior
probabilities for the different trajectories.[10] If such probabilities are high, it
means on average that the fit of the street segments to that trajectory is very
good. Nagin (2005) recommends that the posterior probabilities for specific
trajectories be above 0.70. The majority of the within-group posterior probabilities in our model are above 0.90, and the lowest posterior probability
is 0.77.

Figure 3.4 illustrates the 22-group model we obtained using the group-based
trajectory approach. The figure presents the actual average number of crime
incident reports per street segment found in each trajectory group each year
over the 16-year time period. The figure also lists the number and proportion
of street segments found in each trajectory. The main purpose of trajectory
analysis is to identify the underlying heterogeneity in the population. What is
most striking, however, in our analysis is the tremendous stability of crime at
street segments over a long period of time. While there are, as we discuss below,
important developmental patterns, for the vast majority of street segments in
our analysis, there is a relative stability of crime patterns over time.

CRIME TRAJECTORIES: STABLE PATTERNS

To simplify our description we divided the trajectory groups from figure 3.4
into eight developmental "patterns" representing the main levels of crime and
crime trends we observe. The first pattern represents simply the street segments
in our study that can be seen as relatively "crime free" during this period (see
figure 3.5). Almost half of all of the street segments we studied can be classified
in this trajectory pattern. Though there are differences between the specific trajectory groups included—between those places that have no crime at all and
those with very infrequent events at distant intervals of time—they represent
more generally the fact that about half of the street segments in Seattle have
little or no crime and that this pattern is stable over time.

The fact that half of all street segments in Seattle experienced almost no
crime during the study period reinforces the observation we introduced in

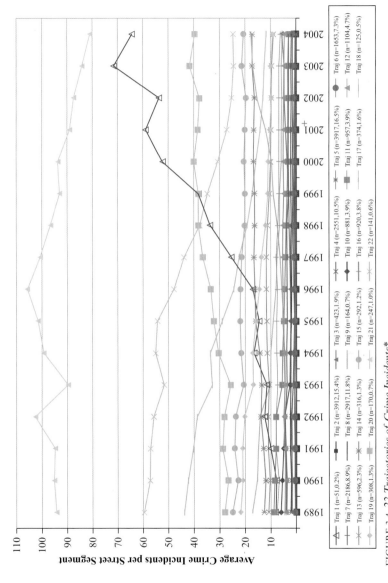

FIGURE 3.4 *22 Trajectories of Crime Incidents**

*Percentages refer to percentage of total street segments in that trajectory group.

chapter 1 that crime is tightly coupled to place, or in this context, that there are places where there is little connection between crime and place. If crime simply moved from place to place in the city, then we would expect crime concentrations to move across the city landscape. The fact that almost half the places in the city experience virtually no crime year after year during the study period suggests that they have characteristics that discourage crime. Of course, as a policy prescription, the identification of those characteristics is important. If we can identify why these streets do not experience crime, we can try to use that knowledge to develop crime prevention interventions for other streets where large numbers of crimes occur. This is a theme we will return to in more detail when we examine policy implications of our study in chapter 8.

An additional 30 percent of the street segments are associated with what we have termed a "low-stable" trajectory pattern (see figure 3.6). As with the relatively crime-free segments, these places evidence stable crime trends. While they cannot be defined as crime free, they certainly should not be categorized as

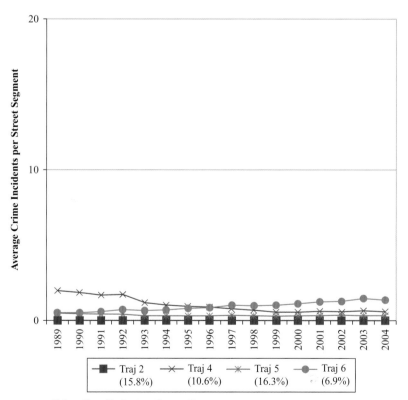

FIGURE 3.5 *Crime-Free Trajectory Pattern**

*Percentages refer to percentage of total street segments in that trajectory group.

crime hot spots. Street segments in three of the trajectory groupings that are included in this pattern (comprising about 22 percent of the street segments in Seattle) have on average consistently fewer than five crime incidents per year. Undoubtedly, this represents meaningful lower levels of crime. But whatever the level of crime for this trajectory pattern, it is clearly the case that these analyses more generally reinforce the simple descriptive finding that most places in the city have no crime or relatively low rates of crime.

What we term the "moderate-stable" trajectory pattern, including 1.2 percent of the street segments in Seattle, evidences much more serious levels of crime (see figure 3.7). At the same time, crime rates are again very stable across the 16 years of study. These street segments average between 20 and 25 crime incidents across the study period.

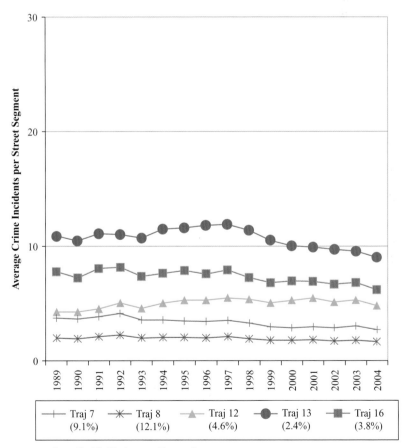

FIGURE 3.6 *Low-Stable Trajectory Pattern**

*Percentages refer to percentage of total street segments in that trajectory group.

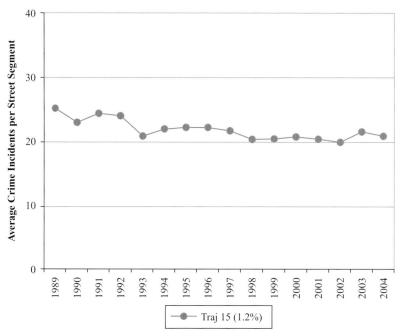

FIGURE 3.7 *Moderate-Stable Trajectory Pattern**
*Percentage refers to percentage of total street segments in that trajectory group.

What we term the "chronic-crime" pattern can be defined as the most serious crime hot spots in the city (see figure 3.8). While there is a slight declining trend for this crime pattern, the average number of crimes per segment is consistently more than 80 crime incidents per year. Between 1989 and 2004, the average number of crimes in the chronic hot spots decreased about 14.2 percent. But this was composed of a slight crime rise between 1989 and 1996 and a larger decline between 1996 and 2004. Importantly, whatever the variability across the observation period, street segments in this pattern were by far the most serious crime hot spots at the start of our study period and at the end. One percent of the street segments are found in this pattern, meaning that there are 247 street segments in the city with this very high and chronic level of crime activity. These 247 street segments account for fully 22 percent of the crime incidents in Seattle between 1989 and 2004.

We draw two key conclusions from our discussion so far. The first is that crime is very concentrated at a very small number of places in the city. In Seattle, just 247 street segments out of over 24,000 account for more than one-fifth of all crime incidents over a 16-year period. Eighty percent of street segments have little or no crime on them during the study period. As we will discuss in more detail in chapter 8, these data reinforce recent efforts to focus crime prevention on hot spots of crime (e.g., Braga 2005, 2007; Braga and Bond, 2008; Braga and Weisburd, 2010; Braga et al., 1999; Sherman and Weisburd, 1995; Weisburd and Green, 1995; Weisburd and Braga, 2006). Crime is not a problem endemic to the city; it is a problem concentrated at a small number of places.

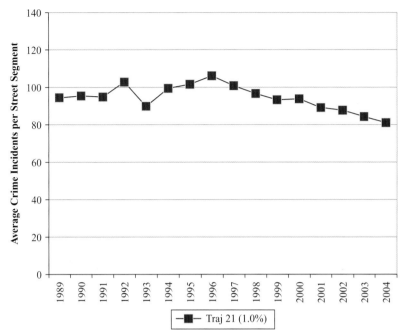

FIGURE 3.8 *Chronic-Crime Trajectory Pattern**

*Percentage refers to percentage of total street segments in that trajectory group.

The second conclusion is just as important and brings us back to our discussion in chapter 1 of the coupling of crime to place. Traditionally, criminologists have thought that crime was "loosely coupled" to place, and accordingly that the concentration of criminal justice agents at places was not likely to lead to strong crime prevention outcomes. While the concentration of crime at place suggests that assumption is wrong, our findings regarding the stability of crime, and in particular the stability of crime at crime hot spots, provide another strong piece of evidence that crime is "tightly coupled" to place. In Seattle, a single set of places evidenced the most serious and chronic crime trends across the study period. Especially if we assume that the police naturally would focus on such high-crime places, it seems particularly telling that the chronic street segments remained among the hottest crime spots across a long time series. This certainly suggests that there are specific characteristics of those places that link crime to place.

In this same context, we think it significant that half of the street segments in the city have virtually no crime throughout the study period. Again, as we noted earlier, this would suggest that there are different characteristics, in this case perhaps discouraging crime, or at least not attracting crime. At this point, our purpose is to simply describe the concentration and patterns of crime at place. In chapter 7, we will begin to identify risk and protective characteristics of places that seem to either attract or discourage crime.

The four remaining trajectory patterns include only about one in five street segments in the city. But nonetheless, they represent interesting trends that help us, as we detail below, to understand the overall trend of crime in Seattle in this period. They also reinforce the importance more generally of recognizing the heterogeneity of crime trends within larger geographic units such as a city.

STRONGLY DECREASING TRAJECTORY PATTERNS
AND THE CRIME DROP

Two of the trajectory patterns evidence markedly decreasing crime trends during this period. The "low rate-decreasing" pattern includes three trajectory groups (see figure 3.9) that account for almost 10 percent of the street segments in the city. The three trends are very similar, and the patterns have relatively lower thresholds of crime (as compared with high-rate or chronic patterns in our study). Street segments in trajectory group 17 began with an average of almost eighteen crime incidents. Street segments in trajectory group 11 began with about nine crime incidents per year and those in trajectory 10 began with about six crime incidents per street segment per year. Importantly, by the end

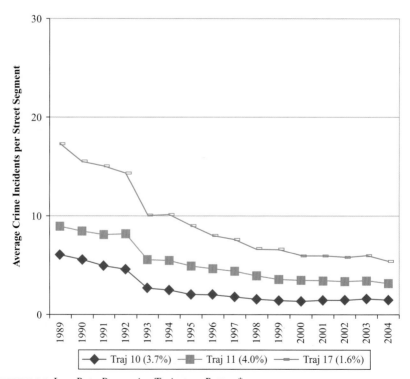

FIGURE 3.9 *Low Rate-Decreasing Trajectory Pattern**

**Percentages refer to percentage of total street segments in that trajectory group.*

of the study period the average number of events per year in each of these groups had declined to about one-third of the crime averages evidenced at the outset.

Similarly, the street segments in the crime trajectories that are part of what we term the "high rate-decreasing" pattern evidence dramatic crime declines during the study period (see figure3.10). Here the base levels of crime in 1989 are much higher, ranging between 20 and 60 crime incidents on an average street segment, though only about 2.4 percent of the street segments are found in this trajectory pattern. However, the crime declines in the study period are very large, leading in 2004 to average observed yearly crime levels less than half of those found in 1989.

These trajectory patterns point to the importance of recognizing developmental trends in studying crime at place. But they also allow us to illustrate why studying crime at a micro geographic level is essential if we are to develop a fuller understanding of the crime problem. A review of broader citywide trends leads us, as we noted above, to focus upon a general crime drop in Seattle, as it

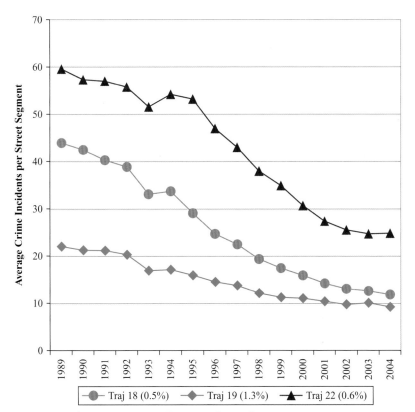

FIGURE 3.10 *High Rate-Decreasing Trajectory Pattern**

*Percentages refer to percentage of total street segments in that trajectory group.

has led scholars to focus on a large crime drop in American cities more generally during this period (Blumstein and Wallman, 2000; Levitt, 2004). Our data suggest a very different understanding of crime trends during this period, one that recognizes that different places in a city will experience crime in different ways. This view of the crime problem in turn recognizes that overall crime trends may mask important variation of crime at place.

In figure 3.11, we show the contribution of each trajectory pattern to the crime drop at street segments in Seattle. Looking at this figure, it is clear that absent these two decreasing trajectory patterns, the overall crime rate at the end of the period would have been similar to what it was at the beginning. If we compare the number of crime incidents at Seattle street segments at the outset of the study and at the last year of observation, we find a difference of 28,545 crimes. This is the crime drop for street segments in Seattle contrasting the first and last observation periods in our data. Looking just at the high-decreasing pattern street segments there is a decline of 12,770 crimes between 1989 and 2004. If we add to this number the crime decline in that period in the low-decreasing pattern street segments (13,972 incidents), we gain a total crime decline for these two patterns of 26,742 incidents. Together,

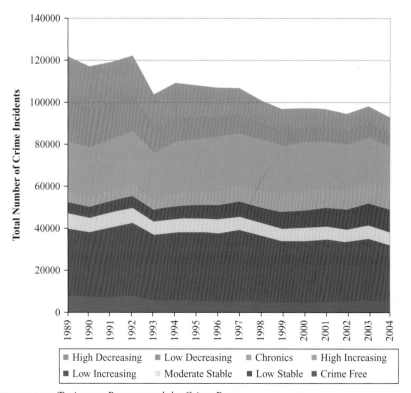

FIGURE 3.11 *Trajectory Patterns and the Crime Drop*

this means that the decline in just 12 percent of street segments in the city was roughly equivalent to the entire crime drop in Seattle. If we add to this the relatively modest proportional decline in the chronic hot spots resulting in a reduction of 4,000 incidents between 1989 and 2004, we can see that the crime drop in Seattle was clustered in just 13 percent of the street segments in the city.

In this context, most places in Seattle, and we suspect elsewhere during the same period, did not experience a crime decline at all during the 1990s. Most places had very stable, often low levels of crime throughout this period. This portrait of overall crime rates in Seattle not only points to the importance of specific places in understanding broader crime trends, but also suggests that we will miss significant trends if we fail to examine crime at a micro place level. During the crime drop, most places in Seattle did not experience a significant change in crime levels.

This means as well that the key to understanding the crime drop may not lie in the units of American cities, but in the changes occurring at specific places in the city. It is common to consider how changes in the economics of a city, or in its overall demographics, or indeed in the general changes in these factors in the United States overall during the 1990s led to a crime decline. But if the crime decline was limited to a small number of places in a city, then we are led naturally to ask how those places changed. The relevant question given our data is how the declining-pattern street segments changed in this period, not how cities overall changed. How did the economic growth in this period affect these places? In turn, are there growth periods where such places are not affected, for example where there would be changes only on streets that are relatively free of crime? Our data push the level of our analysis and interests to a much lower level of geography than has interested most criminological scholars to date. This is a radical change in orientation but one that we think is suggested by our data.

It is interesting to note in this regard that the variability we observe across street segments in Seattle reflects broader trends in crime and violence across American cities. While the national trends illustrate an overall decrease in crime during the 1990s, there was a good deal of variability across cities (Blumstein and Wallman, 2000; Travis and Waul, 2002). When looking at specific crimes there has also been acknowledgement of important differences across populations. For example, Cook and Laub (1998, 2002) observe that the youth violence epidemic was concentrated among minority males who resided in poor neighborhoods, used guns, and engaged in high-risk behaviors such as gang participation (see also Braga, 2003). We are not surprised by this variability and see it more generally as reinforcing the importance of digging more deeply into the phenomenon of overall crime trends. But whatever the trends across cities, or across specific populations, our data suggest the importance of focusing in on crime at very small units of geography.

CRIME WAVES IN A PERIOD OF CRIME DECLINES

The two remaining trajectory patterns are particularly interesting in light of the overall crime decline in Seattle. We term the first, a "low rate-increasing" pattern (see figure 3.12). About 4 percent of the street segments fall in crime trajectories reflecting this pattern. Importantly, there are markedly increasing trends of crime for these trajectory patterns. Note, for example, trajectory group 9 where the crime average for each street segment is more than three times greater at the end of the series than at the outset in 1989. The second, the "high rate-increasing" pattern, shows a similar markedly increasing trend but with higher overall rates of crime (see figure 3.13). One of the trajectory groups in this pattern, including just 51 street segments (trajectory group 1), presents a particularly startling increase, with the average number of incidents per segment going from less than 10 crime incidents a year in 1989 to more than 60 crime incidents a year at the end of the study period.

These trajectory patterns suggest that even when a city overall is experiencing a crime drop, many places are experiencing "crime waves." Street seg-

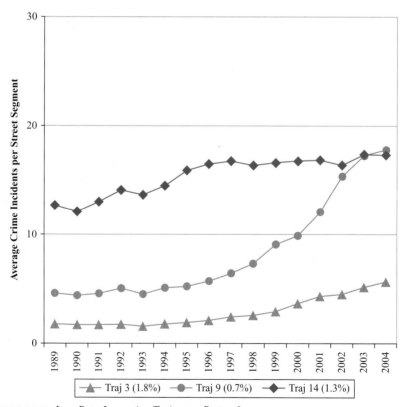

FIGURE 3.12 *Low Rate-Increasing Trajectory Pattern**
*Percentages refer to percentage of total street segments in that trajectory group.

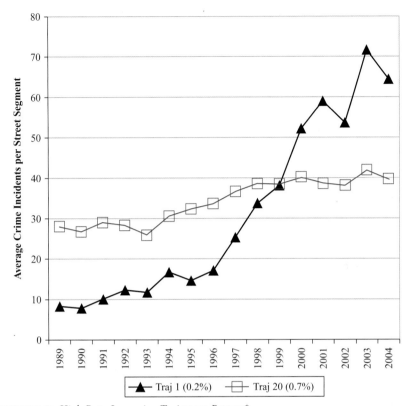

FIGURE 3.13 *High Rate-Increasing Trajectory Pattern**

*Percentages refer to percentage of total street segments in that trajectory group.

ments in trajectory groups with increasing patterns evidenced an average increase in crime of almost 95 percent during the study period. This means that during the period of the crime drop in Seattle, 1,124 street segments not only did not benefit from the overall crime decline in the city, but actually suffered serious increases in crime.

Of course, a key question is what can lead to such strong increases in crime during a period when most places have overall stable or decreasing crime trends? The crime waves experienced here suggest that "something happened" that distinguishes these places from others in Seattle. Increasing crime trajectories could represent places where crime opportunities have increased, perhaps as a result of the introduction of new targets through urban renewal, or motivated offenders through the introduction of easy transportation access. Or, perhaps, there have been major social or structural changes in these places—for example, less advantaged populations moving onto the block, or sudden changes in employment patterns or housing values. While we can only speculate at this juncture, we will return to these issues using data about street segments in chapter 7.

Our observation that there were crime waves on specific street segments in a city during a period when the city overall experienced a crime drop is a new and intriguing insight. It is also an important observation as we consider how to deal with crime in the city. Can we really continue to speak primarily of city-wide crime trends when there appears to be such variability in crime trends at the street segment level of analysis? To do so, for example, may lead the police and other criminal justice agents to ignore places that are in serious need of help. Speaking of the crime drop in American cities may give an overall sense of well-being to city residents, but it is not consistent with the reality of the distribution of crime in the city. Most places did not experience a crime drop in Seattle in the 1990s, and indeed many places experienced a "crime wave." This is an important reality of the crime problem, and one that should not be ignored in assessing crime trends or our ability to do something about crime.

Conclusions

Our analyses confirm prior research showing that crime is concentrated in specific places in urban areas and that most places evidence little or no crime. Importantly, our data also reveal a "law of crime concentrations" at place across time within Seattle. And the similarity of clustering of our data in any given year to data in other studies in other cities suggests that this law of concentrations applies across cities as well as within them. These findings raise intriguing questions about the "normal" levels of crime at places in urban areas. Are there mechanisms at work in cities that limit crime to a specific proportion of places irrespective of the crime levels in a city? What are those mechanisms and do they change, for example, during periods of economic or social stress? We will return to these questions in our conclusions in chapter 8 when we have a fuller understanding of the correlates of crime at place.

Our finding that crime is not only strongly concentrated at crime hot spots, but that such concentrations are relatively stable over the course of our study, provides solid support for the view that crime is tightly coupled to place. As we noted in chapter 1, the strong coupling of crime to place is a key assumption of the criminology of place. Tight coupling suggests that there are characteristics of places that make them more or less attractive to crime, or more or less resistant to crime problems. It also suggests that crime will not move easily around the city, because only certain places are conducive for the emergence or development of crime problems. Our data here reinforce the position that crime is tightly and not loosely coupled to place. In chapter 7, we will return directly to this question, by identifying the specific characteristics of places that are related to crime concentrations and crime patterns.

We have also illustrated in this chapter that analyzing crime trends at a very low level of geography, like the street segment, is central to our interpretation and understanding of more general trends in crime. We found that a relatively small group of places were responsible for the bulk of the crime drop in Seattle. If the trends in Seattle are common to other cities, the crime drop should be seen not as a phenomenon general to all places in a city but rather to a specific and limited group of places. This pushes our effort to understand crime trends to specific places in a city. Explanations in this context would focus not on why cities have changed, but why specific places in the city have changed. This is a very different perspective for understanding crime trends, but one that is warranted by our data.

{ 4 }

The Importance of Street Segments in the Production of the Crime Problem

In chapter 3, we saw that crime was concentrated at street segments, and that relatively few street segments are responsible for most of the crime in Seattle. But so far, we have not discussed the geography of the street segments. Are the chronic-crime pattern street segments all in one area, or are they spread throughout the city? More generally, do street segments near each other evidence very similar developmental patterns of crime? These questions are critical ones for our work because they raise important questions about the unit of analysis we should use in the study of crime at place. If the most serious chronic-crime street segments in Seattle, for example, were found in just one part of town, the focus on micro units of analysis might not add a good deal to our study of crime. However, if chronic hot spot street segments were dispersed throughout the city, then a micro-place approach would likely contribute important new insights to our understanding of the crime problem. A key issue we address in this chapter is whether and to what extent the use of the street segment as our unit of analysis adds important new information to our understanding of crime beyond more traditional units like neighborhoods or communities.

In order to address this question, we develop a number of different types of analyses of spatial patterns of crime trends at street segments in Seattle. We begin with a simple visual description of the geographic distribution of our data. When we look at the geography of the developmental patterns of street segments, can we see evidence of spatial heterogeneity of patterns, or clusters of certain types of patterns in specific areas? We then examine whether the street segments of the same trajectory pattern tend to cluster together in larger areas. For example, are chronic-crime hot spots more likely to be found at short distances one from another? Are street segments adjacent to each other likely to be of the same pattern, or is there significant street-to-street variability in crime patterns? Finally, we explore whether street segments of different trajectory patterns are likely to be spatially attracted, independent, or repulsed one from another. If, for example, we find strong evidence of spatial repulsion (as opposed to spatial attraction), it would suggest that specific patterns (e.g., chronic-crime hot spots or crime-free street segments) are unlikely to be found in the same areas.

Our analyses in this chapter are critical ones for justifying the importance of the criminology of place, because they allow us to put street segments of differing crime patterns in their place in the geography of the city. For the criminology of place to add new information to our understanding of the crime problem, it must be the case that there is significant variability of crime patterns within larger areas. Absent such variability, we would have to conclude that information about crime at macro units of geography such as communities or neighborhoods is likely to provide most of our understanding of the crime problem. Earlier perspectives in geographic criminology tended to ignore the very micro geographic approach that the criminology of place emphasizes. In this chapter, we critically examine to what extent the "action of crime at place" is at very micro levels of geography.

Mapping Trajectory Patterns

The simplest way to examine the geography of the eight trajectory patterns identified in chapter 3 is to look at the locations of the segments on street maps of the city. At the same time, because of the large number of street segments in the city, putting all 24,023 street segments on one map would make it very hard to visually discern the patterns. Accordingly, we divided the city into three sections, representing the three main geographic areas, the Northern (see figure 4.1), Southern (see figure 4.2), and Central (see figure 4.3) areas of Seattle. Each of these maps presents large geographic areas that include many neighborhoods. There is also overlap among the maps to allow for visual continuity among the areas.

These maps offer an easy visualization of the distribution of patterns. All the low-crime groups are represented by thinner lines and the high-crime groups by thicker lines. Crime-free street segments are yellow and thin. Chronic-crime hot spot street segments are represented as thick, dark red lines. Overall, the darker and thicker the lines on the map, the more crime observed during the study period.

In the Northern section of the city, we can see clearly the dispersal of the highest crime trajectory patterns. Dark red lines are found throughout these areas of the city, though there is interesting clustering. For example, in the northern central area of the map there is evidence of high-crime streets following a main or arterial road. We will come back to this finding later in chapter 7, when we show the importance of arterial roads in explaining crime at place. In

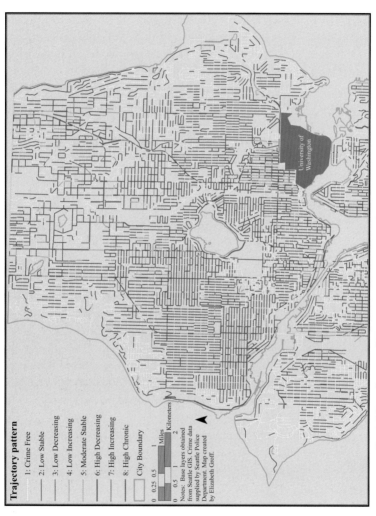

Trajectory pattern

1: Crime Free
2: Low Stable
3: Low Decreasing
4: Low Increasing
5: Moderate Stable
6: High Decreasing
7: High Increasing
8: High Chronic

City Boundary

University of Washington

0 0.25 0.5   1
                Miles
0   0.5   2
            Kilometers

Notes: Base layers obtained from Seattle GIS. Crime data supplied by Seattle Police Department. Map created by Elizabeth Groff.

FIGURE 4.1 *Spatial Distribution of Trajectory Patterns (Northern Seattle)*

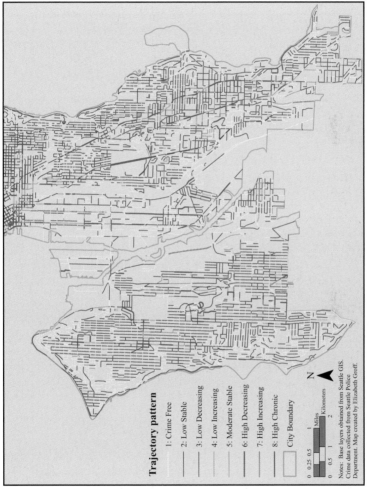

Trajectory pattern

1: Crime Free
2: Low Stable
3: Low Decreasing
4: Low Increasing
5: Moderate Stable
6: High Decreasing
7: High Increasing
8: High Chronic

City Boundary

Notes: Base layers obtained from Seattle GIS.
Crime data collected from Seattle Police
Department. Map created by Elizabeth Groff.

FIGURE 4.2 *Spatial Distribution of Trajectory Patterns (Southern Seattle)*

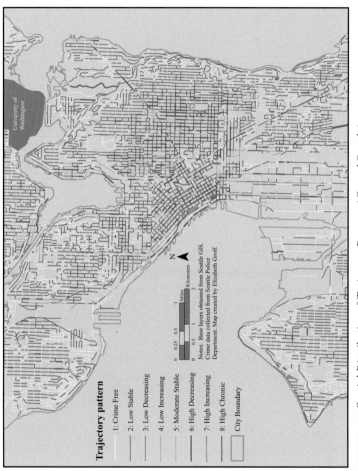

FIGURE 4.3 *Spatial Distribution of Trajectory Patterns (Central Seattle)*

the southeastern part of the map, there is also a noticeable clustering of darker lines near the University of Washington (UW) campus (see figure 4.1). This area is a well-known entertainment district catering to college students and young professionals.

But even here, there is a good deal of street segment-by-street segment variation in trajectory patterns. The area near UW includes about 50 street segments, but within that area all of the higher rate trajectory groups are represented and are neatly surrounded by crime-free and low-stable trajectory pattern segments. This is particularly interesting given the concerns we raised at the outset, because it suggests that even though there are many higher crime streets in this area, they evidence very different crime patterns over time, from moderate-stable patterns to high rate-increasing patterns to high rate-decreasing patterns. While we might hypothesize that some more general community or area characteristics (such as large numbers of students or entertainment facilities) are increasing crime rates here, the fact that the patterns of crime differ strongly across the segments raises the question of whether there are specific characteristics of street segments in this area producing specific crime patterns.

Very apparent in this map of the Northern part of the city is that there are large areas dominated by crime-free and low-stable patterns. This is not surprising, however, given the very large number of street segments that evidence these patterns citywide. About four of every five street segments in the city belong to these two trajectory patterns (12,033 and 7,696 street segments respectively). What is significant here is that other trajectory patterns break up the large areas of crime-free and low-stable crime patterns, thus suggesting dispersal of crime patterns in the Northern part of the city.

The Southern section of the city (figure 4.2) reflects closely the patterns in the Northern section. Once again, we see areas of low-crime and crime-free segments with the other trajectory patterns interspersed. The influence of arterial roads is even greater here, and it is easy to note visually that many high-crime street segments are found on main thoroughfares that traverse this area. The spread of the chronic-crime street segments in the city is particularly striking in this map. These street segments are not limited to one area, but are dispersed across the map. Local area or neighborhood conceptions of the city would miss this broad dispersion of high-crime hot spots.

Turning to the Central area of the city (figure 4.3), which includes the downtown area and some of the city's most densely populated neighborhoods, we see a larger number of high-crime street segments.[1] The "downtown" area in the center of the map shows a very strong degree of clustering of the highest rate crime patterns. But even here there is significant street-by-street variability. Note the presence of high rate-decreasing crime patterns in this area as evidenced by thick, blue street segments, or even the low rate street segments represented by thinner, green or yellow tints. Accordingly, even in this area that shows a strong clustering of chronic-crime hot spots, there are street segments with little crime.

These maps overall suggest the importance of examining crime at a micro-geographic level. We find chronic-crime hot spots dispersed throughout the large geographic areas represented in the maps. Many of these hot spots would be missed if we analyzed our data only in terms of macro geographic units such as communities. At the same time, even when there are clusters of high-rate trajectory street segments, there is often heterogeneity in the patterns observed, for example with moderate-stable, high-decreasing, high-increasing, and chronic-crime hot spot patterns interspersed in an area. In turn, even when there is visual clustering of high-rate crime street segments, we find low-rate segments in the same areas, often interspersed among the high-rate segments.

Statistical Clustering of Trajectory Patterns

Our observations regarding the dispersal and heterogeneity of trajectory patterns within large areas do not rule out the possibility that the patterns are clustered more than would be expected by chance. For example, we have found the spread of crime hot spots throughout the city, but we also noted areas of greater concentrations. These observations suggest that despite the variability we observe in the spatial distribution of trajectory patterns, there appears to be greater clustering of certain patterns in larger areas. To examine this question more carefully, we have to move from a visual description of the data to spatial statistical analyses.

We use a statistic called Ripley's K to examine clustering of the locations of street segments in the same developmental trajectory patterns. Ripley's K describes the proximity of street segments in the same trajectory patterns to one another. For each street segment, it counts the number of street segments of the same trajectory pattern that fall within a specified distance band and then repeats for each distance band in use. Our use of the K-function allows us to test whether the observed pattern is significantly different than what would be expected from a random distribution (Bailey and Gatrell, 1995).

Ripley's K is calculated and then compared to a reference line that represents complete spatial randomness (CSR). It is important to note that the large number of data points in our study means that even small departures are likely to be significantly different from the randomness assumption. This is why it is useful to consider not only whether the data are significantly clustered, but also at what specific geographic distances. In appendix 2, we display the analysis and provide statistical detail. Here we want to focus on our main findings and how they add new information to our understanding of the geography of trajectory patterns.

It is important to consider what would be the interpretation of our data if we observed complete spatial randomness for all of the trajectory patterns. If this occurred, it would imply that street segments of specific temporal patterns arise without regard to larger macro-area pressures. For example, if chronic-crime pattern segments evidenced spatial randomness at all distances, we would conclude that there is no area pattern in the geographic distribution of chronic-crime hot spots—they are just as likely to be found in one neighborhood or community as another. On the other hand, a finding of clustering could indicate micro- or macro-level influences are at work depending on the scale of the clustering. Accordingly, these analyses provide an opportunity for us to observe area trends in our data.

Our findings suggest clustering rather than complete spatial randomness in the trajectory patterns, though the degree of clustering varies by the rate of crime. Trajectory patterns consisting of high-rate crime street segments were the most clustered at all distances. In other words, if the crime rate on a street segment is high, it tends to be near (but not necessarily adjacent to) other segments that are also exhibiting a similar high-crime developmental pattern. Only three trajectories patterns—crime-free, low-stable, and low-increasing—do not exhibit clustering at all distances up to three miles.

Among the higher rate trajectory patterns, chronic-crime street segments have the greatest clustering at just under a mile (5,280 feet) from one another. The high-increasing group exhibits a slower rise in clustering as distances increase and peaks at about 5,500 to 6,500 feet before dropping off steeply. The high-decreasing pattern does not hit its peak clustering until about 8,500 feet and remains stable until about 12,500 feet. The moderate-stable pattern is the least clustered. It peaks at about 6,000 feet and then stays at that level until it begins declining at just over 9,000 feet.

At the other end of the spectrum, among low-rate trajectory patterns, it is the low-increasing street segments which are the most clustered until about 3,500 feet, when the low-decreasing become more clustered and remain more clustered than spatial randomness until just under two miles. The crime-free and low-stable street segments are the least clustered, though they are more clustered than would be expected under an assumption of spatial randomness. The crime-free segments remain more clustered than random until approximately 3,000 feet. The low-stable trajectory segments remain more clustered than CSR until about 6,700 feet.

It may be confusing to distinguish between the significant clustering of trajectory patterns we observe here and the heterogeneity and dispersion we noted earlier. But it is important to recognize that we are adding new information to the portrait of the distribution of crime we provided in the previous section. Street segment–by–street segment variability within small areas is not inconsistent with these results. For example, the strongest clustering for the high-rate crime street segments occurs at about a mile. This suggests that high-rate street segment patterns are significantly more clustered within this distance than one would expect by chance, but it does not mean that other patterns are not interspersed with these street segments. It is also important to recognize that a mile or more in the city is a large distance.

What these data show us is that larger geographic forces are at work in the production of the crime problem at street segments. This is not a new observation and is very much consistent with the very substantial research literature on the importance of communities in understanding crime (e.g., see Boggs, 1965; Bursik and Grasmick, 1993; Bursik and Webb, 1982; Byrne and Sampson, 1986; Chilton, 1964; Kornhauser, 1978; Reiss and Tonry, 1986; Schuerman and Kobrin, 1986; Skogan, 1986; Stark, 1987). Indeed, if we did not find any clustering of our data at distances that reflected larger areas effects we would be led to ask why Seattle differs from other places that have been studied at larger geographic levels.

The Heterogeneity of Street Segment Patterns

While Ripley's K provides important information about the strength and geographic scale of clustering of segments within the same trajectory pattern, it does not allow us to examine the heterogeneity of trajectory patterns within areas. To some degree we examined this problem when reviewing the descriptive maps of crime patterns in Seattle. But spatial statistics allow us to draw more formal conclusions about the relationship of patterns of street segments in the city. For example, looking across the city, are we likely to find significant street-by-street variation in trajectory patterns? Or are the same trajectory pattern street segments located one next to another throughout the city? If the latter were true, our data would not only suggest clustering of specific types of street segments within larger areas, but that specific areas are characterized by specific trajectory patterns. This would argue against formulating theories at the microplace level.

We use Anselin's local indicators of spatial autocorrelation (LISA) (Bailey and Gatrell, 1995; Rowlingson and Diggle, 1993) to answer the question of whether the members of one trajectory pattern are found near one another or whether they are found near the members of other developmental patterns (e.g., are chronic-crime street segments consistently found near other chronic-crime segments, or near other patterns?).[2] We consider only those street segments within one quarter of a mile (1,320 feet or approximately 3–4 city blocks) of each street segment. The LISA maps provided below tell us whether the crime pattern on one street segment is similar to or different from the developmental patterns of crime on nearby streets. Only street segments that have a statistically significant relationship to nearby street segments are depicted on the map.[3] If the crime pattern on one street segment is similar to the crime patterns on adjacent street segments, the two are positively spatially autocorrelated. If the developmental crime pattern on a street segment is significantly different from the patterns on adjacent streets, the street segments are negatively spatially autocorrelated.

CRIME-FREE AND LOW-STABLE TRAJECTORY PATTERNS

Figure 4.4 presents our findings in visual terms for the crime-free and low-stable trajectory patterns. At first glance, it may seem confusing, but taking a specific example will make interpreting these representations easier. In figure 4.4a, our main concern is whether the street segments have a dark red, pink, or light blue color. The dark red color represents street segments in the crime-free pattern that are likely to be located next to other crime-free pattern segments. The pink color shows cases where crime-free segments are likely to be next to other patterns. Finally, the light blue color shows street segments of other patterns that are likely to be near crime-free pattern street segments.

It is not surprising in this visualization that there are many areas that are dark red. Crime-free pattern segments make up about 50 percent of the street segments in Seattle, and thus simply by chance we would expect many of these to be surrounded by other crime-free segments. But notice in figure 4.4a how many light blue and pink street segments are either near to or interspersed with the dark red street segments. In turn, there are many areas in which pink or light blue lines are dominant, and where dark red lines (suggesting contiguous patterns of crime-free streets) are uncommon. This suggests the heterogeneity of patterns even when we are examining a pattern of street segments that is common in the city.

Figure 4.4b, depicting the low-stable pattern, reinforces this description. Again, reflecting in part the large number of street segments in this pattern (20 percent of the total), there are a number of areas where dark red lines are dominant (suggesting positive spatial autocorrelation). Once more, pink and light blue lines are interspaced or close to these areas, and there are many areas in which light blue and pink lines (reflecting negative spatial autocorrelation) are common. This suggests that there are many areas in which low-stable crime pattern street segments are interspersed with street segments representing other patterns.

Returning to our discussion of the crime-free pattern, it is interesting to take a closer look at the central business district of the city, which we noted earlier has much higher concentrations of high-crime street segments than other areas (see figure 4.5). Notice the large number of pink street segments, in this case reflecting negative spatial autocorrelation. These are cases where crime-free streets are near streets that are not crime free. Thus there seem to be pockets of "safe" streets even in an area where there are high-crime street segments overall.

(a) Crime Free Segments   (b) Low Stable Segments

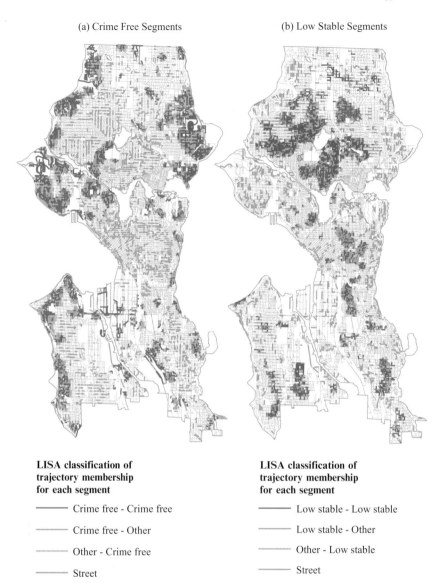

**LISA classification of
trajectory membership
for each segment**

——— Crime free - Crime free

——— Crime free - Other

——— Other - Crime free

——— Street

**LISA classification of
trajectory membership
for each segment**

——— Low stable - Low stable

——— Low stable - Other

··· Other - Low stable

——— Street

Note: Crime data were provided by Seattle Police Department but were
unavailable for the University of Washington across all years so it was excluded
from the study. All geographic base files were obtained from Seattle GIS.
Univariate LISA calculated in GeoDa 9.5i. Low-Low significant autocorrelations
are not depicted to improve map legibility. Map created by Elizabeth Groff.

FIGURE 4.4 *LISA for Crime-Free and Low-Stable Trajectory Patterns*

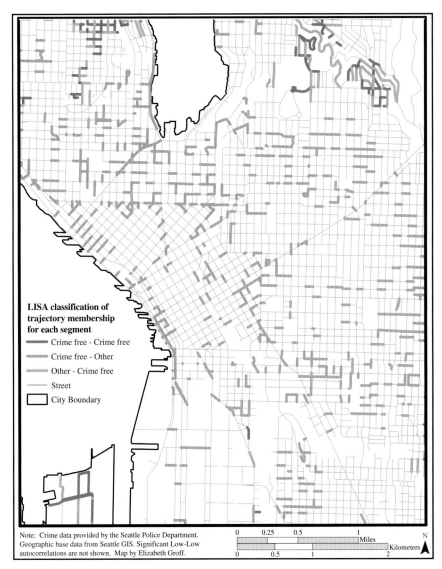

FIGURE 4.5 *LISA for Crime-Free Pattern in the Central Business District*

LOW-DECREASING AND LOW-INCREASING TRAJECTORY PATTERNS

The low-decreasing pattern includes about 9 percent of the street segments in the city. Here we still can see a large cluster of spatial autocorrelation in the center of the city (see figure 4.6a). But more generally, there is strong evidence of negative spatial autocorrelation. For example, notice the large number of light blue streets even in the clustered area of dark red segments. Moreover, there is evidence of negative spatial autocorrelation throughout the city, as indicated by the areas of light blue and pink street segments throughout the map.

The importance of spatial heterogeneity is reinforced when we examine the low-increasing pattern (see figure 4.6b). This pattern includes only about 4 percent of the streets in the city, and we would not expect in this context to see as much positive spatial autocorrelation as in the previous maps simply because there are many fewer streets of this pattern. There is in this map some indication of positive spatial autocorrelation. At the same time, there is a good deal of evidence of negative spatial autocorrelation, especially as represented by the light blue lines. Low-increasing patterns are in this context often interspersed with other trajectory pattern street segments.

MODERATE-STABLE AND HIGH-DECREASING TRAJECTORY PATTERNS

This pattern is continued when we review the moderate-stable and high-decreasing segments (see figure 4.7). The moderate-stable pattern includes about 1 percent of Seattle street segments. The high-decreasing pattern includes 2.4 percent of the segments. Again, there is some evidence of positive spatial autocorrelation, but a good number of streets shaded light blue or pink suggest much greater negative spatial autocorrelation. Moderate-stable and high-decreasing pattern street segments are very likely to be surrounded by other crime pattern street segments. This suggests that these patterns are not simply concentrated in specific areas, but rather that they are interspersed with other trajectory patterns throughout areas of the city.

HIGH-INCREASING AND CHRONIC-CRIME STREET SEGMENT TRAJECTORY PATTERNS

The final two trajectory groups represent the high-increasing and chronic-crime hot spot patterns, each including about 1 percent of the street segments in Seattle (figure 4.8). The heterogeneity of street segment patterns is accented even more in these figures. While there are areas where high-increasing segments are likely to be found near other high-increasing segments (in the downtown area and near the University of Washington, to name just two of the clusters) as represented by the dark red lines in figure 4.8a, much more common in these maps are the light blue lines representing significant negative spatial autocorrelation. In this case, other crime pattern street segments are likely to be near to high-increasing segments. The chronic and most serious hot spots in the city also evidence a high degree of negative spatial autocorrelation (see figure 4.8b). While there are more dark red lines here, indicating cases where chronic-crime street segments are likely to be near to other chronic-crime street segments, the dominant pattern is again the light blue color, and there are many

(a) Low Decreasing Segments (b) Low Increasing Segments

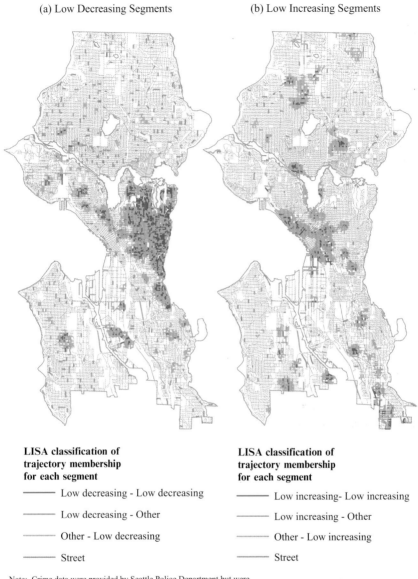

LISA classification of
trajectory membership
for each segment

——— Low decreasing - Low decreasing

——— Low decreasing - Other

——— Other - Low decreasing

——— Street

LISA classification of
trajectory membership
for each segment

——— Low increasing- Low increasing

——— Low increasing - Other

——— Other - Low increasing

——— Street

Note: Crime data were provided by Seattle Police Department but were
unavailable for the University of Washington across all years so it was excluded
from the study. All geographic base files were obtained from Seattle GIS.
Univariate LISA calculated in GeoDa 9.5i. Low-Low significant autocorrelations
are not depicted to improve map legibility. Map created by Elizabeth Groff.

FIGURE 4.6 *LISA for Low-Decreasing and Low-Increasing Trajectory Patterns*

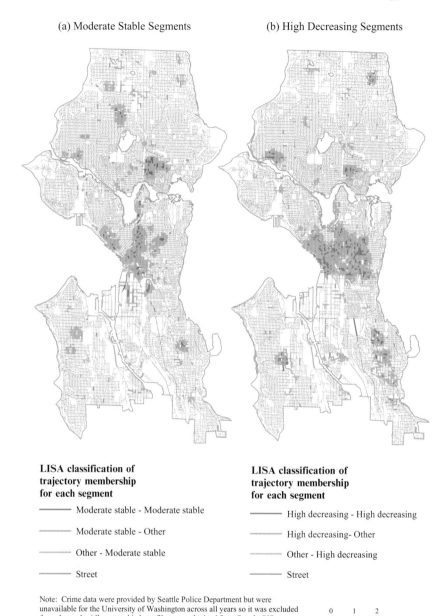

(a) Moderate Stable Segments   (b) High Decreasing Segments

**LISA classification of
trajectory membership
for each segment**

――― Moderate stable - Moderate stable

――― Moderate stable - Other

――― Other - Moderate stable

――― Street

**LISA classification of
trajectory membership
for each segment**

――― High decreasing - High decreasing

――― High decreasing- Other

――― Other - High decreasing

――― Street

Note: Crime data were provided by Seattle Police Department but were
unavailable for the University of Washington across all years so it was excluded
from the study. All geographic base files were obtained from Seattle GIS.
Univariate LISA calculated in GeoDa 9.5i. Low-Low significant autocorrelations
are not depicted to improve map legibility. Map created by Elizabeth Groff.

FIGURE 4.7 *LISA for Moderate-Stable and High-Decreasing Trajectory Patterns*

(a) High Increasing Segments   (b) Chronic Segments

**LISA classification of
trajectory membership
for each segment**

——— High increasing - High increasing

——— High increasing - Other

------- Other - High increasing

——— Street

**LISA classification of
trajectory membership
for each segment**

——— Chronic - Chronic

——— Chronic - Other

------- Other - Chronic

——— Street

Note: Crime data were provided by Seattle Police Department but were unavailable
for the University of Washington across all years so it was excluded from the study.
All geographic base files were obtained from Seattle GIS. Univariate LISA calculated
in GeoDa 9.5i. Low-Low significant autocorrelations are not depicted to improve map
legibility. Map created by Elizabeth Groff.

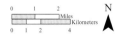

FIGURE 4.8 *LISA for High-Increasing and Chronic-Crime Trajectory Patterns*

pink lines indicating cases where chronic-crime pattern street segments are near to other patterns.

These maps, as well as others reviewed in this section, reinforce the spatial heterogeneity at the street segment level that we illustrated with simple descriptive maps earlier in the chapter. Street segments of one pattern are very likely to be surrounded by street segments of a different crime trajectory pattern. While there is evidence of clustering, or positive autocorrelation of trajectory patterns (especially for crime-free and low-stable crime patterns that include a large proportion of the street segments in the city), our analyses overall suggest that crime patterns are interspersed throughout the city.

Are Street Segments of Specific Trajectory Patterns Attracted, Repulsed, or Independent?

In the previous section, we examined the extent to which street segments of a specific pattern were spatially clustered. But another approach, the cross-K analysis, allows us to directly examine how segments of each trajectory pattern are related to every other pattern (e.g., how low-decreasing pattern segments are related to high-decreasing pattern street segments) (Bailey and Gatrell, 1995; Rowlingson and Diggle, 1993). There are three potential relationships that can be observed: significant spatial attraction, significant spatial repulsion, or independence. A finding that two patterns exhibit attraction to one another provides evidence that there is a significant likelihood of their being found in the same larger area, and accordingly that there is spatial heterogeneity of developmental patterns of crime in that area. Independence similarly would also suggest heterogeneity, or at least that the two crime patterns are not significantly dispersed one from another. A finding of repulsion would suggest homogeneity of crime patterns examined in larger areas, or at least that street segments with two specific patterns are unlikely to be found near to one another.

We conduct a series of pairwise comparisons to evaluate the patterns of each group as compared to those of every other group (i.e., crime-free to low-stable, crime-free to low-increasing, crime-free to low-decreasing, etc.) at distances of up to 2,800 feet (about 7 blocks in Seattle).[4] Each trajectory pattern was individually compared to every other trajectory pattern. We summarize our findings in figure 4.9.

The most interesting finding is simply illustrated in figure 4.9. None of the pairs of patterns evidence significant spatial repulsion at any of the distances we examined. This is a very important finding, because it suggests that whatever the strength of the influences on crime that are brought by larger geographic units such as communities or neighborhoods, local influences are producing strong variability of crime patterns at the street segment level.

	2 – Low Stable	3 – Low Decreasing	4 – Low Increasing	5 – Moderate Stable	6 – High Decreasing	7 – High Increasing	8 – Chronic
1 – Crime Free				<= 1,200			
2 – Low Stable							<= 800 ft
3 – Low Decreasing						<= 1,200 ft	<= 400 ft
4 – Low Increasing							
5 – Moderate Stable							
6 – High Decreasing							
7 – High Increasing							

Attraction ☐ Independence ☐ Repulsion ■

FIGURE 4.9 *Spatial Attraction, Repulsion, and Independence of Trajectory Patterns*

It is worthwhile to consider for a moment why we might hypothesize spatial repulsion. Let us say that we considered a neighborhood as being a high-crime area, what is sometimes colloquially referred to as a "bad neighborhood." One might expect that we would observe in this neighborhood spatial repulsion of crime-free street segments, meaning that the neighborhood context made it very difficult for such a pattern to emerge in that area. We have already seen the interspersion of chronic-crime street segments in areas with many crime-free and low-stable pattern street segments in maps earlier in the chapter, so this hypothesis is not consistent with our prior results. Nonetheless, the fact that we do not see evidence of significant spatial repulsion for any of the pairwise comparisons of the developmental crime patterns provides statistical support for our emphasis on the importance of local processes, such as those operating at the street segment level.

Reinforcing this argument is the number of patterns that evidence significant spatial attraction. Twenty one of the 28 pairwise comparisons in figure 4.9 show significant spatial attraction at all distances. This includes pairs that have crime trends as different as the high- increasing/high-decreasing, and low-stable trajectory patterns. This means that most of the patterns we observe appear to move together in space, a situation that provides the strongest evidence of spatial heterogeneity in our data. The visual description we provided at the beginning of the chapter is accordingly reinforced by these spatial statistics.

What of the three pairwise comparisons that evidence spatial independence? This is true for the relationship of the crime-free pattern with the high-increasing, high-decreasing, and chronic-crime hot spots patterns. Importantly, independence is not repulsion, and what this shows is that these patterns neither spatially attract nor repulse each other in our data. If repulsion had been the outcome, we would have concluded that the crime-free pattern and the most serious crime pattern street segments are effectively being "repulsed" from each other within larger areas. This is not reflected in our statistical analysis. If significant spatial attraction had been found between these patterns, we would have concluded that they are more likely than we would expect by chance to be interspersed one with another. Our data suggest that they are simply interspersed in ways that we would expect by chance given the prevalence of these street segments in the city.

Conclusions

We began this chapter by asking whether and to what extent the use of the street segment as our unit of analysis adds important new information to our understanding of crime beyond more traditional macro units of geography like neighborhoods or communities. Our analyses suggest overall that there is tremendous street-by-street variability in developmental patterns of crime at street segments in Seattle. For example, simple descriptive maps pointed to the spread of crime hot spots across Seattle. Though certain areas, like the downtown center of the city, evidenced larger numbers of chronic crime hot spots, hot spot street segments were generally dispersed throughout the city. An approach that assumed that they were clustered only in a few "very bad" neighborhoods would misrepresent the spread of such problems in the city.

Similarly, drawing conclusions from spatial statistics we found that trajectory patterns are interspersed, for example, with crime-free street segments often likely to be bounded by higher-crime street segments, or chronic hot spots near to street segments evidencing less serious developmental crime patterns. Importantly, the main pattern of relationships we observe across the eight crime patterns is spatial attraction. This reinforces the idea of the heterogeneity of patterns at the street segment level. The fact that no repulsion was evidenced in our data reinforces the idea that looking at crime data in large geographic areas is likely to miss important local area trends. The action of crime in this sense begins at a very micro level of geography, in this case the street segment.

But it would be a mistake to draw from our analyses the conclusion that larger area forces have no influence on the trends we observe in very small geographic areas. We found significant spatial clustering at distances of a mile for many of the trajectory patterns. This means that there is not a random distribution, for example, of chronic-crime hot spots across the city, but that in certain large areas more such hot spots are identified. We think this conclusion is very much consistent with prior research on communities and crime (e.g., see Boggs, 1965; Bursik and Grasmick, 1993; Bursik and Webb, 1982; Byrne and

Sampson, 1986; Chilton, 1964; Kornhauser, 1978; Reiss and Tonry, 1986; Schuerman and Kobrin, 1986; Skogan, 1986; Stark, 1987), as well as our common everyday observations of life in the city. Some neighborhoods certainly are more likely to have chronic crime hot spots than others. This is a well-known fact and one that our data reflect. But our analyses suggest that within such large geographic areas there is a tremendous degree of spatial heterogeneity of crime patterns. This would be missed if we began our study with the neighborhood or other large area. This chapter reinforces the idea that we must look beyond neighborhood effects to the dynamics of crime at a micro place level. This is not the only level of geography important in understanding crime, but it has been virtually neglected in criminological understandings of crime until recent years. Our analyses suggest that such neglect leads us to miss a great deal of the action of crime at place.

{ 5 }

Concentrations of Crime Opportunities

The identification of variation in crime patterns at the micro level raises the question of whether there are similar variations in opportunities for crime. From the outset, the criminology of place has been informed by theoretical perspectives that emphasize crime opportunities. Situational prevention (Clarke, 1983, 1995), environmental criminology (Brantingham and Brantingham, 1981), and routine activity theory (Cohen and Felson, 1979) all place emphasis on the situation and context that provide opportunities for crime. They do not ignore criminal motivation, but rather place it as only one element in the crime equation. The key question that these theories raise is how situational and contextual factors influence a crime event (Eck and Weisburd, 1995).

If opportunity theories are correct in their emphasis on situational opportunities for crime at place, then we should observe variation of factors affecting crime opportunities at a very low level of geography. For example, if crime patterns differ street to street in a city, then a theory that saw routine activities as key to that patterning would also predict variation in motivated offenders, suitable targets, or capable guardians at the same level. Put more directly, if there are hot spots of crime, there should also be hot spots of crime opportunities. This is the focus of our interest in this chapter. Our data provide an opportunity to critically evaluate a key assumption in the criminology of place. Do crime opportunities vary at a micro level of geography? If they do not, then the importance of the opportunity perspective for understanding the criminology of place would be challenged.

Identifying Retrospective Longitudinal Data on Places

Identifying retrospective longitudinal data on crime opportunities represented a major challenge for our study, as did the identification of measures of social disorganization in the next chapter. Unlike crime data, which are routinely collected by police agencies, there is not a single repository for information on the key theoretical concerns we have raised in previous chapters. Indeed, a major critique of police information systems in recent years has focused on the fact that there has not been a concerted effort to systematically collect data on opportunity characteristics of places that have been identified as important in the production of crime problems (Block, 1997; Weisburd, 2008).

In turn, social data on geographic areas that are relevant both to opportunity theory (e.g., see residential population later) and to social disorganization theory are not released by the U.S. Census at the street segment level because of fears of identifying individuals and accordingly violating confidentiality. While some data are available at the census block level,[1] such information would not have been helpful for our study. Our study emphasizes the importance of street-by-street variability in the city. The census block is defined as the four block faces on a square street block. This would include one side of the street each for four different street segments as we have defined them in our study. Given our findings of strong street segment–to–street segment variation in crime, the use of data on the census block would be inappropriate for assessing characteristics of street segments.

This meant that we had to draw information for our study from available data sources, collected often for reasons having little to do with crime or crime theory, that reflected as best as possible the concepts and perspectives that inform our work. In some sense, we embarked on a "treasure hunt" across the many databases that are routinely collected in Seattle and that code information geographically to identify information on key concerns of opportunity and social disorganization theories (see appendix 4 for details of the data collection process). We went to city agencies such as the Department of Transportation, the Department of Planning and Development, the Seattle Housing Authority, Seattle Parks and Recreation, and the public utility companies (e.g., Seattle City Light). We sought out records from the public schools, from the Yellow Pages, and from private companies like InfoUSA. As will be apparent in the next two chapters, we were able to collect a wealth of data reflecting opportunities for crime and social disorganization at places using archival records. Nonetheless, in some cases, as we detail in our discussion below and in chapter 6, we could not measure directly key dimensions of either opportunity or social disorganization. This is an important limitation of our study, and one which we will return to in chapter 8 when we summarize our findings and discuss their implications for future research and public policy.

Motivated Offenders

One factor that links opportunity theories with more traditional theoretical perspectives in criminology is the importance of motivated offenders for understanding the crime problem. For more traditional approaches, the criminological contribution has been in trying to understand why certain people are more motivated to commit crime than others (e.g., see Akers, 1973; Gottfredson and Hirschi, 1990; Hirschi, 1969; Raine, 1993). For opportunity theories, motivation itself has not been the key subject of empirical inquiry, but rather the extent to which crime opportunities are increased when motivated offenders are found at places. For example, in the crime triangle developed by Cohen and Felson (1979; see also Felson, 1994), it is assumed that a crime event necessitates a "motivated offender" who would take advantage of the presence of a suitable target and the absence of a capable guardian. The mere presence of suitable targets without capable guardians at a place would not lead to a crime unless there was someone present who was willing to make the decision to become involved in crime (Clarke and Cornish, 1985, 2001).

There is, it should be noted, some theoretical confusion among scholars in this area regarding the extent to which environments act upon individuals to become "offenders" and the extent to which offenders enter a crime situation with such motivations. In the original presentation of routine activity theory (Cohen and Felson, 1979), criminal motivation was seen as a given, simply one of the parts of a crime triangle (including as well "suitable targets" and "capable guardians"). Similarly, situational crime prevention scholars relied on rational choice theories, which saw criminal motivation as something that was developed before a motivated offender entered the crime situation (Clarke and Cornish, 1985). Once crime becomes a viable alternative, potential offenders are seen as susceptible to situational factors related to particular crime opportunities. A similar approach is taken more recently by P.-O. Wikström (2004) in his formulation of "situational action theory," where criminal decisions are seen as the result of both preexisting individual characteristics of the offender and contextual characteristics of the crime situation.

Brantingham and Brantingham (1993a), in contrast, argue directly that the backcloth of a place and situation will influence the motivations of individuals leading them to become more or less likely to commit a crime. Felson and Clarke (1998) have taken the model of opportunities influencing motivation a step further, suggesting simply that "opportunity makes the thief." In this context, motivation itself becomes less problematic, as it is assumed that there are large numbers of people that might in certain circumstances be motivated to commit a crime. In a study of white-collar offenders, Weisburd, Waring, and Chayet (1995) provide empirical support for a model which sees opportunities leading otherwise conventional individuals to crime. They argue that much white collar crime is committed by "opportunity takers" and "crisis responders" who come to situations without evidence of prior criminality, but who are either enticed by specific opportunities or responding to crises that lead them to violate legal norms. Nonetheless, even in that study of white collar crime, there was a small group of offenders who fulfilled stereotypes of long-term involvement in crime and deviance that led them to seek out criminal opportunities.

Whatever the extent of prior criminal motivation that is important for understanding crime events, there is broad recognition in opportunity theories that the presence of "motivated" offenders will increase the likelihood of a crime's occurrence (e.g., see Hollinger and Dabney, 1999). Measuring motivated offenders directly at the street segment level is a difficult problem, as it would require us to be able to identify who lives on each block in the city, and what their orientation to criminality is. Such data are not presently available in Seattle or other cities. An alternative approach might have been to locate the residences of all arrested offenders in the city and then to estimate from that the number of individuals with a criminal record who live on each street segment. While this data would have told us how many "criminals" live on each block, it would have by necessity confounded being officially charged with committing a crime with "criminal motivation." Moreover, address data are not consistent on arrest reports, and it would have been difficult to be sure that people who committed crimes lived on street segments at any specific period.

In our search for data on motivated offenders, we thought that information gathered from the public schools provided a particularly useful source. There is a long history of research that documents the importance of juveniles in the production of crime (Baumer et al., 1998; Bernasco and Nieuwbeerta, 2005; Bursik and Grasmick, 1993; Chilton, 1964; Gordon, 1967; Schmid 1960a, 1960b; Schmitt, 1957; Shaw and McKay, 1942 [1969]), and their importance for generating crime at place (Stephenson, 1974; Turner, 1969; Weisburd, Morris, and Groff, 2009). Moreover, the Seattle Public Schools were able to provide us with geographic data on students from 1992 until the end of our study period. In the school database made available to us, there was information both on truancy and low academic achievement, two measures that have been linked strongly to the commission of crimes in prior studies (Dryfoos, 1990; Catalano et al., 1998; Robins and Ratcliff, 1978; Snyder and Sickmund, 2006). In Seattle, students who are absent 10 or more times during an academic year are considered to be truant. The schools define specific students as "low academic achievers" when they are in the bottom quartile in results from standardized academic achievement tests and in "in school" academic performance.[2]

We combined these two measures into a single indicator representing "high-risk juveniles." If a student is either defined as a truant or designated as a low academic achiever or both, he or she is included in our measure of total high-risk juveniles who live on the street segment. It is important to note that our measure does not ask whether juveniles come to a specific place in the context of their routine activities. We will examine facilities that might bring potential offenders to a place later in the chapter. Rather, our concern here is whether juveniles who are likely to be of high risk of involvement in deviant behavior live on a street segment.

In the 1992–1993 academic year, there were 5,366 students that were classified as high-risk juveniles out of a total student population of 34,525. The number of high-risk juveniles declined steadily between the school year of 1992–1993 (n = 5,366) and 2004–2005 (n = 4,383). Interestingly, these figures follow a more general juvenile crime drop noted in the United States in other studies (see Butts, 2000; Cook and Laub, 2002), and the specific drop in juvenile crime identified in Seattle (see Weisburd, Morris, and Groff, 2009). This occurred over a time period when the number of public school students per year was fairly stable and even rising slightly, ranging from 34,525 in 1992–1993 to 36,153 in 2004–2005.

High risk juveniles tend to be concentrated on particular street segments rather than spread evenly across them (see figure 5.1). In Seattle, 50 percent of high-risk juveniles are consistently found on between 3 and 4 percent of the total number of Seattle street segments. This seems to follow closely our findings regarding crime in the city, where approximately 5 percent of the street segments accounted for 50 percent of crime each year. Accordingly, there appear to be hot spots of high-risk juveniles, as there are hot spots of crime. All of the high-risk juveniles are found on between 18 and 23 percent of the total street segments. As there are only about one-fifth as many high-risk juveniles per year as street segments, this relatively low proportion is not surprising. This percentage peaks in 1998–1999 and then declines.

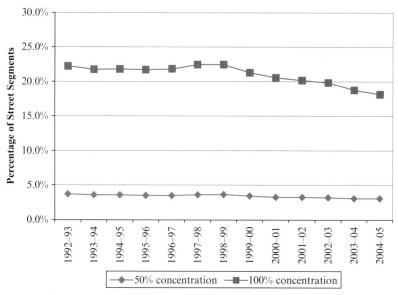

FIGURE 5.1 *Concentration of High-Risk Juveniles at Street Segments*

A question we asked in our examination of crime concentrations is whether patterns of crime varied within larger areas. This was an important question because it focused on the key issue of whether crime patterns were common to large areas, or rather reflected micro-level geographic influences. We found evidence of strong micro-geographic trends as reflected by the tremendous street-by-street variability in crime patterns found in our data. We also found evidence of wider area trends, as reflected in the fact that some areas had larger numbers of serious crime pattern segments. Are high-risk juveniles also distributed in similar ways in Seattle?

We examine the concentration and variability of characteristics across space for our measure of motivated offenders and other opportunity characteristics in this chapter, in similar ways to our examination of the distribution of crime across geography. We first provide a simple descriptive map showing where concentrations lie. For ease of interpretation, we focus in on the street segments that include 50 percent of the high-risk juveniles in the city. We then examine the spatial pattern of the data statistically, in this case using Anselin's local indicators of spatial autocorrelation (LISA) described in chapter 4. We use the LISA statistic to assess whether the number of high-risk juveniles on a street segment is similar, different, or unrelated to the amount of the same characteristic on nearby street segments. While we have data on high-risk juveniles across 14 years, we present maps here only for 1992–1993 year. We do this for the sake of parsimony in our descriptions. In the case of high-risk juveniles, as for other characteristics we examine in this chapter, the basic conclusions we reach regarding the concentration and distribution of crime across geography are similar across the time periods we observe.[3]

A map of the street segments that account for 50 percent of all high-risk juveniles indicates that hot spots of high-risk juveniles are spread throughout Seattle, though there are areas of much higher concentration (see figure 5.2a). One cluster of high-risk juveniles is in the east central portion of the city. Two other linear clusters are in the southeastern section and in the eastern section of the southwestern area of the city. But it is also clear that there is significant variability in the relative number of high-risk juveniles, even among the 4 percent of street segments that include 50 percent of high-risk juveniles in the city. Note the varying shades of concentration even when an area has many more streets with high-risk juveniles living on them.

The results from a LISA analysis (see figure 5.2b) show that high-risk juveniles are not only concentrated on a small number of street segments, but that there is a good deal of street-by-street variability in this characteristic. The visual representation of the LISA statistic shows us whether street segments high or low on this motivated-offender measure are highly likely to be located near to similar or different streets (i.e., high next to low, or low next to high). Note that the high-concentration area in the southeastern part of the city, for example, is not uniform but rather has street segments with high numbers of

(a) 50% Spatial concentration   (b) Spatial autocorrelation

Number of high-risk   LISA classification of
juveniles per street   high-risk juveniles per
segment in 1993   street segment in 1993

——— 9–93   ——— High-High

——— 6–8   ——— High-Low

——— 4–5   ——— Low-High

——— Street   ——— Street

Note: All base geographic base files were obtained from Seattle GIS.
Juvenile data were supplied by Seattle Public Schools. Map (a) depicts
only the 3.74 percent of street segments that account for 50 percent
of all high risk juveniles. Significant Low-Low autocorrelations are not
displayed on map (b) to improve legibility. Map designed by Elizabeth
Groff and produced by Julie Hibdon.

FIGURE 5.2 *Spatial Concentration and Spatial Autocorrelation of High-Risk Juveniles*

high-risk juveniles in close proximity to other street segments with high numbers (dark red) but also street segments with low numbers of high-risk juveniles near streets with high numbers (as represented by the light blue lines). There are also many pink lines throughout the map (especially in the northern half of Seattle), also indicating negative spatial autocorrelation, in this case streets with higher numbers of high-risk juveniles surrounded by streets with relatively low numbers of high-risk juveniles. Accordingly, the number of high-risk juveniles varies across street segments rather than being uniformly high or low.

Suitable Targets

Suitable targets are a second major dimension of opportunity theories. In regard to place, the assumption is that specific places that include more attractive or larger numbers of potential victims or targets are likely to have more crime (Eck and Weisburd, 1995; Felson, 1994). Do street segments vary significantly in the nature of suitable targets? Again, are there hot spots of suitable targets in Seattle?

One problem in measuring the presence or attractiveness of suitable targets is that it is often difficult to distinguish "suitable targets" from offenders or even guardians. For example, a number of studies have documented that victims in one context may become offenders in another (Braga et al., 2001; Lauritsen, Sampson, and Laub, 1991). And capable guardians in one context, such as doormen or local business owners, may become victims in another. Despite these complexities, it has generally been assumed by opportunity theorists that larger numbers of people that are potential victims in places are related to higher crime rates (Cohen and Felson, 1979).[4] We measure this potential through three estimates indicating the population of people who work, visit, or live on street segments. We also assess the attractiveness of street segments as targets by the extent of retail business that is done there.

EMPLOYMENT

Quantifying the number of people who work at a place provides an important foundational element for understanding crime opportunities (Brantingham and Brantingham, 1995). People who work on a street segment are not only potential victims when they come to work or leave or when they take breaks from work to shop or eat; they also may drive cars to work, which may also become suitable targets for offenders. People who work on a street segment, moreover, may receive paychecks or even cash payments that provide another potential attraction to offenders.

In Seattle, we were able to obtain data about the entire spectrum of businesses for four specific years between 1998 and 2004. One attribute of the

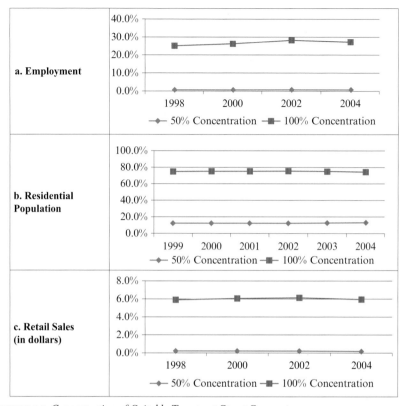

FIGURE 5.3 *Concentration of Suitable Targets at Street Segments*

business data is the number of employees who work at each business. In 1998, our data showed there were 360,736 employees in Seattle, and in 2004 there were 364,036 employees. Between 1998 and 2004, half of all the employees in the city were located on about 0.8 percent of Seattle street segments (see figure 5.3a). Employment accordingly is very concentrated at employment hot spots in Seattle. All employment was concentrated on between 25 and 28.5 percent of total street segments over the study period. The total number of street segments with employees increased slightly from 1998 to 2002 and then showed a slight decline in 2004. These figures point to the concentration of most employment on relatively few street segments.

Figure 5.4a reveals that those street segments making up 50 percent of all employment in Seattle are dispersed across the city, with concentrations in the downtown center and with a few high-employment clusters in the industrial area of the southern sector and scattered locations in the northern sector. The LISA map shows that there is strong street-by-street variability even in those areas (figure 5.4b). For example, in the central areas of the city note that light

(a) 50% Spatial concentration   (b) Spatial autocorrelation

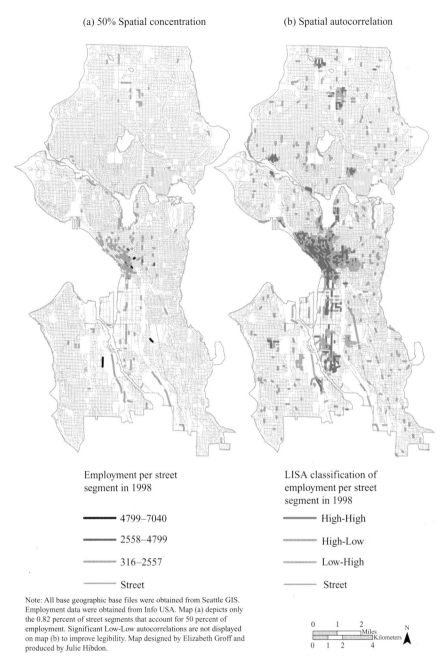

Employment per street   LISA classification of
segment in 1998   employment per street
                                         segment in 1998

———— 4799–7040   ———— High-High

———— 2558–4799   ———— High-Low

———— 316–2557   ———— Low-High

———— Street   ———— Street

Note: All base geographic base files were obtained from Seattle GIS.
Employment data were obtained from Info USA. Map (a) depicts only
the 0.82 percent of street segments that account for 50 percent of
employment. Significant Low-Low autocorrelations are not displayed
on map (b) to improve legibility. Map designed by Elizabeth Groff and
produced by Julie Hibdon.

FIGURE 5.4 *Spatial Concentration and Spatial Autocorrelation for Employment*

blue lines are interspersed with the dark red lines. This shows that there is significant negative spatial autocorrelation, or low-employment areas interspersed with high-employment areas, even in an area with very high employment overall.

PUBLIC FACILITY–RELATED CRIME GENERATORS
AND ATTRACTORS

Public facilities play a key role in attracting suitable targets. If a hospital is on a block, for example, many people will end up visiting there both as patients and to visit family or friends. During these visits, they become potential targets, that is, people who may become the victims of motivated offenders in these areas. Roman (2002), for example, found that middle and high schools act as a crime generator in blocks surrounding schools during the time students are in class (Monday through Friday, 10:00 AM–2 PM). Cromwell, Alexander, and Dotson (2008) apply situational crime prevention to libraries, noting that levels of vandalism and theft have become a bigger problem in and around libraries, as have "problem patrons," who include the homeless, the mentally ill, and disorderly youth.

   In Seattle, the public facilities on the street segments included community centers, hospitals, libraries, parks, and middle and high schools.[5] The total number of public facilities in Seattle ranged from 379 in 1989 to 419 in 2004.[6] The number of public facilities decreased for the first two years of the study period and then began a steady increase between 1993 and 2002. In 2003, there was a slight decrease before rebounding. These changes were due to both temporary closings for renovations, permanent closings, and relocations, as well as new facilities being added. Community centers (n = 26) and hospitals (n = 13) were stable in number over time. The overall number of public facilities in Seattle increased over the time period largely due to more parks being created (an increase of 44 parks). Schools added two locations and libraries added four.

   Because of the small number of facilities present in Seattle, we operationalized the construct as the average number of public facilities within one quarter of a mile of a street segment rather than the presence of a facility on a specific street segment.[7] This approach is also consistent with prior literature that notes the influence of parks (Crewe, 2001; Coleman, 1989; Evans and Oulds, 1984; Groff and McCord, 2012; Knutsson, 1997; LaGrange, 1999; Wilcox et al., 2004), and community centers (Perkins et al., 1993) on adjacent areas. The majority of street segments (approximately 63 percent) have no public facilities within one-quarter of a mile. Relatively few, less than 12 percent, have more than one facility nearby. In this context, we can also conclude that public facilities—like motivated offenders and employees—are concentrated at or near to specific street segments in the city.

Because a catchment area of 1,320 feet (one-quarter mile) does not allow us to examine the geographic distribution of facilities at street segments, a concentration graph is inappropriate. Instead, we examine in figure 5.5 the simple distribution of facilities within a quarter mile of each street segment in the city. Figure 5.5a shows that facilities are spread throughout the city. Nonetheless, the greatest concentrations are in the central section of Seattle. This spatial dispersion of public facilities is confirmed in our LISA analysis (see figure 5.5b). There are a number of places where streets with high numbers of public facilities are near other streets with high numbers of facilities (represented by dark red lines). However, the dominant pattern is one of negative spatial autocorrelation (as indicated by the light blue and pink lines). That is, there are places with high numbers of public facilities near places with low numbers and places with low numbers of facilities are often located near street segments with higher numbers of facilities.

RESIDENTIAL POPULATION

Residential population is an important environmental backcloth characteristic (Brantingham and Brantingham, 1993a; Felson, 1986). In this context, residents are seen as potential victims, and the larger the number of such victims, the higher the rates of crime that would be expected. Of course, as we noted earlier, a large number of residents could also reflect larger numbers of motivated offenders or even capable guardians in the area (Felson and Boba, 2010).[8]

The natural starting point for estimating residential population is census data. However, as we noted at the outset of the chapter, our focus on the street segment made using census data impossible. In our search for publicly available data that would provide an estimate of residential population at the street segment, we identified two sources. The first comes from our data on public school students. The second comes from a database on registered voters in Seattle. Both of these databases represent the density of specific populations in our study. The public school data tell us about the number of young people who live on street segments in Seattle. It is likely biased toward poorer and younger residents who would on average have more children and would be more likely to send those children to public schools. Our indicator of population density from the data on registered voters is biased toward more affluent populations, who are the most likely to participate in elections. While we recognize the shortcomings of this measure, we think their combination provides an indicator that is scaled toward actual resident concentrations at the street segment level.[9] To assess this relationship, we aggregated up our street segment estimates to census block groups for the year 2000.[10] We then estimated a correlation between our data and the census estimates. We found a highly significant correlation of 0.70,

(a) Spatial concentration   (b) Spatial autocorrelation

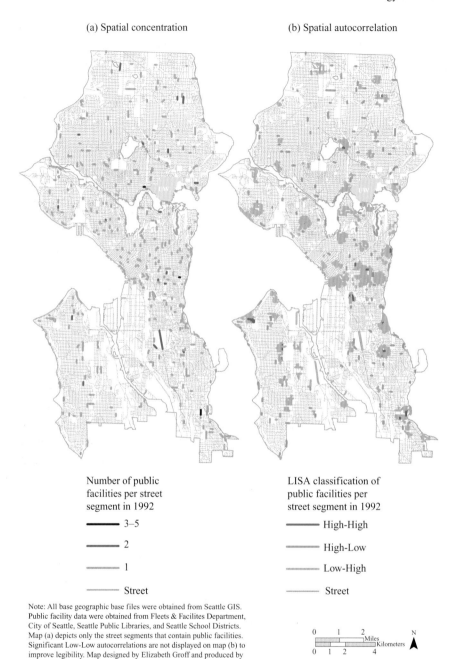

Number of public   LISA classification of
facilities per street   public facilities per
segment in 1992   street segment in 1992

——— 3–5   ——— High-High

——— 2   ——— High-Low

——— 1   ——— Low-High

——— Street   ——— Street

Note: All base geographic base files were obtained from Seattle GIS.
Public facility data were obtained from Fleets & Facilites Department,
City of Seattle, Seattle Public Libraries, and Seattle School Districts.
Map (a) depicts only the street segments that contain public facilities.
Significant Low-Low autocorrelations are not displayed on map (b) to
improve legibility. Map designed by Elizabeth Groff and produced by
Julie Hibdon.

FIGURE 5.5 *Spatial Concentration and Spatial Autocorrelation for Public Facilities*

indicating that there is a degree of error in our measure, but that overall it fits fairly well to the actual population estimates of areas in Seattle.

In 1999, 75.4 percent of the streets in Seattle had at least one resident using our population index. In the same year, the average number of residents on a Seattle street segment using our index was just under 18 and no street had more than 513 residents. By 2004, there were fewer streets with at least one resident (74.8 percent), and the average number of residents had declined to approximately 16 with a maximum of 409 residents. Looking first to the concentration of residents on street segments, figure 5.3b reveals that 50 percent of the residential population consistently lives on between 12 and 14 percent of Seattle street segments. Thus, there are strong concentrations of people living on a relatively small proportion of the streets. The densest residential areas are found in the central and northern areas of the city (see figure 5.6a). There are also areas of high population density in the southeastern and southwestern parts of the city, but they are fewer, and the distance between them is greater.

The results of the LISA analysis (see figure 5.6b) indicate large swaths of the city with positive spatial autocorrelation of residential population as represented by the dark red lines. Nonetheless, even in the midst of these areas there are light blue lines suggesting significant negative autocorrelation, or areas in which low residential population street segments are interspersed with high residential population segments. This could be a sign, for example, of apartment complexes that are among single-family residential units. Whatever the cause, the pattern suggests heterogeneity at those places. In the southeastern areas of the city, there is strong evidence of a dominant pattern of negative spatial autocorrelation, as represented by the pink lines. Here the street-by-street variability of residential population appears particularly pronounced.

BUSINESS-RELATED CRIME GENERATORS AND ATTRACTORS

Businesses located at a place have been found to play a key role in attracting suitable targets.[11] People who shop at stores may have money when they enter or goods that can be stolen when they leave. In turn, businesses themselves are often attractive targets for offenders. To measure this characteristic, we added up the total sales for all the retail businesses on the street segment. We purchased data from InfoUSA for four different years: 1998, 2000, 2002, and 2004.[12] Between 1998 and 2004, 50 percent of all retail sales in Seattle were consistently found on about 0.2 percent of the total street segments in Seattle (see figure 5.3c). Clearly, retail sales are concentrated in retail-sales hot spots. For 100 percent of total retail sales, the trend line again shows a fairly consistent trend at about 6.0 percent of all street segments. These figures also show that approximately 94 percent of streets have no retail business sales in any given year.

(a) 50% Spatial concentration   (b) Spatial autocorrelation

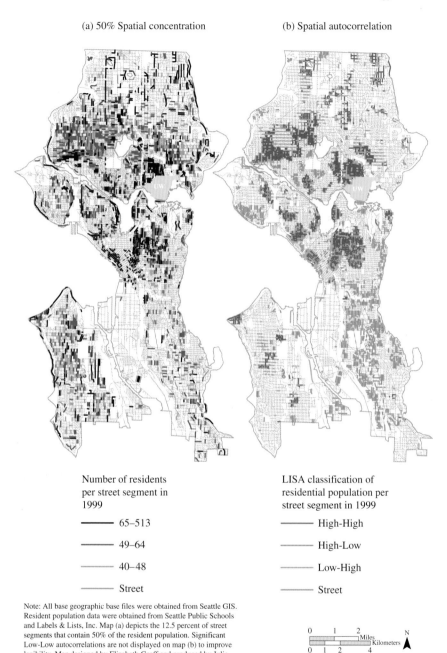

Number of residents   LISA classification of
per street segment in   residential population per
1999   street segment in 1999

—————— 65–513   —————— High-High

—————— 49–64   —————— High-Low

—————— 40–48   ———————— Low-High

—————— Street   —————— Street

Note: All base geographic base files were obtained from Seattle GIS.
Resident population data were obtained from Seattle Public Schools
and Labels & Lists, Inc. Map (a) depicts the 12.5 percent of street
segments that contain 50% of the resident population. Significant
Low-Low autocorrelations are not displayed on map (b) to improve
legibility. Map designed by Elizabeth Groff and produced by Julie
Hibdon.

FIGURE 5.6 *Spatial Concentration and Spatial Autocorrelation for Residential Population*

The street segments making up 50 percent of retail business sales are scattered across Seattle (see figure 5.7a). While we expected to see clusters of those street segments in the downtown core area and in major shopping areas, we were surprised by the extent of the concentration and the scattered geographic pattern of the segments. Retail sales are clustered along major arteries and in business districts such as the downtown area and the industrial area south of downtown.

The LISA for retail businesses emphasizes the strong street-by-street variability of this characteristic (see figure 5.7b). The downtown core has many street segments with high retail sales near other street segments with high retail sales. However, there are also many streets with low retail sales interspersed within those high-sales street segments as indicated by the light blue lines. Finally, there are individual street segments (found in all parts of the city) where a street has significantly lower retail sales than the streets around it (the pink lines). These clusters represent the residential street segments where commercial places are found in the midst of residential areas.

Accessibility/Urban Form

Accessibility and urban form have long been an interest of criminologists concerned with crime opportunities at places. Indeed, even before the development of more recent opportunity theories, urban planners and criminologists have been interested in what is now often termed *Crime Prevention through Environmental Design* (e.g., see Jeffery, 1971; Newman, 1972). A key element of this perspective is the accessibility of offenders and victims to commit crimes in specific places.[13] Just as an accident can occur on a deserted road but is more likely on a crowded urban street, crime can occur on less traveled roads and ones with fewer transportation nodes, but is assumed by opportunity theorists to be more likely to occur on arterial roads and places where there is easy public transportation access (Felson, 2006). Prior studies at the street segment level of analysis have established the relationship between traffic flow and accessibility (defined by type of street and connectivity) for both property crime (Beavon, Brantingham, and Brantingham, 1994; Bevis and Nutter, 1977; Brantingham and Brantingham, 1993a, 1993b; Johnson and Bowers, 2010) and robbery (Bernasco and Block, 2011).[14] We identified two key measures of urban form and accessibility in Seattle: bus stops and type of street.

BUS STOPS

Bus stops are often used as a measure of public transportation accessibility. Previous studies have examined crime near bus stops (LaGrange, 1999; Levine and Wachs, 1986; Loukaitou-Sideris, 1999), while others have used the presence

(a) 50% Spatial concentration   (b) Spatial autocorrelation

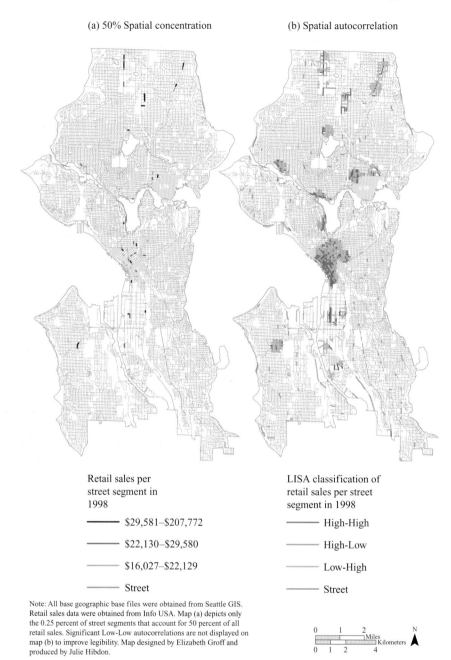

Retail sales per
street segment in
1998

———— $29,581–$207,772

———— $22,130–$29,580

———— $16,027–$22,129

·········· Street

LISA classification of
retail sales per street
segment in 1998

———— High-High

———— High-Low

———— Low-High

·········· Street

Note: All base geographic base files were obtained from Seattle GIS.
Retail sales data were obtained from Info USA. Map (a) depicts only
the 0.25 percent of street segments that account for 50 percent of all
retail sales. Significant Low-Low autocorrelations are not displayed on
map (b) to improve legibility. Map designed by Elizabeth Groff and
produced by Julie Hibdon.

FIGURE 5.7 *Spatial Concentration and Spatial Autocorrelation for Retail Sales*

of bus stops as part of a composite measure of "busy places" (Brantingham and Brantingham, 1981; Wilcox et al., 2004). One study focused on school bus stops and crime, finding that census blocks with higher numbers of school bus stops are associated with higher crime (Roman, 2005). These studies have indicated that bus stops on a street segment contribute to "setting the stage" for criminal events.

We were able to gain information on bus stops from King County Metro Transit. We focus just on bus service within the city of Seattle. The average number of bus stops across streets in Seattle is relatively stable at about 4,000 per year between 1997, the first year these data were available, and 2004. The average number of streets with at least one bus stop is 3,026. About one-third of those streets experienced a change in the number of bus stops over the time period (some gained or lost service completely). The total number of bus stops has decreased slightly since 1997, but the number of streets with bus stops is almost identical. This is not to say that there were not changes in the particular streets with a bus stop, only that the overall picture was relatively stable. Roughly 95.4 percent (n = 23,077) of street segments in the city had no change in the number of bus stops (e.g., if they had none at the start of the period, they did not get any over the period).

The concentration of bus stops on streets is extremely high. Between 1997 and 2004, 50 percent of the total bus stops were consistently found on about 4 percent of Seattle street segments (see figure 5.8). All of the bus stops were located on between 12 and 13 percent of the total street segments, indicating a fairly stable global trend over time.

Figure 5.9a shows that streets including 50 percent of the bus stops are dispersed across the city. But nonetheless, they are concentrated on major arteries or through streets. It is interesting to note that we observed in chapter 3 a concentration of crime on major arteries as well, appearing to confirm the

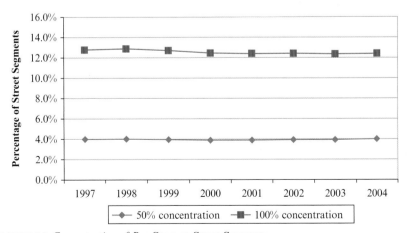

FIGURE 5.8 *Concentration of Bus Stops at Street Segments*

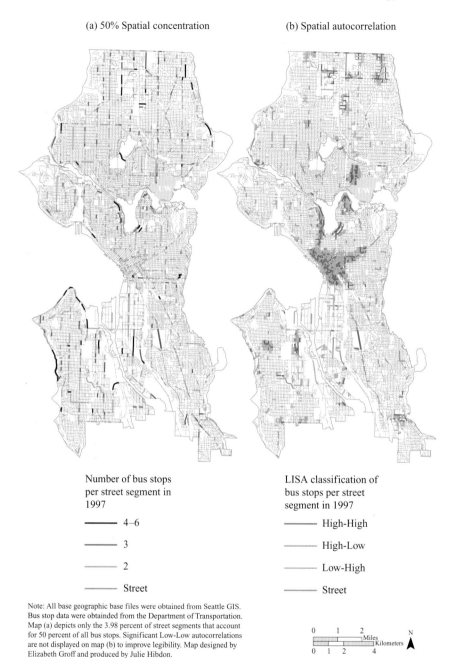

FIGURE 5.9 *Spatial Concentration and Spatial Autocorrelation for Bus Stops*

relationship between accessibility and crime. In chapter 7, we will examine the correlation of these factors with crime more carefully in the context of an analysis that controls for other measures that may also be concentrated across major arteries in the city (e.g., business sales).

The LISA results for bus stops are in line with findings from the other maps (figure 5.9b). There is significant variation across streets in many areas of the city, and especially in downtown Seattle. Note, for example, the large number of light blue and pink lines representing negative spatial autocorrelation across the city. The clustering of bus stops tends to follow a continuous linear pattern rather than the clustered pattern seen for most other variables. In a continuous linear pattern, the streets that are connected end to end (for example, two different street segments of the same avenue) tend to have similar amounts of a characteristic (in this case bus stops), while quantities on streets one street over are unrelated. The exceptions to this pattern occur in high-bus-service areas such as downtown and near the University of Washington.

TYPE OF STREET

Perhaps the most important component of the accessibility of offenders, victims, and guardians to places is determined by the street network itself. We consider in this context only two street types, arterial roads and non-arterial roads. Arterial streets are through streets that carry larger volumes of traffic. The non-arterial roads consist of residential streets and walkways.[15] Residential streets run through neighborhoods and are designed to carry only neighborhood traffic. Walkways are non-vehicular paths or stairways that typically connect two residential streets.

Arterial streets are of particular interest to this study because of their role in increasing accessibility and serving as change points across the urban landscape. A number of studies have shown a relationship between street type and crime. In Los Angeles, one study found that the 10 highest crime bus stops were situated in commercial areas at the intersections of multilane roads (Levine and Wachs, 1986; Loukaitou-Sideris, 1999). In New York City, street segments with more lanes experienced more reported Part I and quality-of-life crimes (Perkins et al., 1993).[16] Non-arterial streets are the largest category of streets in Seattle. They account for 73.4 percent (n = 17,628) of all streets in the study. Arterial streets are 26.6 percent (n = 6,395) of all streets. Measures of variability across time were not applied to this variable since the same street segments were used for the entire study period.[17]

Since Seattle is a mature city, it is not surprising that the residential road network covers the majority of the land surface that is not covered by water (see figure 5.10). Water is a major factor in shaping transportation in Seattle because it acts as a barrier. The "blank" areas of the city depicted on figure 5.10 are major water bodies. The spatial distribution of streets by type is as would be

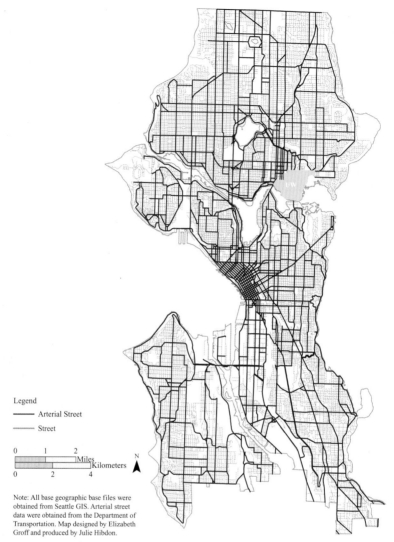

Legend

——— Arterial Street

------- Street

0   1   2
        |Miles
                |Kilometers
0   2   4

N

Note: All base geographic base files were
obtained from Seattle GIS. Arterial street
data were obtained from the Department of
Transportation. Map designed by Elizabeth
Groff and produced by Julie Hibdon.

FIGURE 5.10 *Distribution of Arterial Roads*

expected. The arterial streets tend to be near other arterial streets (near in this
case is a linear concept since streets are connected at their ends; see figure 5.10).
There is a marked concentration of arterial streets in the downtown area.

Guardianship

Guardianship has been a particularly important component of routine activity
theory (Felson, 1987; Osgood et al., 1996) and has been the focus of recent
crime prevention efforts such as hot spots policing (Braga and Weisburd, 2010;

Braga and Bond, 2008; Sherman and Weisburd, 1995; Weisburd and Green, 1995). At the outset of our study, we tried to gain a measure of police guardianship, but found it impossible to construct such a measure in an accurate way. It is very surprising in some sense that the police do not "keep track" of where they patrol and the types of patrol employed. But this is the case in Seattle and nearly all other American police jurisdictions. Only over the last few years have some innovative agencies begun to use automated vehicle locator systems (AVL) to track the presence of police in their cities, and such programs are still in their experimental phases.[18] We tried to use emergency crime call data, which lists the times when police are responding to calls as a way of tracking police presence, but we were able to gain data only for four years of our study period, and those data were, not surprisingly, extremely highly correlated with crime incident data.[19] We concluded that the data overall reflected not police patrol at places, but police response to crimes at specific places, many of which were later identified as the locations of crime incidents. The collinearity of these data with crime, and the short time frame available to us, led us not to include them in our analyses here. At the same time, we think the absence of strong data on where the police are provides an important limitation to our study, which we will return to in chapter 8.

While we were not able to measure police presence, we were able to include an indicator that reflected the location of police and fire stations. In some sense, this should be an important indicator of official guardianship, since we would expect the visibility of police and firefighters to be greatest in these areas. This is both because this is where they are stationed and because they routinely depart and return to these places. We also measure the percentage of vacant land as an indicator of guardianship. Other studies have noted that vacant land represents the presence of a consistent hole in the fabric of informal social control on a street segment (Rice and Smith, 2002). Vacant land is not typically a destination for legal activities, and it has no place managers at all; thus, it decreases the potential for informal social control. Finally, the amount of street lighting captures the visibility at a place during evening hours. It has often been assumed that good street lighting is a deterrent to crime (e.g., Farrington and Welsh, 2002; Painter and Farrington, 1997). Lighting has also been hypothesized to represent the investment of a city in a place (Groff and LaVigne, 2001).

POLICE AND FIRE STATIONS

Together there were a total of 39 streets that had an emergency station on them during the study period from 1989–2004. The number of emergency stations was very stable. For most of the time period, there were 37 stations (1989–2002), only four of which were police stations. When one police station moved from one location to another, there were 36 active stations in 1999 and then 37 again in 2000. In 2003, a new police station opened in southwest Seattle, which brought the number up to 38 emergency stations.[20]

Using the same methodology that was used for public facilites, we develop a measure reflecting "average number of fire and police stations within one-quarter of a mile" to capture the influence of fire/police stations on nearby places.[21] We use this approach both because of the small number of emergency stations in the city, and the fact that we would expect the impact of the stations to extend beyond the immediate street segments on which they were located. As expected given the small numbers, the majority of street segments (approximately 93 percent) have no fire/police facilities within one-quarter of a mile over the entire time period. Relatively few, approximately 6 percent, have one facility and less than 1 percent have two.

Because of our use of catchment areas, a concentration graph is inappropriate. However, as with public facilities, it is possible to examine the geographic distribution of exposure to fire and police stations at the street segment level (see figure 5.11). Mapping of the fire and police stations indicates they are very uniformly distributed across Seattle. In this context, guardianship as reflected by police and fire stations strongly varies at a local geographic level.

PERCENTAGE OF VACANT LAND

Percentage of vacant land is defined from the parcel data for Seattle, which has a land-use code that identifies parcels that are vacant. The category includes developable land that is currently vacant (land uses such as cemeteries, parks, easements, etc. are not included in this measure). Previous research shows that at the street segment level, vacant/parking lots are significantly related to increased auto theft (Taylor et al., 1995). Streets with more vacant land have also been found to have more Part I and quality-of-life crimes (Kurtz, Koons, and Taylor, 1998), higher levels of physical deterioration (Loukaitou-Sideris, 1999), higher levels of litter and vandalism, as well as increased calls for service (Evans and Oulds, 1984; Herbert, 1982). Vacant lots have also been found to be significantly related to street robbery (Kurtz et al., 1998).

Between 1989 and 1998, 50 percent of the vacant parcels in Seattle are consistently found on between 2 and 2.5 percent of the total Seattle street segments (see figure 5.12a). In 2004, there is a decline down to 1.7 percent of street segments. The concentration line for 100 percent of the vacant land shows a slight increasing trend from 1989 to 1998, moving from 6.4 to 8.0 percent of total street segements. There is a dramatic decline down to 4.7 percent of street segments in 2004. A substantial decrease in total vacant parcels explains the drop in 2004. Overall, these data suggest that vacant land is consistently concentrated on a small number of street segments in the city.

The geographic pattern of the concentration of places accounting for 50 percent of vacant land parcels indicates that this characteristic is spread widely

(a) Spatial concentration   (b) Spatial autocorrelation

Police/Fire station
locations in 1992

—— Presence

········ Street

LISA classification of
police/fire stations per
street segment in 1992

—— High-High

—— High-Low

—— Low-High

—— Street

Note: All base geographic base files were obtained from Seattle GIS. Police and
Fire station data were obtained from the Fleets and Facilities Department. Map
(a) depicts street segments that contain a police or fire station. Significant
Low-Low autocorrelations are not displayed on map (b) to improve legibility. Map
designed by Elizabeth Groff and produced by Julie Hibdon.

FIGURE 5.11 *Spatial Concentration and Spatial Autocorrelation for Fire and Police Stations*

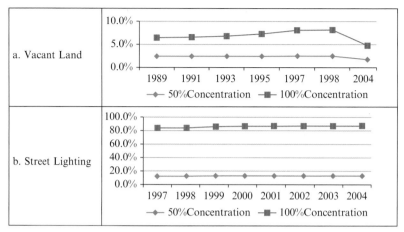

FIGURE 5.12 *Concentration of Guardianship at Street Segments*

throughout the city (see figure 5.13a). Importantly, there is not evidence here of large areas that are composed only of vacant land. The LISA statistics for vacant land parcels tell the same story, emphasizing street-by-street varaiability (see figure 5.13b). There is evidence of positive spatial autocorrelation (or dark red lines) in certain areas, but those areas also include many pockets of negative spatial autocorrelation (light blue and pink lines), indicating streets with low levels of vacant land are near streets with high levels.

STREET LIGHTING

Street lighting is measured using total number of watts per street segment[22]. As mentioned above, the amount of street lighting has been shown to be related to crime levels. One study found eight of the ten highest crime bus stops lacked adequate street lighting (Loukaitou-Sideris, 1999). Another demonstrated that "gas drive-offs" (i.e., where people drive away from the gas station without paying) could be reduced by as much as 65 percent with increased lighting at convenience stores (LaVigne, 1994). British studies fi nd that increased street lighting decreases crime (Painter and Farrington, 1997, 1999). An early review of the literature concluded that targeted increases in street lighting were more effective than general ones and that improved lighting decreases fear of crime (Pease, 1999). A more recent meta-analysis of street lighting and crime found a reduction in crime when lighting is increased (Farrington and Welsh, 2002; Welsh and Farrington, 2008).

Looking at the city as a whole, between 1997 and 2004, 50 percent of the total street lighting was consistently found on between 11.5 and 13 percent of Seattle street segments (see figure 5.12b). All of the street lighting was located

(a) 50% Spatial concentration   (b) Spatial autocorrelation

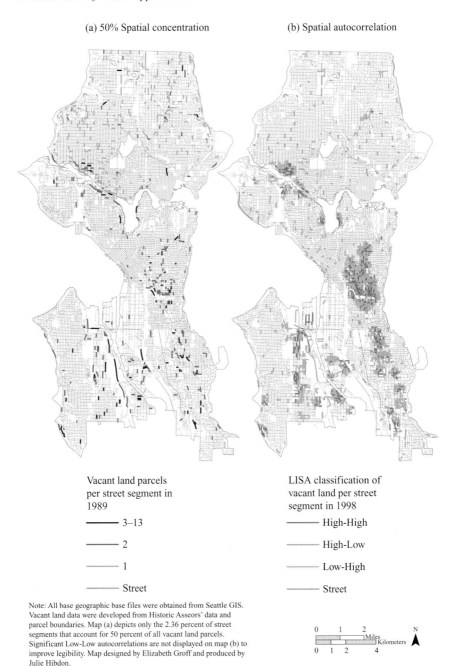

Vacant land parcels
per street segment in
1989

——— 3–13

——— 2

——— 1

——— Street

LISA classification of
vacant land per street
segment in 1998

——— High-High

——— High-Low

——— Low-High

——— Street

Note: All base geographic base files were obtained from Seattle GIS.
Vacant land data were developed from Historic Asseors' data and
parcel boundaries. Map (a) depicts only the 2.36 percent of street
segments that account for 50 percent of all vacant land parcels.
Significant Low-Low autocorrelations are not displayed on map (b) to
improve legibility. Map designed by Elizabeth Groff and produced by
Julie Hibdon.

FIGURE 5.13 *Spatial Concentration and Spatial Autocorrelation for Vacant Land*

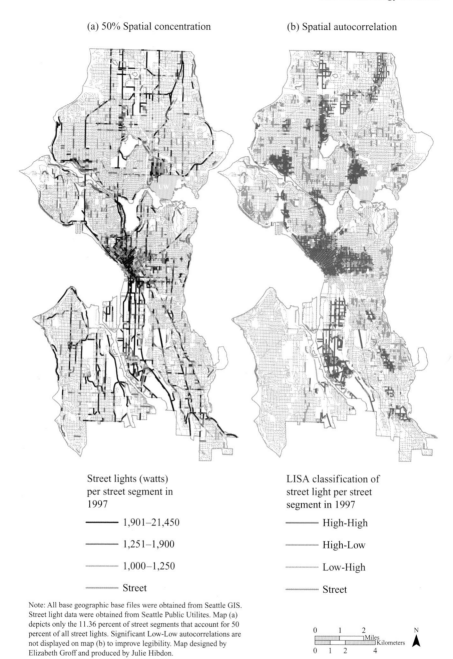

(a) 50% Spatial concentration   (b) Spatial autocorrelation

Street lights (watts)
per street segment in
1997

——— 1,901–21,450

——— 1,251–1,900

——— 1,000–1,250

——— Street

LISA classification of
street light per street
segment in 1997

——— High-High

——— High-Low

——— Low-High

——— Street

Note: All base geographic base files were obtained from Seattle GIS.
Street light data were obtained from Seattle Public Utilites. Map (a)
depicts only the 11.36 percent of street segments that account for 50
percent of all street lights. Significant Low-Low autocorrelations are
not displayed on map (b) to improve legibility. Map designed by
Elizabeth Groff and produced by Julie Hibdon.

FIGURE 5.14   *Spatial Concentration and Spatial Autocorrelation for Street Lighting*

on between 84 and 87 percent of the total street segments. Both trend lines are fairly stable over time. This follows a pattern of concentration at relatively few places but widespread presence across most places. Between 13 and 16 percent of streets have no lighting in any given year.

Geographically, the concentration of streets accounting for 50 percent of street lighting follows the major arterial roads and illustrates the difference between downtown (which is extremely well lit) and the rest of the city (see figure 5.14a). An examination of the spatial dependency in street lighting from street to street reinforces this observation, departing from previous analyses in this chapter (see figure 5.14b). The pattern, as indicated by dark red lines, reflects the overwhelming concentration of street lighting in the downtown area and then in major population areas of the north. The industrial part of the southeastern section of the city also has many places with high amounts of lighting, which are surrounded by other streets of high street lighting. Outside of these areas, the dominant pattern of street lighting is linear and follows major roads. This suggests that there are areas of low street lighting divided by individual streets with higher amounts and that street-by-street variability is not as great as observed for other opportunity measures. This means that street lighting, though concentrated on a relatively small number of street segments, represents more of an area than local process, at least in Seattle. As we will see in chapter 7, this has important implications for its use as a measure for explaining variability in crime patterns at street segments.

Conclusions

Our examination of the concentration and variability of opportunity factors at street segments in Seattle provides initial confirmation of the assumption in opportunity theories that factors that provide opportunities for crime are concentrated at specific places, and that concentration is at a very low geographic level. Motivated offenders (operationalized as high-risk juveniles) are concentrated on individual segments and evidence significant variability from street segment to street segment. Examination of the concentration and geographic variability of suitable targets, as measured by employment, public facilities, residential population, and business sales, tells a similar story of strong concentration in hot spots, yet variability at the street segment level. Indicators of urban form and accessibility, as reflected by type of road and bus stops, also follow this pattern. In the case of our indicators of guardianship, street segments with vacant land and emergency stations are dispersed and isolated, representing distributed concentration. Street lighting departs most significantly from the other patterns, with some homogeneous areas of concentration and other areas that have relatively low and similar levels of lighting. In many cases, the low levels of lighting were divided by major roads on which quite a lot of lighting exists. These patterns evidence area rather than micro-geographic-level processes.

Accordingly, for most of the characteristics of street segments we examined in this chapter there are strong geographic concentrations at a very low geographic level. We have identified hot spots of crime opportunities, just as in the previous chapters we identified hot spots of crime. There is also significant street-by-street variability in these characteristics, as with crime, suggesting the importance of examining street segment as contrasted with community or larger area trends. At the same time, for many of the traits identified here we also saw concentrations in larger areas, suggesting as we had seen with the distribution of crime at street segments that larger area effects are at play in influencing the distribution of certain opportunity characteristics in areas of the city.

One additional finding from this chapter is perhaps not surprising, but is likely to have important impacts on our understanding of variability in crime at place over time. The traits we examined in this chapter generally stayed relatively stable over the periods for which we had data available. This suggests that opportunity characteristics at place are relatively stable over time. In some sense, this is not surprising, reflecting the fact that characteristics of places, unlike characteristics of people, may be likely to change only over relatively long periods of time. In the next chapter, when we examine the concentration and distribution of characteristics of social disorganization, we will gain a more general view regarding whether this applies across different theoretical constructs.

We think it important before concluding to also mention again that our data are necessarily limited and that we could not identify some key components of opportunity theories. For example, as we noted earlier, we were not able to identify a valid measure of police guardianship. Nonetheless, ours is the most comprehensive and systematic collection of data we are aware of in the criminology of place, and we have been able to carefully identify the concentration and variability of opportunity measures in ways that have not been possible in prior studies.

We have now established that there is concentration and variability of opportunity characteristics of crime at place. This provides a strong basis for examining whether such concentration and geographic patterning at a micro geographic level are related to the patterns of crime we observed in chapter 3. Are hot spots of crime opportunities strongly related to hot spots of crime itself? Do changes in such opportunities at specific street segments across time relate to changes in crime patterns over time? These are key questions that have not been systematically examined in prior studies. But before we turn to them in chapter 7, we explore in the next chapter whether measures of social disorganization also have relevance for the criminology of place.

{ 6 }

Are Processes of Social Disorganization Relevant to the Criminology of Place?

As we described in chapter 2, social disorganization theories have played an important part in the study of crime at place. Beginning with the Chicago School (Park, 1925 [1967]; Shaw, 1929), and more recently with contributions to the study of communities and crime (Reiss and Tonry, 1986), criminologists have long recognized that the social organization of communities and neighborhoods is an important factor in understanding the crime problem. According to social disorganization theorists, a community with a high crime rate is usually disorganized with dilapidated buildings, high infant mortality rates, abandoned cars, boarded windows, and population heterogeneity (Bursik, 1984; Shaw and McKay, 1942 [1969]). In recent years, researchers have emphasized intervening mechanisms of social disorganization, reflecting the degree to which people who live in communities can exercise social control over the behavior of residents and visitors. Such mechanisms and their relationship to crime have been documented in studies of participation in local organizations, willingness (or perception of responsibility) to intervene in public affairs, local friendship networks, mutual trust, and unsupervised teens (Sampson and Groves, 1989; Sampson, Raudenbush, and Earls, 1997; Taylor, Gottfredson, and Brower, 1984; Taylor, Kelly, and Salvatore, 2010; Wilcox, Madensen, and Tillyer, 2007).

But the impact of social disorganization on crime has been described at much larger units of analysis than our interests in the study of crime and place in Seattle. Social disorganization theorists have focused their concerns on "communities" and "neighborhoods," not on street segments or even small groups of street segments. Even Shaw and McKay (1942 [1969]), who began their investigation of juvenile delinquency with the addresses of the youths they studied, focused their theoretical interests on the general patterns of delinquency in large areas of the city. The criminology of place, in turn, has been linked strongly to the opportunity theories that we examined in the previous chapter.

There has been relatively little interest in applying social disorganization theories to micro units of place such as street segments (for exceptions, see Kurtz, Koons, and Taylor, 1998; Perkins et al., 1990; Rice and Smith, 2002; Smith, Frazee, and Davison, 2000).

In our view, this neglect of social disorganization theory in the criminology of place has hindered the development of theory and empirical analysis in this area. The founders of the social disorganization perspective sought to bring into our understanding of crime the important social dynamics that occur within communities in urban areas. They were concerned with the face-to-face interaction of community members and the ways in which communities differed in their abilities to control misbehavior. We think that the idea of behavior settings, which we have used in defining the street segment, is consistent in many ways with the concept of community as presented in the social disorganization perspective. Behavior settings are micro communities, or "small scale social systems" (Wicker, 1987: 614), evidencing many of the characteristics that defined neighborhoods and communities for the Chicago School or later theorists in this area. We noted in chapter 1 that people who frequent a street segment get to know one another and become familiar with each other's routines, they develop certain roles they play in the life of the street segment, and norms about acceptable behavior emerge and are often shared (Taylor, 1997, 1998). The street segment in this context can be seen as a type of community, much smaller than that which has focused the interests of social disorganization theorists, but nonetheless a social system where social disorganization may have salience for understanding crime problems.

The focus of this chapter is to examine whether social disorganization theory is relevant to the criminology of place. Do characteristics of social disorganization cluster at a very local level of geography? Are there hot spots of social disorganization as there are hot spots of crime and crime opportunities? Perhaps most important, do characteristics of social disorganization vary within larger areas of geography such as communities and neighborhoods? If characteristics of social disorganization vary only at higher geographic units, then the theory's salience for understanding the variability at micro units of geography would be limited. But if such traits vary greatly within neighborhoods and across street segments, then social disorganization theory must be considered as a potential explanatory perspective in the criminology of place.

Structural Variables

In the specification of social disorganization theory developed at the Chicago School, structural characteristics of neighborhoods and communities were seen as a key element in the production of crime. In this conception, a neighborhood that was poorer, more disadvantaged, more heterogeneous in the types of people who lived there, and more urbanized was more vulnerable to crime and other social problems. These are described as structural characteristics because they tell us about the overall structure and social fabric of communities, and an important contribution of the Chicago School theorists was to emphasize that these structural characteristics shaped the behavior of the people in these areas. We were able to identify a number of indicators that reflect structural dimensions of social disorganization at the street segment level (see appendix 4 for details of the data collection process). Nonetheless, we think it important to emphasize here, as we did in chapter 5, that our measures by necessity are defined by the data sources available to us.

SOCIOECONOMIC STATUS

In the original version of social disorganization theory, Shaw and McKay (1942 [1969]) contended that the concentration of industries and businesses in the downtown area makes it an undesirable place to live. People who could not afford to move out of town ended up in the transitional zone—the area between the industrial center and the residential area. Thus, the transitional area tends to contain low-socioeconomic-status residents, high crime rates, and other social illnesses. In social disorganization theory, the socioeconomic status (SES) of residents is an important indicator of crime-ridden areas. Even in recent social disorganization theory, SES is still used widely as an indicator of the resources and capabilities of residents to invest in the community where they live (e.g., see Bellair, 1997; Bursik and Grasmick, 1993; Sampson, 1993; Sampson and Groves, 1989; Veysey and Messner, 1999).

We measure SES by using the average property values of housing on each street segment, and the extent to which there is public housing assistance. The value of residential property is a good micro-level indicator of the socioeconomic status of people who live on a street segment, because it is factored into both the price of homes for sale and into the rent that is paid by non-home owners (Smargiassi et al., 2006; Connolly, O'Reilly, and Rosato, 2010). Public assistance for housing identifies a somewhat different dimension of SES, because it focuses on places where there are concentrations of truly disadvantaged populations (see below).

Residential Property Values

Using data from the city planning office and the tax assessor's office, we were able to identify information about residential property values for six years over the study period: 1991, 1993, 1995, 1997, 1998, and 2004.[1] About 72 percent of the streets have detailed records about housing values. Among the streets with at least one residential property, 16,166 street segments have at least one single-family house at some point during the study period (93.11 percent). Multifamily buildings are more concentrated in the city. For example, in 1989, out of the 17,150 streets with any residential building, 16,052 streets had single-family houses while only 3,480 streets had multifamily residential buildings.

One complication of using the raw property value data for the residential areas is that it includes both single-family housing and multifamily dwellings. If we simply compare property values without addressing the differences between single-family houses and multi-dwelling buildings, the results will be misleading. Single-family houses tend to be worth less than high-rise buildings simply because of the size of the land or physical construction; however, people who live in single-family houses are more likely to own their homes and accordingly are likely to be of higher socioeconomic status. To take into account the impact of both single-family dwellings and multifamily dwellings, we rank single-family housing and multifamily housing separately and then create a composite score to represent the SES of the street segment.[2]

As in the previous chapter, our first question is whether there is concentration in SES at the level of street segments in Seattle. Our answer to this question is not as clear as in many indicators examined in the previous chapter. Fifty percent of residential property wealth, as measured by our index, is concentrated at between 30 and 31 percent of street segments with any residential property throughout the observation period (see figure 6.1a). While the concentration of property values at street segments remained constant over time, the overall value of property at street segments increased.[3]

Figure 6.2a shows the streets that include the top 50 percent of property values using our index. As in chapter 5, we present maps only for the first year

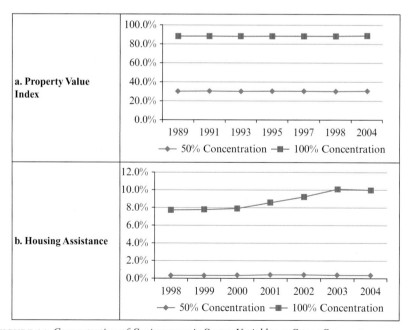

FIGURE 6.1 *Concentration of Socioeconomic Status Variables at Street Segments*

(a) 50% Spatial concentration   (b) Spatial autocorrelation

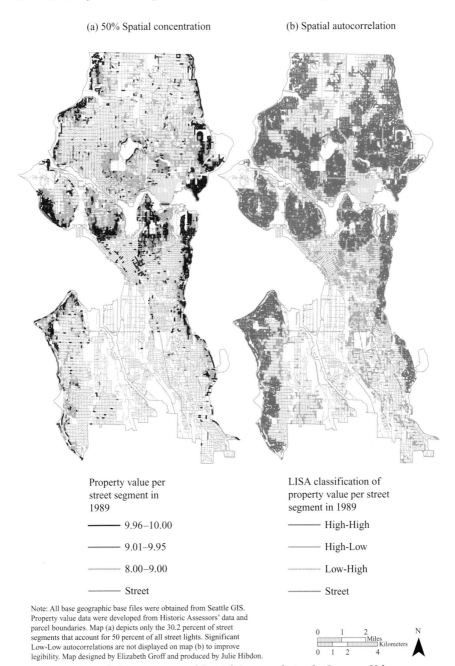

Property value per
street segment in
1989

———— 9.96–10.00

———— 9.01–9.95

———— 8.00–9.00

———— Street

LISA classification of
property value per street
segment in 1989

———— High-High

———— High-Low

·········· Low-High

———— Street

Note: All base geographic base files were obtained from Seattle GIS.
Property value data were developed from Historic Assessors' data and
parcel boundaries. Map (a) depicts only the 30.2 percent of street
segments that account for 50 percent of all street lights. Significant
Low-Low autocorrelations are not displayed on map (b) to improve
legibility. Map designed by Elizabeth Groff and produced by Julie Hibdon.

FIGURE 6.2 *Spatial Concentration and Spatial Autocorrelation for Property Value*

of available data to simplify our presentation. Again, we do not find mean-ingful differences in the geographic distribution of the measures across time.[4] Clearly there are strong area effects indicated in this map. For example, there are strong concentrations of the highest value residential street segments along the coasts and in the northern sections of the city. This would not have been a surprise to the Chicago School theorists, who argued that greater wealth and socioeconomic status would be found farther away from the central business and industrial parts of the city (Burgess, 1925 [1967]). Perhaps the concentration of wealth on the coasts also represents the desire of urban residents to be near scenic views and open areas. But note that there are also concentrations of wealth in the central city areas, reflecting, in this case, the fact that specific places in the city center can be attractive for modern urban residents. More generally, though there is clearly area clustering, there is also considerable spread of higher value residential street segments, and also a good deal of var-iability within areas.

Reinforcing these observations, the LISA map shows large areas of gener-ally positive and significant spatial autocorrelation (see figure 6.2b). The LISA analysis confirms the concentration of high-value street segments along the coasts and in the northern part of the central section and the northern sections of the city. But note too that there are often street segments dominated by low-value properties sprinkled among them (as indicated by the light blue lines). There are as well areas that are dominated by negative spatial autocorrelation, especially as indicated by the pink lines in the southern areas of Seattle showing that high SES streets are often interspersed with low SES streets.

Housing Assistance: Public Housing and Section 8 Vouchers

A second measure of SES in our data is the extent to which there is evidence of public assistance for housing on street segments. In Seattle, as in other American cities, public housing and assistance for housing is provided to the most disad-vantaged populations.[5] Concentrations of public assistance have long been connected to social disorganization (Kubrin and Weitzer, 2003) and have been seen to further amplify the effects of other neighborhood disadvantages (Bursik, 1989; Wilson, 1987).

For example, McNulty and Holloway (2000) point out that black commu-nities with public housing projects have higher crime rates than black com-munities without public housing projects, while the latter have crime rates comparable to white communities. Nonetheless, we want to emphasize that a place with a disadvantaged population still can have high levels of social con-trol or collective efficacy if residents share close relationships and trust each other. The determinants of collective efficacy of places will be reviewed in a later section. We combine two measures that indicate public housing assistance (public housing and Section 8 vouchers) into a single variable. The distribution of the public-housing-assistance variable represents the locations where the economically disadvantaged live.

To qualify for public housing in Seattle, households must earn 80 percent or less of the median Seattle-area income. Public housing in Seattle includes both high-rise communities (approximately 75–300 units per building) and garden communities (community style; approximately 525 units). High-rise buildings were built in the 1970s; garden communities were built in the 1940s, and some have been renovated and redeveloped over time. The structures and locations of public housing in Seattle have been fairly stable, especially within our study period. However, when change did occur, the magnitude was very large. For example, the total number of units decreased from 5,856 in 1989 to 3,896 in 2004. Importantly, public housing is very concentrated in Seattle. Less than 1 percent of street segments (around 200 streets) in Seattle have public housing units on them.[6]

Housing vouchers, termed Section 8 vouchers because they were first instituted in Section 8 of the 1974 U.S. Housing and Community Development Act, are provided only to low-income families and individuals. Recipients in this case must earn 30 percent of the area's median income or less to qualify. Section 8 vouchers can be used to rent any market-rate apartment for a reduced cost (at apartments where the management accepts the vouchers), with the voucher making up the difference in cost. The number of vouchers used in Seattle increased slowly for the first three years of our study period, from 3,583 in 1998 to 3,869 in 2000, but then almost doubled between 2001 and 2004. The average number of vouchers per year over the whole time period was 4,670.

Public housing assistance is extremely concentrated in what might be termed public-assistance hot spots. Indeed, 50 percent of housing assistance is consistently found on about 0.4 percent of the street segments in Seattle (see figure 6.1b). The concentration line for 100 percent of the housing-assistance variable shows a gradual increasing trend from 1998 to 2003, moving from 7.7 to 10.1 percent of total street segements, followed by a leveling off in 2004. The increase in the 100 percent concentration line of the housing-assistance variable is mainly the result of increases in Section 8 housing vouchers after 2001.

When we view the street segments in the city that include the top 50 percent of housing assistance, we can see that such assistance is not only concentrated but widely spread across Seattle (see figure 6.3a). Public-assistance hot spots accordingly are not simply concentrated in a few specific areas or communities. Indeed, the LISA map (see figure 6.3b) reinforces the idea that there is very strong heterogeneity of this characteristic within areas. While there are some pockets of high public housing assistance in the southern areas of Seattle (as indicated by the dark red lines), negative spatial autocorrelation, as indicated by pink and light blue lines, is much more common across the map. This means that there is a good deal of interspersion of street segments with different levels of housing assistance in most areas. The pink lines indicate where streets with

(a) 50% Spatial concentration   (b) Spatial autocorrelation

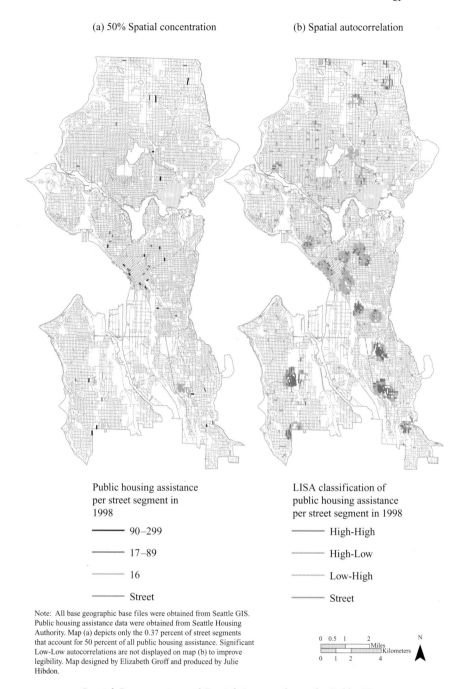

Public housing assistance
per street segment in
1998

────── 90–299

────── 17–89

────── 16

────── Street

LISA classification of
public housing assistance
per street segment in 1998

────── High-High

────── High-Low

────── Low-High

────── Street

Note: All base geographic base files were obtained from Seattle GIS.
Public housing assistance data were obtained from Seattle Housing
Authority. Map (a) depicts only the 0.37 percent of street segments
that account for 50 percent of all public housing assistance. Significant
Low-Low autocorrelations are not displayed on map (b) to improve
legibility. Map designed by Elizabeth Groff and produced by Julie
Hibdon.

FIGURE 6.3 *Spatial Concentration and Spatial Autocorrelation for Public Housing
Assistance*

high levels of public housing assistance are near to streets with generally low levels of public housing. The light blue lines depict isolated street segments with low levels of public housing assistance which are surrounded by streets with higher levels.

MIXED LAND USE

Type of land use has also been argued to vary across communities and influence community crime rates in the social disorganization perspective (e.g., see Sampson and Groves, 1989). Communities with a mixture of different land uses are assumed to be less likely to have strong ties among residents, while communities with mainly residential units are expected to evidence stronger ties among residents and have significantly lower crime rates (Roncek, 2000; Stark, 1987). Several theorists argue that land use is related to the strength of social control (Jacobs, 1961; Taylor, 1997; Wilcox et al., 2004). Public places must contend with more strangers, and there is a higher level of anonymity in such areas that reduces the level of community social controls.

We were able to measure this dimension of the social disorganization perspective by looking at data from the Planning Department in Seattle. At the outset of our data collection period (1989), about 83.6 percent of the street segments in Seattle were defined by the Planning Department as used at least partially for residential purposes.[7] Only 3.6 percent of street segments were used exclusively for commercial purposes.

A key issue in assessing mixed land use is the lack of consensus on what level of mixture of land use is required to reach a tipping point that creates a high risk of increasing crime. For example, should mixed land use be defined as something close to equal residential and business presence on a street, or would the social disorganization associated with mixed land use begin as soon as any commercial use is added to a residential street segment? A number of scholars have taken the latter approach, defining any area with less than 100 percent of total area used for residential purposes as including mixed land use (e.g., see Sampson and Groves, 1989; Wilcox et al., 2004). We thought a more conservative measure of mixed land use was warranted for street segments. A single small business, for example, on a street with a number of large apartment buildings did not seem to us enough of a disruption of the social fabric of a street segment to warrant the mixed land use definition. Accordingly, we defined a street segment as having mixed land use if residential or commercial properties accounted for between 25 percent and 75 percent of all land use on the street.

Mixed land use is an extremely concentrated phenomenon and very stable over time in Seattle. As shown in figure 6.4, about 3 percent of street segments each year account for 50 percent of segments with mixed land use across the observation years available.[8] All the segments meeting the definition of mixed land use are found on between 5–6 percent of streets in Seattle each year.

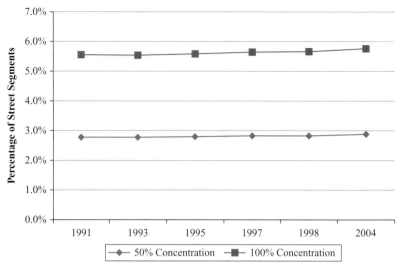

FIGURE 6.4 *Concentration Graph of Mixed Land Use at Street Segments*

The results of geographic analyses are presented in figure 6.5. Figure 6.5a is a simple descriptive map that shows where the streets with mixed land use are located. Not surprisingly, there are greater concentrations of streets classified as mixed land use in the central business district of the city, and there is a clear relationship between the street patterns and land use. More street segments classified as mixed land use are found on arterial or through streets in Seattle. This likely reflects the advantages that such streets provide merchants in generating business through easy access and greater street traffic.

The LISA map (see figure 6.5b) indicates a great deal of spatial heterogeneity in mixed land use across the city. Streets with mixed land use are widely distributed across Seattle but occur in isolated pockets of mixed land use (as reflected by the small number of dark red lines in the map). At the same time, streets with primarily a single purpose of usage are nearby streets with mixed usage (as indicated by the light blue lines). Accordingly, not only is mixed land use concentrated at specific street segments in the city, but also those concentrations evidence a great deal of variability from street to street in the city.

RACIAL HETEROGENEITY

In social disorganization theory, racial heterogeneity has long been considered an important predictor of crime (Bursik and Grasmick, 1993; Kornhauser, 1978; Sampson and Groves, 1989). An area with a more heterogeneous racial composition is in this perspective likely to be considered less cohesive and have lower levels of community social control. Racial differences can sometimes become a barrier for people to communicate and identify with each other. Thus,

(a) Spatial concentration   (b) Spatial autocorrelation

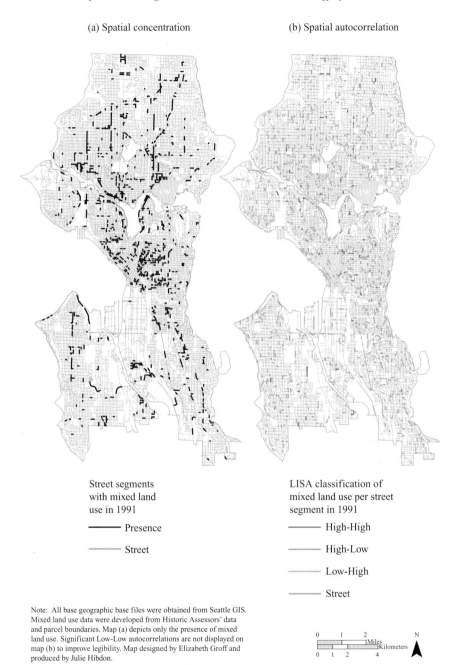

Street segments   LISA classification of
with mixed land   mixed land use per street
use in 1991   segment in 1991

———— Presence   ———— High-High

········· Street   ———— High-Low

                                  ········· Low-High

                                  ———— Street

Note: All base geographic base files were obtained from Seattle GIS.
Mixed land use data were developed from Historic Assessors' data
and parcel boundaries. Map (a) depicts only the presence of mixed
land use. Significant Low-Low autocorrelations are not displayed on
map (b) to improve legibility. Map designed by Elizabeth Groff and
produced by Julie Hibdon.

FIGURE 6.5 *Spatial Concentration and Spatial Autocorrelation for Mixed Land Use*

residents are less likely to develop strong ties, and as a result, the population turnover rate is also likely to be high. This can also be a result of a natural selection process, as places with more racial heterogeneity tend to have more rental properties or affordable housing. Consequently, crime tends to occur at places that are more heterogeneous, even if the racial make-up itself might not lead to a high crime rate (Sampson, Raudenbush, and Earls, 1997; Shaw and McKay, 1942 [1969]).

In prior studies, the percentage of blacks (or minority residents) has traditionally been used as an indicator of racial heterogeneity (see Blau and Blau, 1982; Messner, 1983). Williams (1984) challenged the idea and showed that the relationship between the percentage of blacks and homicide rates is actually an inverted-U shape, not linear. The explanation is straightforward: when an area has a high percentage of minority residents relative to whites (the commonly used reference group), it is actually more homogeneous than heterogeneous, as minorities become the dominant group at that place. After passing the tipping point, the high percentage of minority residents actually leads to a more stable social control system and a lower crime rate. To support this argument, Williams reanalyzed data from Messner (1983) and Blau and Blau (1982) with the new specification and the performance of models improved substantially (variance explained increased 14 percent).

However, using only the percentage of blacks can be a flawed approach. With the changes of population composition in the United States, population heterogeneity has become a more complex phenomenon. Indeed, as of the year 2000, Hispanics had surpassed blacks and become the largest minority group in America. Additionally, Seattle has a disproportionately larger Asian population compared to the nationwide average (see chapter 1). To account for these changes, and the particular racial and ethnic composition of Seattle, we adopt an approach developed by Smith, Frazee, and Davison (2000) and Smith and Jarjoura (1988) and define racial heterogeneity using a probability-based model.[9] The overall index measures the level of heterogeneity of each street segment including white, black, Hispanic, and Asian population characteristics. Each street is assigned a score where the lowest possible value is 0, indicating no racial heterogeneity on the street, and the highest possible value is 0.1875, which represents a scenario of an extremely heterogeneous environment. After examining the data carefully, a cut-off point of 0.12 was chosen to distinguish streets that we consider racially heterogeneous from streets that are more homogeneous.

Because census data, as we discussed in chapter 5, are not available at the street segment level, we draw information on racial composition from data provided by the public schools in Seattle. We recognize at the outset that these data do not provide an exact accounting of the overall racial composition of Seattle residents. For example, Seattle was estimated to be about 70 percent white in 2000 by the Census Bureau. In our data, about 40 percent of the students are defined as white in the same year. Nonetheless, our interest is not in identifying an accurate portrait of the overall weighting of race in the city, but rather the extent to which there is heterogeneity of race at the street segment level. Such racial heterogeneity is likely to be indicated broadly by the student population.

We could not in this case describe the number of street segments accounting for a specific percentage of racial heterogeneity, since our measure is an index for each street segment. Accordingly, to gauge concentration we look at the proportion of street segments that reach the cut-off point of 0.12, which we define as reflecting high racial heterogeneity. Only between 6 and 7.5 percent of the street segments in Seattle reached this threshold during the study period (see figure 6.6). It is also apparent that there is a good deal of spread of this characteristic across the city (see figure 6.7a), though one area of the central southern part of the city appears to have little evidence of racial heterogeneity. The LISA map (see figure 6.7b) suggests that while there are larger concentrations of racial heterogeneity in many areas, there is also evidence of significant negative spatial autocorrelation in the same areas. This is indicated by the light blue lines indicating low racial heterogeneity streets surrounded by high racial heterogeneity streets. In turn, there are many areas, for example in northern and southeastern Seattle, where negative spatial autocorrelation is the dominant pattern.

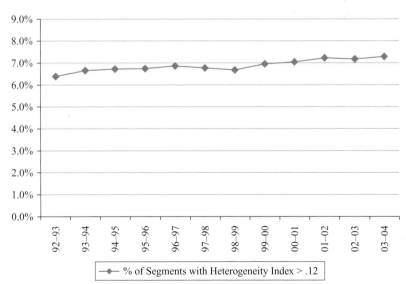

FIGURE 6.6 *The Trend of Racial Heterogeneity from 1992/1993 to 2003/2004 (school years)*

(a) 50% Spatial concentration   (b) Spatial autocorrelation

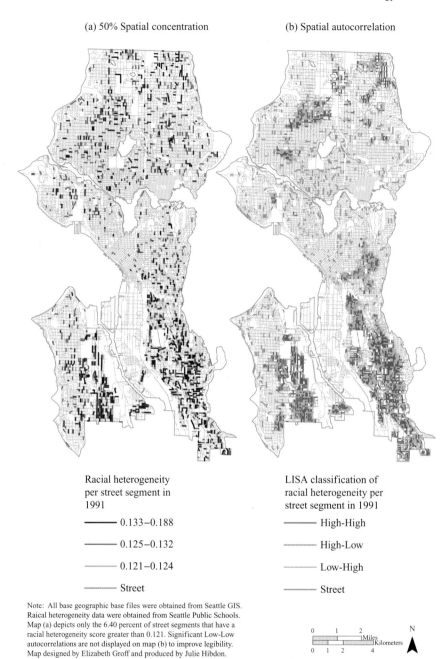

Racial heterogeneity
per street segment in
1991

——— 0.133–0.188

——— 0.125–0.132

——— 0.121–0.124

——— Street

LISA classification of
racial heterogeneity per
street segment in 1991

——— High-High

——— High-Low

——— Low-High

——— Street

Note: All base geographic base files were obtained from Seattle GIS.
Raical heterogeneity data were obtained from Seattle Public Schools.
Map (a) depicts only the 6.40 percent of street segments that have a
racial heterogeneity score greater than 0.121. Significant Low-Low
autocorrelations are not displayed on map (b) to improve legibility.
Map designed by Elizabeth Groff and produced by Julie Hibdon.

FIGURE 6.7 *Spatial Concentration and Spatial Autocorrelation for Racial Heterogeneity*

DISTANCE TO CITY CENTER (URBANIZATION)

Distance from the city center was a key element of the early presentations of social disorganization theories. Ernest Burgess, for example, developed a concentric zone model for the distribution of social problems in cities (Burgess, 1925 [1967]). Social disorganization theorists more generally have suggested that areas nearest the central core of a city are impacted more greatly by social problems and particularly delinquency and crime (Macionis and Plummer, 2005, Schmid, 1960a, 1960b). These were the areas where new immigrants and poorer residents were concentrated, where social control was weak, and juvenile delinquency and crime problems would accordingly be concentrated (Thrasher, 1927 [1963]).

Concepts of concentration of street segments and variability within areas are not relevant to this aspect of the social disorganization perspective. For our study, street distance was calculated from the geographic center of Seattle to every street segment. This method takes into account the road network when calculating distances.[10] A visualization of distance to the city center is provided in figure 6.8.

PHYSICAL DISORDER

Another important measure of social disorganization in our study assesses the physical condition of street segments. Social disorganization theory argues that a disorganized place includes litter, broken windows, abandoned buildings, and the like (Shaw and McKay, 1942 [1969]; Perkins et al., 1990). Thus, physical conditions can be viewed as proxies for the level of social organization of areas. Some scholars have argued that disorder is less an indicator of social disorganization than its product, much as crime is viewed as being the result of low social control in communities (Sampson and Raudenbush, 1999). We discuss this concern more generally regarding structural variables below, but note it here because the causal link between disorder and crime has been challenged in a number of recent studies (Corman and Mocan, 2005; Geller, 2007; Harcourt and Ludwig, 2006; St. Jean, 2007; Yang, 2010; see also Bratton and Kelling, 2006; Xu, Fiedler, and Flaming, 2005 for different opinions).

Data on physical disorder were provided by Seattle Public Utilities and contained information from 1993 to 2004. The database included the frequency and volume of physical disorder reported to the authority on each street. Physical disorder indicators include the number of incidents of illegal dumping, litter, graffiti, weeds, inoperable cars on the street, junk storage, exterior abatement, substandard housing, and minor property damage. The sources of information included residents' reports, inspectors' reports, and other agencies' information filed to Seattle Public Utilities.

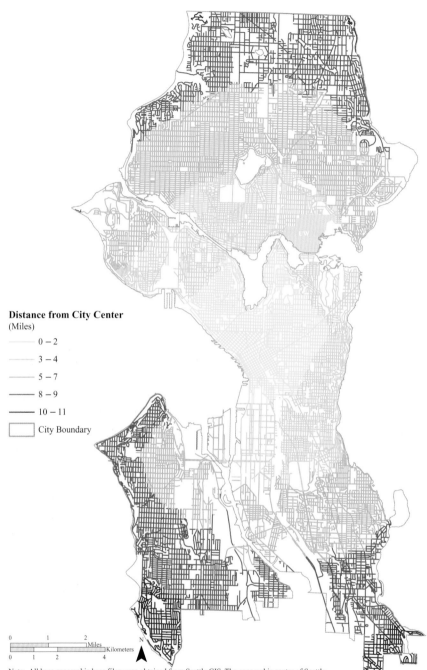

Note: All base geographic base files were obtained from Seattle GIS. The geographic center of Seattle
used was 331 Minor Ave N. Distances were measured using ArcGIS™ Network Analyst. Map by Elizabeth Groff.

FIGURE 6.8 *Distance to the Center of Seattle*

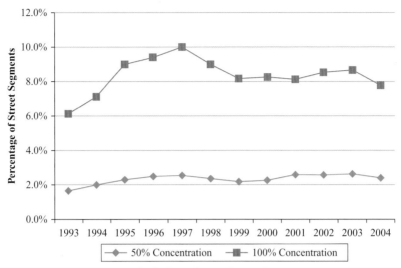

FIGURE 6.9 *Concentration Graph of Physical Disorder Incidents at Street Segments*

Physical disorder incidents are found to be strongly concentrated and relatively stable over time (see figure 6.9). Over 50 percent of incidents were found on just between 1.5 and 3 percent of street segments across the study period. Clearly there are hot spots of physical disorder as there are hot spots of crime in Seattle. The concentration line for 100 percent of the physcial disorder measure shows more variation over time, ranging from 6.1 percent in 1993 to 10.0 percent in 1997. Overall, the percentage of street segments with physical disorder shows an increase from 1993 to 1997, then a decline to 1999, and a fairly stable trend until 2004.

Hot spots of physical disorder are spread throughout the city, though they are more concentrated in the center and southeastern areas of the city (see figure 6.10a). But even where there is concentration, there is significant within area variability. This is reinforced by the LISA map (see figure 6.10b). Note the large numbers of light blue and pink lines across the maps, indicating significant negative spatial correlation in patterns from street to street. In some of these areas, street segments with high numbers of phyiscal disorder incidents are significantly associated with the presence of low incidence physical disorder street segments (pink lines). The opposite is also true; streets with low numbers of phyiscal disorder incidents are surrounded by streets with high numbers (light blue lines).

Intermediating Variables

As mentioned earlier, recent conceptualizations of social disorganization theory draw distinctions between the structural characteristics of places and the medi-

(a) 50% Spatial concentration   (b) Spatial autocorrelation

Physical disorder per
street segment in
1993

——— 3–16

——— 2

——— 1

——— Street

LISA classification of
physical disorder per
street segment in 1993

——— High-High

——— High-Low

——— Low-High

——— Street

Note: All base geographic base files were obtained from Seattle GIS.
Physical disorder data were obtained from Seattle Public Utilities.
Map (a) depicts only the 1.65 percent of street segments that account
for 50 percent of all physical disorder. Significant Low-Low
autocorrelations are not displayed on map (b) to improve legibility. Map
designed by Elizabeth Groff and produced by Julie Hibdon.

FIGURE 6.10 *Spatial Concentration and Spatial Autocorrelation for Physical Disorder Incidents*

ating factors that link the structural factors and outcome variables like crime (see Bursik, 1988; Sampson and Groves, 1989; Sampson and Wilson, 1995). These mediating factors reflect more generally the degree to which people who live in communities can exercise social control over the behavior of residents and visitors. Coleman (1993: 9) argues that the level of social control of a community depends upon "a dense and relatively closed social structure that has continuity over time." The strength of social relationships among residents, also called social capital, determines the extent to which social control functions in such areas (Coleman, 1990; Sampson, 1993). Measures identified in prior studies to operationalize such intermediating factors include participation in local organizations (Perkins et al., 1990; Taylor, Gottfredson, and Brower, 1984; Sampson and Groves, 1989), willingness (or perception of responsibility) to intervene in public affairs (Perkins et al., 1990; Taylor, Gottfredson, and Brower, 1984; Sampson, Raudenbush, and Earls, 1997), local friendship networks (Sampson and Groves, 1989), mutual trust (Sampson, Raudenbush, and Earls, 1997), and unsupervised teens (Sampson and Groves, 1989; Sampson, Raudenbush, and Earls, 1997). These variables are believed to condition the effects of structural disadvantage on local crime problems.

Intermediating variables are seen as particularly important in the social disorganization perspective because they appear to avoid what some have argued is a lack of a clear causal chain for many social disorganization indicators. For example, as we noted earlier, some scholars have suggested that disorder is not a cause of crime but rather disorder, just like crime, is affected by other underlying social problems (Sampson and Raudenbush, 1999). By incorporating the mediating factors, social disorganization theorists argue that social disorganization is now "clearly separable not only from the processes that may lead to it (e.g., poverty, mobility), but also from the degree of criminal behavior that may be a result" (Sampson and Lauritsen, 1994: 58; see Bursik, 1988). In this study, we include the number of unsupervised teens and percent of active voters to represent the levels of local social control and social capital on each street segment.

INFORMAL SOCIAL CONTROL: UNSUPERVISED TEENS

Unsupervised teens as a mediating factor was first conceptualized by Sampson and Groves (1989: 778), who argued that "communities that are unable to control street-corner teenage groups will experience higher rates of delinquency than those in which peer groups are held in check through collective social control." It is not because these street-corner teenagers are all "criminals," but the appearance of unsupervised teens on the street corner is evidence of the lack of social control in a community. Accordingly, a community with fewer kids wandering on a street during school time is better at controlling its residents than a community with many truant students unattended. In this study,

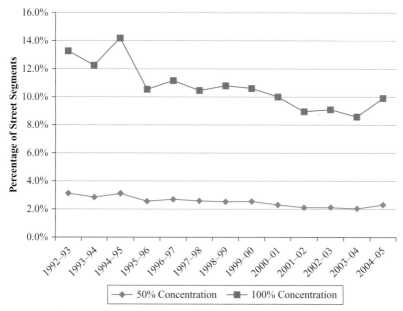

FIGURE 6.11 *Concentration Graph of Truant Students at Street Segments*

we use the number of truant students on each street segment to represent one aspect of informal social control—the presence of unsupervised teens.[11] When identifying truant students, we use the public school student data described in the previous chapter. To define truancy, we followed the definition used by Seattle Public Schools, which considers a student who has more than 10 unexcused absences in a school year to be truant.[12]

From figure 6.11, it is clear that truancy is also a highly concentrated phenomenon. Fifty percent of truant students are consistently found to live on between 2 and 3.5 percent of the total number of street segments in Seattle. All of the truant students are found on between 8 and 14.5 percent of the total street segments over time. The percentage shows a sharp decline from 1994–1995 and then a very slow decline until 2003–2004.

Truant juveniles are found all over Seattle, but there are greater concentrations of truant students in the southern parts of the city, just as there were greater concentrations of poverty and physical disorder in these areas (see figure 6.12a).[13] This, of course, emphasizes the relevance of social disorganization to understanding larger area influences. In this, our data simply confirm prior studies that have linked social disorganization to crime at the community or neighborhood level. But our data also identify significant street-to-street variation, even within areas with relatively higher concentrations of truancy. This is illustrated in the LISA map by the interspersion of both negative (light blue) and positive (dark red) spatial autocorrelation in the high truant areas of

(a) 50% Spatial concentration   (b) Spatial autocorrelation

Truant juveniles per
street segment in
1993

——— 6–35

——— 4–5

——— 2–3

——— Street

LISA classification of
truant juveniles per
street segment in 1993

——— High-High

——— High-Low

——— Low-High

——— Street

Note: All base geographic base files were obtained from Seattle GIS.
Truant juvenile data were obtained from Seattle Public Utilities. Map
(a) depicts only the 3.13 percent of street segments that account for
50 percent of all truant juveniles. Significant Low-Low autocorrelations
are not displayed on map (b) to improve legibility. Map designed by
Elizabeth Groff and produced by Julie Hibdon.

FIGURE 6.12 *Spatial Concentration and Spatial Autocorrelation for Truant Juveniles*

the southern half of the city (see figure 6.12b). The LISA map also reveals the more isolated nature of high truant street segments in areas of the city that have little truancy (as indicated by the pink lines).

COLLECTIVE EFFICACY: WILLINGNESS TO INTERVENE IN PUBLIC AFFAIRS

In a later revision of social disorganization theory, Sampson, Raudenbush, and Earls (1997) extended the concept of social control to emphasize the capacity of a community to realize common values and regulate behavior through cohesive relationships and mutual trust among residents (see also Sampson, 2004). Informal social control, as Sampson, Raudenbush, and Earls (1997) note, is very different from the formal mechanisms of policing and relies "on the effectiveness of informal mechanisms by which residents themselves achieve public order" (918). Sources of the differential ability of communities to regulate their residents are structural characteristics such as poverty and residential mobility, or the ability of neighborhoods to restrain unruly juveniles. Sampson, Raudenbush, and Earls (1997: 919) coined the concept of collective efficacy of communities, or the "willingness [of residents] to intervene for the common good," to emphasize the mechanisms by which a community can prevent crime. One important indicator of collective efficacy is residents' willingness to participate in public affairs (Morenoff, Sampson, and Raudenbush, 2001; Sampson, Raudenbush, and Earls, 1997). We use voting behavior as an indicator of collective efficacy in our study (see also Coleman, 2002; Putnam, 2001). We assumed that active voters would be willing not only to participate in public elections, but also in other aspects of public affairs.

The total number of registered voters has fluctuated in Seattle between 1999 and 2004 (the years for which we were able to identify data), but the magnitude of change is not large. The number increased slowly for the first four years, from 383,226 in 1999 to 418,673 in 2002. After 2002, the total number of registered voters declined, and by 2004 there were 345,671 registered voters in Seattle. An average of 74 percent of streets per year had at least one person registered as a voter. This percentage remains relatively stable throughout the six years. There were on average about 22 voters per street per year considering only the streets with any voters. The majority of streets (about 75 percent) have less than 30 voters. There are few streets with extremely high numbers of voters (i.e., 409–803) and this is probably a result of having high-rise buildings on those streets. Only 5 percent of the streets had just one voter.

We define active voters as people who voted more frequently than the average voter in Seattle. We use a moving average of the two previous years' voting behavior to identify active voters. From 1999 to 2004, the average number of active voters increased slightly and then declined afterwards until the end of the

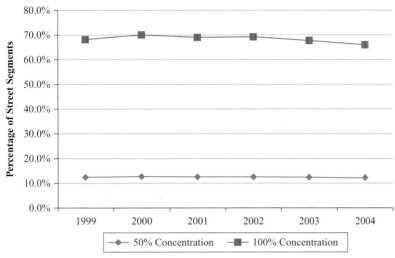

FIGURE 6.13 *Concentration Graph of Active Voters at Street Segments*

series. On average, there are around seven active voters per street. The range of the variable distribution is wide; some streets have more than 300 active voters while many other streets have none. When we identify the concentration patterns of active voters, we find that 50 percent of the total active voters consistently lived on between 12 and 13 percent of Seattle's street segments (see figure 6.13). The percentage of street segments where 100 percent of active voters resided ranged between 68 to 70 percent. In 2003 and 2004, there is a slight decline, but there is no substantial change over time.

In figure 6.14a, we show a concentration map of active voters in Seattle. As is apparent from the map, there are clusters of active voters throughout the city. At the same time, there are areas with very few segments with active voters, for example in the center of the city map. The variability of active voting across streets is illustrated in the LISA map (see figure 6.14b). In the north sector, street segments with high numbers of active voters are often in proximity to other street segments with high numbers of active voters. However, there are often streets with low numbers of active voters interspersed, as evidenced by the light blue lines found throughout these areas. There are also pockets of light blue lines in the southeastern, northern, and central areas, where streets low in the number of active voters are likely to be found near streets with high numbers of active voters. This suggests areas where negative spatial autocorrelation patterns dominate. This is true of the southeastern areas of the city, where pink lines suggest that high active voting streets are likely to be surrounded by streets with low numbers of active voters.

One problem with using the number of active voters on the street as an indicator of collective efficacy is that the number of active voters will be directly related to the overall population density of streets. In this context, 10 active

(a) 50% Spatial concentration   (b) Spatial autocorrelation

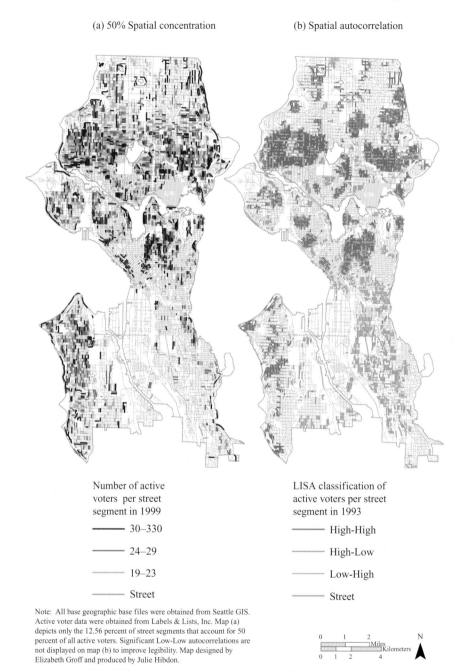

Number of active
voters per street
segment in 1999

——— 30–330

——— 24–29

········· 19–23

········· Street

LISA classification of
active voters per street
segment in 1993

——— High-High

——— High-Low

········· Low-High

········· Street

Note: All base geographic base files were obtained from Seattle GIS.
Active voter data were obtained from Labels & Lists, Inc. Map (a)
depicts only the 12.56 percent of street segments that account for 50
percent of all active voters. Significant Low-Low autocorrelations are
not displayed on map (b) to improve legibility. Map designed by
Elizabeth Groff and produced by Julie Hibdon.

FIGURE 6.14 *Spatial Concentration and Spatial Autocorrelation for Active Voters*

voters on a street with 100 registered voters is not the same as 10 active voters on a street with 10 registered voters. Accordingly, to construct our measure of collective efficacy, we created a variable that reflects the proportion of active voters on a street segment. The mean percentage of active voters on street segments in Seattle ranged over the observation years from 32.19 to 42.29 percent. The mean across the years was 36.64 percent. Figure 6.15 shows the streets in the city map in which more than 75 percent of the voters on a street are active voters (13.24 percent of streets). This map emphasizes the extent to which active voting streets are spread throughout Seattle. At the same time, there is tremendous street-by-street variability as represented by the varying shades in coloring across the map.

Conclusions

Much is known about the distribution of social disorganization and social capital at macro geographic levels across the urban landscape (Bursik and Grasmick, 1993; Sampson, 1985; Sampson and Groves, 1989; Sampson and Morenoff, 2004; Sampson, Raudenbush, and Earls, 1997; Sampson, Morenoff, and Gannon-Rowley, 2002; Shaw and McKay, 1942 [1969]; Shaw, 1929). However, our research is the first we know of to examine this distribution at a micro place level such as the street segment. We have noted throughout the chapter the limitations we faced in identifying measures of social disorganization. In some cases, the measures we have of key concepts are limited, for example in identifying intermediating variables. In others, we had to use imperfect proxies, for example in using school data for gaining an estimate of racial heterogeneity. Nonetheless, despite these limitations, we believe that our findings are groundbreaking. They both suggest a concentration of traits of social disorganization at the micro place level and provide significant evidence of the variability of social disorganization at street segments within larger areas.

Looking both at structural and mediating variables, we find that there are hot spots of social disorganization at the street segment level. Moreover, such hot spots are not found only in specific neighborhoods. Rather, they are often distributed across the city landscape. In turn, we found strong evidence of spatial heterogeneity of social disorganization at street segments. While there are sometimes clusters of street segments with specific traits in larger areas, there is also significant street-by-street variation in such areas.

Together, these findings raise intriguing questions about the relationship between social disorganization and crime at the street segment level. Are hot spots of social disorganization related to hot spots of crime? Does street level variability in social disorganization relate to developmental trends of crime at place?

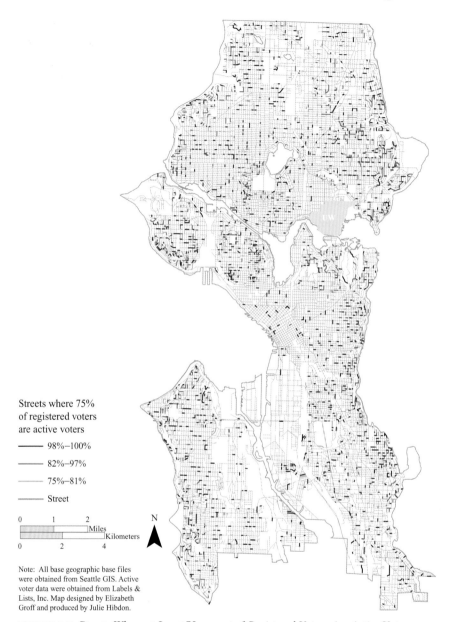

Streets where 75%
of registered voters
are active voters

——— 98%–100%

——— 82%–97%

——— 75%–81%

——— Street

0   1   2
|Miles
|Kilometers
0   2   4

N

Note: All base geographic base files
were obtained from Seattle GIS. Active
voter data were obtained from Labels &
Lists, Inc. Map designed by Elizabeth
Groff and produced by Julie Hibdon.

FIGURE 6.15 *Streets Where at Least 75 percent of Registered Voters Are Active Voters*

In chapter 7, we will explore these relationships between social disorganization and crime at street segments. Those who have studied the criminology of place have generally ignored social disorganization theories in favor of the opportunity and rational choice perspectives we reviewed in chapter 5. Our data so far suggest that it is time to examine whether social disorganization theory is in fact relevant to the criminology of place.

Understanding Developmental Patterns of Crime at Street Segments

In the previous chapters, our interest was primarily in description. We sought to identify how crime and other social and contextual characteristics varied across places and to examine whether the idea of hot spots could be applied not only to crime, but also to social disorganization and opportunity variables that we identified as possible risk and protective factors in understanding the criminology of place. Our data confirm prior studies that crime is concentrated at small geographic units of analysis and that there are distinct developmental trends of crime at place across time. Our analyses in chapter 4 confirmed not only that there are developmental trends, but also that there is significant street-to-street variability in such trends, suggesting the inherent importance of understanding causal processes at the level of street segments. In chapters 5 and 6, we established that there is clustering of social disorganization and opportunity measures at street segments. Simply stated, there are hot spots of crime opportunities and hot spots of social disorganization at a micro geographic level.

In this chapter, we want to focus on whether the variability of characteristics of places representing theories of opportunity and social disorganization is related to developmental crime patterns at street segments. For example, do opportunity measures such as the presence of high-risk juveniles living on a street ("motivated offenders") or large numbers of people working there ("suitable targets") help us to differentiate developmental crime patterns at the street segment level? Is variability in indicators of social disorganization at the street segment level, such as property values, mixed land use, physical disorder, or racial heterogeneity, related to crime at street segments? As we have noted throughout this book, opportunity theories have played the key role in the development of the criminology of place and have generally been the primary perspectives used to explain variability in crime at micro geographic units of analysis. Does social disorganization theory also have relevance to understanding the criminology of place?

The analyses reported upon in this chapter are drawn from an approach that examines opportunity and social disorganization features of street segments within a multivariate statistical model of crime patterns at places. We describe that model in the next section and explain why this type of statistical approach is warranted. We then go on to examine the general level of explanation in our study. How well do we explain crime patterns at street segments using the theoretical dimensions of opportunity and social disorganization that we have identified? How do opportunity and social disorganization perspectives compare in their ability to explain crime at street segments? We then examine the relevance of specific variables in understanding the criminology of place in relationship to two specific questions. What distinguishes the most serious chronic-crime street segments from those that are relatively crime free during the study period? Do changes in opportunity and social disorganization variables over time predict crime wave and crime drop developmental patterns in our data?

An Overall Model for Explaining Developmental Trajectories of Crime at Place

One problem in assessing the relationships between characteristics of places and patterns of crime at street segments, and in particular identifying the most salient and important indicators, is that the characteristics we have examined are often confounded (Greenland, Robins, and Pearl, 1999; Meinert, 1986; Robins, 1989; Weisburd and Britt, 2007). For example, we found in chapter 5 that business activity is concentrated on arterial roads, as is street lighting. If we simply examined the concentrations of these traits and those of crime patterns, it would be difficult to distinguish one from the other, or indeed the relative importance of arterial roads themselves, which have been seen in prior studies as an important component of the opportunity structure of crime at place (Bernasco and Block, 2011; Brantingham and Brantingham, 1993a, 1993b; Felson, 2006; Johnson and Bowers, 2010). Low socioeconomic status, high population heterogeneity, mixed land use, and low collective efficacy all show greater concentrations in the southeastern sections of Seattle, as do many opportunity factors. The problem is that because these features often overlap in space, it is difficult to distinguish which characteristics are in fact most directly related to crime patterns. In order to examine the questions we have raised, we need a statistical approach that allows us to distinguish and identify the specific factors that are most salient in understanding variability in crime patterns at street segments while holding other factors constant.

Accordingly, we use multivariate statistical methods to understand crime at place. Multivariate statistical analyses allow us to include multiple measures (or independent variables) in a single model of crime patterns. Our independent variables in this model are the opportunity and social disorganization measures described in chapters 5 and 6. When the specific estimate of the relationship between a measure and crime patterns is provided, it takes into account or statistically controls for the impact of other measures included in the model. For example, the relationship of retail business sales to crime patterns is "purged" of the potential influence of the street being an arterial road. This approach also allows us to compare the impacts of specific measures one to another, and accordingly to identify the most important variables in understanding the criminology of place.

The phenomena that we want to explain or understand using this approach, or what is termed the "dependent variable" in these analyses, are the eight trajectory crime patterns identified in chapter 3: crime-free, low-stable, low-decreasing, low-increasing, moderate-stable, high-decreasing, high-increasing, and chronic-crime patterns. Our use of trajectory patterns that are nominal categories creates an additional statistical complexity for our analyses. Traditional statistical approaches to categorical- or nominal-level dependent variables have generally constrained the dependent variable to two choices (Agresti, 1996; Long, 1997; Reynolds, 1977). Accordingly, we might have conducted a separate statistical analysis for each of the possible comparisons in our study (e.g., crime-free versus low-stable, crime-free versus low-decreasing). But a main question in our study is how well our "model" predicts selection into any of the eight trajectory patterns we have identified.[1]

A technique termed multinomial logistic regression provides a straightforward solution to this problem because it allows a simultaneous examination of all of the different possible comparisons (Agresti, 1996; Begg and Gray, 1984; Long, 1997; Peng and Nichols, 2003; Weisburd and Britt, 2007). It also provides both an overall assessment of the statistical importance of the measures examined in predicting trajectory patterns, as well as a specific set of coefficients for understanding the varying effects of the independent variables in the model.

In defining our model, we included all of the opportunity and social disorganization variables described in chapters 5 and 6. For each measure, we create a variable reflecting the "baseline" estimate, or the mean of the first three years for which we have valid data. This reflects the influence of the initial measurement of a trait on crime patterns. We also include a measure of change over time, when we have valid data available for a long time series and there is evidence of significant change at the street segment level.[2] For example, in the case of truant juveniles, we created a variable that represents the change in the number of truant juveniles between the first three years for which we have data (1993–1995) and the last three years (2002–2004). This is often called a difference of moving averages (Baller et al., 2001). This measure in the model assesses whether changes over time in characteristics of street segments affect their likelihood of falling in a trajectory pattern.

We also created a spatial lag term which reflects the average number of crimes on street segments within one-quarter of a mile of the segment examined. A spatial lag term (Anselin, 1988; Anselin et al., 2000) is a variable that contains the weighted averages of the neighboring values of a location.[3] In this sense, it takes into account larger area influences in our model. Spatial lag terms acknowledge directly that the relationships observed at street segments may be affected by the crime levels in the areas surrounding a street segment (Rosenfeld, Fornango, and Rengifo, 2007). Our spatial lag term captures both the initial level and the change in crime rates for the neighboring streets (i.e., within one-quarter of a mile) between the first and last three years of observation. Finally, we include a measure of the exact length of the street segments. We are not substantively interested in this measure, but it allows us to take into account the fact that there may be variability in the number of crimes, or crime patterns, on longer versus shorter streets. The independent variables in our analysis are described in table 7.1.[4]

TABLE 7.1 Description of Variables in the Model

Variable Name	Description
Opportunity Perspective:	
Motivated Offenders:	
High Risk Juveniles	Total number of public school students who are truants or low academic achievers
Suitable Targets:	
Employment	Total number of employees
Public Facilities	Total number of public facilities (community centers, parks, libraries, middle/high schools, hospitals) within one-quarter mile (1,320 feet)
Residents	Total number of residents (sum of the registered voters and public school students)
Total Retail Sales	Total retail sales in dollars (divided by 1,000)
Accessibility/Urban Form:	
Bus Stops	Total number of bus stops
Arterial Road	Is the street segment an arterial road? (yes/no)
Guardianship:	
Police/Fire Stations	Total number of police or fire stations within one-quarter mile (1,320 feet)
% Vacant Land	Percentage of vacant land
Street Lighting	Total number of watts (divided by 100)
Social Disorganization Perspective:	
Structural Variables:	
Socioeconomic Status:	
Residential Property Values	Combination of weighted ranking of single or family housing and multi-family housing of a given street (see endnote 2 in chapter 6)

(continued)

TABLE 7.1 Continued

Variable Name	Description
Housing Assistance	Combination of public housing and Section 8 vouchers
Mixed Land Use	Dichotomous variable, representing whether the place has a mixture of between 25 percent and 75 percent of residential and other types of land use
Racial Heterogeneity	Racial heterogeneity of public school students (see endnote 9 in chapter 6)
Urbanization	Distance of a street to the center of city (divided by 100 feet to adjust the scale)
Physical Disorder	The total number of physical disorder incidents
Intermediating Variables:	
Truant Juveniles	Total number of public school students who are truants
% Active Voters	Percentage of active voters out of all the registered voters
Other Variables	
Segment Length	Total number of feet (divided by 100)
Spatial Lag	Average number of crimes on neighboring street segments within one-quarter of a mile

How Well Does Our Model Predict Variation in Crime Patterns at Street Segments?

Our first question is whether variability in opportunity and social disorganization at the street segment level improves our understanding of crime patterns at places. Is our statistical model doing a good job of predicting trajectory patterns? How do the opportunity and social disorganization perspectives compare in regard to their contribution to explanation of crime patterns at street segments?

One straightforward way of assessing explanation is to look at the "fit" of a model to the patterns that are observed in the dependent variable, in this case trajectory patterns of crime. The higher the statistical fit of the model, the better the model is at explaining or predicting the outcomes examined. Two measures are commonly used for assessing model fit in logistic regression, Cox and Snell's (1989) and Nagelkerke's (1991) Pseudo R^2 statistics (see table 7.2). Both have a general interpretation as the proportion of the overall variability in the dependent variable explained by the variables included in the model.[5] The Pseudo R^2 values produced in our model are 0.63 (Cox and Snell) and 0.68 (Nagelkerke). Cox and Snell's estimate is generally considered overly conservative in cases where the prediction value is high, such as ours (Nagelkerke, 1991).

How well does this suggest we have done in predicting patterns of developmental trajectories of crime at place? In a recent article in the *Crime and Justice* series, Weisburd and Piquero (2008) examined R^2, commonly termed "variance

TABLE 7.2 Multinomial Logistic Regression Measures of Model Fit

Measure of Model Fit	Value	Chi-Square
Full Model		
Cox and Snell	.632	—
Nagelkerke	.684	—
−2 Log Likelihood	37,870	24,000***
Opportunity Variables Only		
Cox and Snell	.605	—
Nagelkerke	.655	—
-2 Log Likelihood	39,550	22,320***
Social Disorganization Variables Only		
Cox and Snell	.470	—
Nagelkerke	.508	—
-2 Log Likelihood	46,640	15,230***

* $p < .05$, ** $p < .01$, *** $p < .01$

explained," in tests of criminological theories in the American Society of Criminology journal *Criminology*. Their results suggest that in comparison to studies more generally, we are doing extremely well in explaining the criminology of place. The median value for R^2 in that review was only 0.36, and a quarter of the studies examined had values of less than 0.20. While the number of Pseudo R^2 statistics examined was relatively small, they had on average even lower R^2 values than variance explained statistics in ordinary regression analyses. The average R^2 value for person-based studies was about 0.30. In this context, our Pseudo R^2 values above 0.60 imply that we have been able to explain a good deal of the variability in trajectory pattern membership. In this context, we can say that much of the variability in the criminology of place can be systematically identified. As we argue in the concluding chapter, this not only suggests that we have considerable understanding already of the factors that influence crime at place, but also that this understanding provides a strong basis for developing effective crime prevention interventions.

It is interesting in this regard to compare the overall degree of explanation of the two theoretical perspectives that we draw from in developing our model of crime patterns at street segments. Accordingly, we ran separate regressions that included only the social disorganization and only the opportunity measures. These results should be viewed with caution for two reasons. First, we were not able to identify every relevant opportunity and social disorganization measure. Accordingly, differences in the overall model fit of these perspectives will reflect to some degree our ability to garner measurement of key dimensions of the theories. Second, and returning to our reasoning for using a single model, the measures for both perspectives are often confounded at places. Such confounding means that estimating models separately will allow for measures reflecting one perspective to spuriously account for variability that may in fact belong in the province of the second perspective.

But despite these limitations, we think that estimating the fit of each perspective separately allows us to gain a general sense of how much each contributes to our understanding of crime patterns at places. If social disorganization variables measured in our study, for example, can provide little explanation for the patterns of crime observed, then the introduction of this perspective in the criminology of place would not seem warranted. In turn, we would expect opportunity theory measures to have very strong explanatory power in these models, given the emphasis on such perspectives in the development of the criminology of place.

We do indeed find a very high level of explanation in the case of the opportunity perspectives model, where the Nagelkerke's R^2 value of 0.66 is almost the same as the value for the full model (see table 7.2). But the value for the social disorganization perspective is also large, at 0.51. We think some initial conclusions can be drawn from these analyses, with the caveats we raised above in mind. The first is that opportunity theories appear to provide stronger consistency with crime patterns at places than the social disorganization perspective. But at the same time, given their neglect in the criminology of place, social disorganization measures are remarkably strongly related to crime patterns at street segments.

The high levels of explanation of the two models suggest to some degree the confounding that we have already noted in the distribution of these characteristics at street segments. That leads to the question of whether in the context of the overall model, variables reflecting both perspectives remain significant in explaining crime patterns. Table 7.3 presents results from an overall test of significance for each measure on the general allocation of street segments into trajectory patterns when all the variables are included in a single statistical model. This table examines whether specific variables explain trajectory pattern "choice" irrespective of the trajectory pattern for a street segment. A statistically significant result means that we can reject the null hypothesis that there is no relationship between the measure and trajectory pattern membership.

Nearly all of the measures examined are statistically significant at the 0.001 level. This means that examined broadly, variation in both opportunity and social disorganization variables are predictive of developmental crime patterns at street segments. Accordingly, the strong explanation found in our measures of model fit is reflected in the large number of variables that are significantly related to trajectory pattern groups. And the salience of both opportunity and social disorganization variables are reflected in this analysis. Variables from both perspectives are meaningful in understanding crime patterns, when they are examined in a single model that controls for confounding of measures across places.

While overall the variables we identified in earlier chapters are significantly related to developmental crime trends at street segments, there are specific

TABLE 7.3 Likelihood Ratio Tests for the Multinomial Logistic Regression

Variable	-2 Log Likelihood	LR Chi-Square
Opportunity		
High Risk Juveniles	37,980	108.287***
High Risk Juveniles (change)	37,900	25.351**
Employees	39,570	1,703.000***
Employees (change)	38,100	229.626***
Public Facilities	37,930	59.751***
Residents	43,100	5,226.000***
Residents (change)	37,980	110.355***
Total Retail Sales	37,880	6.586
Bus Stops	37,920	51.651***
Arterial Road	38,130	257.083***
Police/Fire Station	37,880	11.372
% Vacant Land	37,900	24.828**
% Vacant Land (change)	37,890	17.806*
Street Lighting	38,020	149.097***
Social Disorganization		
Property Value	38,090	215.262***
Housing Assistance	37,940	71.507***
Mixed Land Use	37,870	2.503
Racial Heterogeneity	37,880	9.941
Racial Heterogeneity (change)	37,890	12.921
Urbanization	38,320	449.707***
Physical Disorder	38,340	472.143***
Physical Disorder (change)	38,080	212.081***
Truant Juveniles	37,910	37.331***
Truant Juveniles (change)	37,930	59.490***
% Active Voters	38,010	136.047***
Other Variables		
Segment Length	38,000	128.065***
Spatial Lag	38,360	489.153***
Spatial Lag (change)	38,180	311.866***

df = 7; * p < .05, ** p < .01, *** p < .001

variables that do not have significant impacts. Two of these are from the social disorganization perspective. Neither mixed land use[6] nor racial heterogeneity has a significant impact on the selection into a trajectory group in the overall model, though as we will see later in the chapter, racial heterogeneity significantly influences whether street segments experience crime waves or crime drops. For the opportunity perspective, total retail business sales and whether a street segment is located close to a fire or police station also do not have statistically significant impacts in our model. We will discuss these variables more directly when we examine the direction and magnitude of variable effects in the next section.

Importantly, the effects observed remain significant despite our taking into account spatial lag terms for crime levels, which would indicate and distinguish larger area effects. The fact that the spatial lag terms are significant indicates that there are larger area spatial processes in our data. This is not surprising given our observation of area concentrations in earlier chapters. However, the identification of area effects in our model does not minimize the importance of street segment level characteristics. These remain strongly significant.

Which Variables Are Most Important in Identifying Serious Crime Hot Spots?

While the likelihood ratio test allows us to examine the overall significance of variables in the model, it does not provide a measure of the size or direction of the effect of specific variables examined. For example, we have seen that opportunity and social disorganization measures are significantly associated with trajectory pattern membership, but we do not know from the statistics we have examined so far whether the directionality of these effects is consistent with these theories. In turn, in very large samples such as ours, it is easier to identify small variable effects, because the precision of estimates is aided greatly by the fact that a large number of cases are used for estimation. While this makes it possible to identify the impacts of characteristics we measure, significance here, as in many other studies, does not provide a very good indicator of the strength of specific characteristics in explaining outcomes.

To do this, we have to look at the individual parameters or estimates of the impact of characteristics on trajectory membership. One complication of using multinomial regression is that the parameter estimates are given for each trajectory pattern relative to an excluded or baseline category. In our analysis, the crime-free trajectory pattern is the reference group or excluded category both because it includes the largest number of cases, and thus provides statistical stability to the overall model, and because it provides a logical comparison group in understanding the analysis. In this context, we are comparing the seven other trajectory patterns with some criminal activity to the crime-free pattern. The number of comparisons produced in this analysis is very large (including 210 parameter estimates) because a separate parameter estimate is given for each of the independent variables for each of the seven trajectory patterns (as compared with the crime-free pattern).

We think that discussion of more than 200 parameter estimates in our model would be unwieldy and is not necessary to draw the main insights from our analysis. Instead, we focus on what is the starkest contrast in our data, the comparison between the chronic-crime pattern and the crime-free reference group. This comparison tends to provide the clearest portrait of the influence of the independent variables. It is also the comparison that is most relevant to our concern with the criminology of place, since it focuses directly on the characteristics that are associated with crime hot spots. Table 7.4 gives the results for our analysis comparing the chronic-crime pattern and the crime-free pattern. Appendix 5 gives the full model results of the multinomial regression.[7]

The parameter estimates (b) of the models are difficult to interpret because of the nonlinear nature of the coefficients in logistic regression. Instead, we focus our discussion below on individual change in the "odds ratio." The odds ratio gives the proportional change in the likelihood of being in the chronic-crime pattern (as opposed to the crime-free pattern) associated with a one unit change in the independent variable. Accordingly, if the odds ratio estimate of the independent variable is 1.5, it would indicate that a one unit change in that variable increases the odds of being in the chronic pattern (as compared to the crime-free pattern) by 0.50. While the odds ratio is useful for understanding the specific impact of a variable, it is not helpful in making comparisons between variables in the model. For example, if we wanted to identify the variable with the largest impact on the likelihood of being in the chronic group, we could not use the odds ratio estimate because it is scaled in the units of the independent variable, and the measurement of many of our variables is very different. Accordingly, we also include a standardized measure of variable effect, Beta, in table 7.4.[8] The standardized measure can be compared across variables because it places each variable in a standardized unit of measurement.

OPPORTUNITY MEASURES AND CRIME HOT SPOTS

Motivated offenders have been seen as a key element of the crime triangle, which also includes potential targets and capable guardians (Cohen, 1981; Cohen and Felson, 1979). They also have been a key dimension in crime pattern theory (Brantingham and Brantingham, 1981). Consistent with this component of the opportunity perspective, we find that an increase in motivated offenders, as represented by an increase in high-risk juveniles on a street segment, has a strong and significant impact on the likelihood of being found in the chronic-crime hot spots pattern. Indeed, an additional high-risk juvenile found on a street segment doubles the odds of being in this group as opposed to the crime-free group. A positive change over time in the number of high-risk juveniles on a street segment also increases the likelihood of being in a chronic-crime pattern street segment, though this effect is considerably smaller than that of the baseline indicator. Our result is particularly interesting, because prior studies have often assumed that offenders will not commit crimes immediately adjacent to their home (Brantingham and Brantingham, 1981). Of course, the fact that high-risk juveniles on a street increases crime risk does not mean that these juveniles are the culprits. It may be, for example, their friends who commit crimes on the street in the course of their routine activities (possibly visiting the high-risk juveniles who live on a particular street segment).

TABLE 7.4 Multinomial Logistic Regression Results of Impact of Social Disorganization and Opportunity Variables (Including Change Variables) on Likelihood of Being in Chronic-Crime Trajectory Pattern vs. Crime-Free Pattern

Variable	b	Odds Ratio	Beta	Significance
Opportunity				
High Risk Juveniles	0.797	2.218	1.675	0.000***
High Risk Juveniles (change)	0.217	1.242	0.351	0.002**
Employees	0.072	1.075	9.162	0.000***
Employees (change)	0.031	1.031	3.292	0.000***
Public Facilities	0.212	1.237	0.179	0.014*
Residents	0.216	1.241	5.878	0.000***
Residents (change)	0.053	1.055	0.375	0.000***
Total Retail Sales	0.007	1.007	0.194	0.281
Bus Stops	0.605	1.831	0.309	0.000***
Arterial Road	2.388	10.870	1.055	0.000***
Police/Fire Station	0.441	1.555	0.115	0.045*
% Vacant Land	0.394	1.482	0.040	0.616
% Vacant Land (change)	1.758	5.803	0.139	0.064
Street Lighting	0.085	1.089	0.590	0.000***
Social Disorganization				
Property Value	−0.350	0.704	−1.263	0.000***
Housing Assistance	0.099	1.104	0.457	0.000***
Mixed Land Use	0.448	1.565	0.093	0.256
Racial Heterogeneity	−4.632	0.010	−0.178	0.106
Racial Heterogeneity (change)	−4.723	0.009	−0.171	0.085
Urbanization	0.000	1.000	0.000	0.653
Physical Disorder	3.244	25.634	1.230	0.000***
Physical Disorder (change)	1.820	6.169	0.747	0.000***
Truant Juveniles	0.950	2.585	0.792	0.000***
Truant Juveniles (change)	0.678	1.969	0.468	0.000***
% Active Voters	−3.188	0.041	−1.010	0.000***
Other Variables:				
Segment Length	0.020	1.021	0.050	0.516
Spatial Lag	0.202	1.224	1.057	0.000***
Spatial Lag (change)	0.157	1.170	0.303	0.000***

n = 24,023; * p < .05, ** p < .01, *** p < .001

As we noted in chapter 5, a second key element of opportunity theories is the presence of suitable targets (Brantingham and Brantingham, 1995; Cohen and Felson, 1979).[9] All else being equal, it would be expected that as the number of suitable targets increases, the number of crimes would also increase. We examine four measures reflecting the number and attractiveness of targets on a street segment: employment, public facilities, residential population, and retail sales.

Employment is the single most important variable in explaining the likelihood of falling in the high chronic-crime pattern in our model (as reflected by the standardized regression coefficient). An additional employee on a street segment increases the odds of falling in this pattern by 8 percent. The change in number of employees over time also has a strong and significant impact in the same direction, though of a somewhat smaller magnitude. While the percent change for each additional employee is much smaller than the change noted above for high-risk juveniles, it is important to note that there are many more employees than high-risk juveniles in our data, meaning that even though the impact of each employee is smaller than that observed for each additional high-risk juvenile, the overall impact of the variable on being a chronic hot spot is much larger.

The presence of public facilities within a quarter mile of a street segment also significantly increases the probability of being in the chronic-crime pattern. Having a public facility such as a community center, park, library, middle and high school, or hospital, within a quarter mile increases the odds of being in the chronic-crime pattern (as contrasted with the crime-free pattern) by almost 25 percent.

Residential population also has a very strong impact on the likelihood of being a crime hot spot in our data. Indeed, it is the second most important predictor behind employment (as indicated by the Beta coefficient). As would be expected by opportunity theory, the larger the residential population, the more likely a street segment is to be in the chronic-crime pattern. In contrast, our measure of retail sales, while in the expected direction (with higher sales leading to a greater likelihood of being in the chronic pattern), is not statistically significant. It may be that the amount of retail sales does not reflect the number of patrons or visitors to the street, or that after accounting for employment, public facilities, and residential population, we have captured most of the variability in suitable targets that exists on street segments. Whatever the explanation of the nonsignificant effect of retail business sales , the presence of suitable targets as indicated by employees, facilities, and residential population is a key factor in understanding crime hot spots. Indeed, the two most important measures in our analysis, as indicated by the standardized regression coefficients, are found in this dimension of opportunity theories.

Accessibility and urban form also are significant variables in predicting that a street segment will be a crime hot spot. For every additional bus stop on a street, the odds of being in the chronic-crime pattern as contrasted with the crime-free pattern almost doubles. A strong and statistically significant effect is also found in the case of arterial roads. Even after accounting for confounded variables like employment and bus stops, being an arterial road starkly increases the likelihood of a street segment being in the chronic-crime pattern as opposed to the crime-free pattern.[10]

Our findings for guardianship are less clear than those for motivated offenders, suitable targets, and accessibility and urban form. This may result in part from the fact that we could not measure a key component of guardianship, police activity at street segments. We did measure whether a police or fire station was within a quarter of a mile of a street segment as a proxy for governmental guardianship more generally. But our measure, while statistically significant, is not in the expected direction. The presence of a police or fire station increases the likelihood of a street segment being in the chronic-crime pattern. This effect is significant at the 5 percent level, though it is important to note that as mentioned earlier (see table 7.3), the overall effect of police/fire stations in the model is not statistically significant. This means that we should be cautious in drawing strong inferences from a specific finding in this comparison (Weisburd and Britt, 2007). We might speculate that the increased risk of crime hot spots being located near police stations may relate to decisions by cities to place such facilities in parts of town where crime is a more serious problem but this does not apply to fire stations which are placed to minimize response time for the entire city.

We argued in chapter 5 that vacant land reflects an absence of capable guardianship. Overall, our model supports this finding, as indicated in table 7.3, where both percentage of vacant land and change in vacant land over time are statistically significant. Nonetheless, in the case of the specific comparison between chronic-crime street segments and crime-free segments examined here we do not gain statistically significant results, though the effects are in the expected direction. We do find that vacant land is significantly related to selection into the low activity crime segments (as contrasted with the crime-free segments; see appendix 5). We suspect that the relationship between vacant land and crime is complex. Vacant land may on the one hand decrease capable guardianship, while on the other decrease the number of potential targets. This would explain its significance in predicting presence in lower crime street segments, as vacant land may act as a risk factor but have relevance to a relatively smaller number of targets.

Our final measure of guardianship is street lighting. Street lighting has a strong and significant effect in our model, but not in the expected direction. More wattage on a street is associated with a higher likelihood of being a crime hot spot. Remember that we have already taken into account the road network (and accordingly the fact that arterial roads are likely to have higher wattage lighting), and many other characteristics of the street segments that might be related to street lighting (e.g., residential population or employment). It may be that the long-held assumption that street lighting increases guardianship and reduces crime (Welsh and Farrington, 2008) is spurious at the street segment level. But we suspect that the relationship of lighting to crime is too complex to be accurately parsed using total crime over both daytime and nighttime hours. Moreover, street lighting was found in our data (see chapter 5) to operate most strongly as a large area effect. It may be, that lighting is generally increased in areas where crime problems are seen as more serious.

SOCIAL DISORGANIZATION AND CRIME HOT SPOTS

We identified a series of variables reflecting structural components of social disorganization in chapter 6 (see table 7.1). A key measure of this aspect of social disorganization is socioeconomic status (SES). We measured SES both by assessing the value of residential property on a street segment, and the amount of housing assistance. We find that both of these measures are strongly and significantly related to a street segment falling in the chronic-crime pattern.

Consistent with social disorganization theory, a unit increase in rank in residential property value (in a scale ranging from 0 to 10) is associated with a 30 percent decrease in the odds of being in the chronic-crime pattern. Housing assistance is also a significant and strong predictor of crime hot spots, though the magnitude of this effect is smaller than residential property values. Again consistent with social disorganization theory, a one unit increase in housing assistance leads to an increase of 10 percent in the odds of being a chronic-crime street segment as opposed to a crime-free street segment.

Two key structural dimensions reflecting social disorganization are mixed land use and racial heterogeneity. Both of these measures were not statistically significant in the overall model test (see table 7.3) and were not statistically significant in the comparisons between the chronic-crime and crime-free patterns. Another structural component of social disorganization theories—distance from the city center—has an overall impact on our model (see table 7.3) but does not influence the likelihood of a street segment being in the chronic-crime pattern. This reinforces our observation in chapter 3 that chronic-crime-pattern street segments intersperse with crime-free segments in the city.

Physical disorder is the most direct indicator of social disorganization, and its relationship to developmental trajectories of crime at street segments is very strong. In our sample, a street segment is much more likely to be in the chronic-crime pattern as opposed to the crime-free pattern if it has additional reports of physical disorder incidents. Interpretation of the very large odds ratio should be made with caution, as most streets in the city are not reported as having physical disorder problems.[11] The overall impact of this variable in the model is similar to that of residential property values. Change in physical disorder is also strongly related to trajectory pattern membership, with increases in incidents associated with higher likelihoods of being in the chronic-crime pattern.

Mediating variables that reflect the ability of communities, or in this case the small social systems of street segments, to regulate behavior are also important in the social disorganization framework (Bursik and Grasmick, 1993; Sampson, Raudenbush, and Earls, 1997; Sampson and Groves, 1989). A key variable in this context is truant juveniles, as the presence of truant juveniles represents the lack of regulation on the given street. We find that truant juveniles on a street segment significantly increase the likelihood of it being a crime hot spot.[12] Indeed, an additional truant juvenile more than doubles the odds of a street being in the chronic-crime pattern. The change variable also significantly influences the likelihood of a street segment being in the chronic-crime pattern, as contrasted with the crime-free pattern.

We used percentage of active voters as an indicator of collective efficacy at the street segment level. Overall, the measure follows what would be expected from social disorganization theory. In the case where there are no active voters as contrasted with a situation where all registered voters are active voters, the odds ratio of being in the chronic-crime trajectory group compared with the crime-free pattern decreases almost 96 percent. It seems accordingly that the more involved the residents are in public affairs, the less likely the streets are to have chronic crime problems. The overall impact of this measure in the model is statistically significant and is similar in magnitude to that of property values and physical disorder (as indicated by the standardized regression coefficients).

SUMMARY

Our examination of the direction and magnitude of influence of specific variables in the analysis reinforces our general examination of model explanation. A large array of opportunity and social disorganization measures influence the likelihood of a street segment being in the chronic-crime pattern as contrasted with the crime-free pattern. Both opportunity and social disorganization perspectives are important in this context in understanding the criminology of place. The single most important effects in the model are found in the case of two opportunity measures reflecting suitable targets: number of employees and number of residents. But a series of other variables reflecting both opportunity and social disorganization also have large impacts in the model. These include public facilities in the opportunity perspective as well as measures of SES (property value), physical disorder, and collective efficacy (as reflected in the number of active voters) from the social disorganization perspective.

Do Changes in Opportunity and Social Disorganization at Street Segments Impact upon Crime Waves and Crime Drops?

Our analyses so far have focused on how variables reflecting opportunity and social disorganization perspectives affect the overall "choice" of trajectory-pattern membership and the specific choice of being in a chronic-crime pattern versus a crime-free pattern. It is also important to consider directly how change in the independent variables over time influences developmental crime patterns at street segments. For example, in chapter 3 we observed that there were "crime waves" as well as "crime drops" at Seattle street segments. That is, there were in Seattle during the period of study groups of street segments that evidenced markedly opposing crime trends. The low-decreasing pattern street segments, for example, evidenced a 69.3 percent crime drop during this period, while the low-increasing segments experienced a 95.7 percent crime wave. For the high-decreasing pattern, the percent drop was 62.1, while for the high-increasing pattern there was a 93.4 percent crime wave. These contrasts provide an opportunity to see whether there were corresponding increases and decreases in social disorganization and opportunity measures at these street segments during this period.

Our main focus in these analyses is on how change over time in the independent variables influences change in the developmental patterns of crime at street segments over time. Accordingly in our analyses below we are primarily concerned with the influence of change variables on crime patterns. However, one important limitation in our study is that we could not collect such information for some measures, and for many, the time periods we observed were only partial. Because of these limitations in our data, we think caution should be exercised in drawing overly strong conclusions from our analyses. Nonetheless, as we describe below, the overall relationships we find are strongly consistent with the theoretical perspectives we examine.

We estimate two separate models: one comparing low-decreasing to low-increasing trajectory patterns, and one comparing high-decreasing to high-increasing patterns. The regressions include all of the baseline measures from table 7.1 as control variables. We include all of the possible change variables.[13] The full models are presented in appendix 5. In table 7.5, we provide an overall summary of the findings regarding the change measures.[14]

What stands out most in table 7.5 is the fact that opportunity variables representing change seem to have relatively weak relationships with crime waves and crime drops. For the low crime comparisons, only employees and number of residents have strong and statistically significant relationships with these contrasts. In both cases, as opportunity theories would predict, increasing numbers of employees and residents are related to crime waves and decreasing numbers on a street segment, to crime drops. Only the number of employees was a statistically significant predictor in the analysis of the high crime comparisons.

One explanation for the lack of significant findings regarding the opportunity perspective might be simply that the number of cases in these analyses is relatively smaller than those described earlier, and as we noted earlier, models including larger numbers of cases are more likely to observe significant effects than models that include fewer cases. The model for the low crime comparison has 3,105 cases while the model for the high crime comparison includes 793

TABLE 7.5 Summary of Findings for Comparisons of Increasing and Decreasing
Trajectory Patterns

Change Variables	Low Decreasing (−)/ Low Increasing (+)	High Decreasing (−)/ High Increasing (+)
Opportunity		
High Risk Juveniles	+	−
Employee Population	+ **	+ *
Residential Population	+ ***	+
Total Retail Sales	+	+
Bus Stops	−	−
% Vacant Land	−	+
Street Lighting	+	+
Social Disorganization		
Property Value	− **	−
Housing Assistance	+ ***	+
Mixed Land Use	+	+
Racial Heterogeneity	+	+ *
Physical Disorder	+ ***	+ **
Truant Juveniles	+ ***	+ **
% Active Voters	− *	− **

"+" indicates variable is associated with an increased likelihood of being in the increasing pattern; "−" indicates
variable is associated with an increased likelihood of being in the decreasing pattern

n = 3,105 for low decreasing/low increasing; n = 793 for high decreasing/high increasing;

* p < .05, ** p < .01, *** p < .001

cases. At the same time, as is apparent from table 7.5, and discussed below, there are a number of statistically significant findings observed in the case of change variables for social disorganization.

We think that a more straightforward explanation for the relatively weaker impact of opportunity measures here relates to a finding in our study described in chapter 5. There appears overall to be relatively little variation during the time period we studied for many of the opportunity-perspective variables. Bus stops and vacant land, for example, did not evidence very much change during the study period. This perhaps is part of a more general principal, at least in mature cities, that the structure of situational opportunities at street segments is likely to remain relatively stable across time. As we argued earlier, many aspects of the urban landscape may change over long periods of time, but are less likely to change dramatically in the time period of 16 years that we observe in this study. Importantly as well, we argued that the stability of crime at place may be a reflection in good part of the stability of crime opportunities.[15]

Our discussion here is speculative because we are limited in the time period we study, and many of the change measures we include are even more limited than our data on crime. Nonetheless, especially given the very strong impacts of variables reflecting the opportunity perspective earlier in the chapter, we do not think that one should draw from these findings a conclusion that changes in situational opportunities have only limited impact on crime waves and crime drops at street segments. Our findings reflect in good part the limitations of our data (in regard to tracking these variables over time) and the slow pace of change for many elements of the opportunity perspective.

In terms of the social disorganization perspective, four of the structural measures of change that were included in the model are significantly related to increasing and decreasing patterns. Property values and housing assistance are both strong and significant variables in distinguishing crime waves and crime drops in the low crime comparison. As would be expected from social disorganization theory, decreasing property values and increasing public assistance at street segments are related to crime waves. While racial heterogeneity was not found to be important in predicting developmental crime patterns more generally in our data, it is statistically significant in the high crime comparison model, with greater heterogeneity being related to crime waves. Physical disorder is again strongly and significantly related to crime trends. In both the high and low crime comparisons, increases in physical disorder over time are related to increased crime trends.

As we noted earlier, a number of scholars have argued that measures like physical disorder are strongly confounded with crime and may be the result of common underlying problems. Mediating social disorganization variables have been assumed to be less vulnerable to such criticism. We find very strong and significant impacts for change over time both for truant students and for voter participation. Increasing collective efficacy (as reflected by the percentage of active voters on a street segment) is related to crime drops, and increasing numbers of unsupervised teens (as reflected by truant students) is related to crime waves.

SUMMARY

Our analyses of contrasts between crime waves and crime drops in our data suggest that changes over time in opportunity and social disorganization are salient for understanding this aspect of the criminology of place. Changes in structural and mediating social disorganization measures have particularly strong relationships to change patterns in crime. This finding is consistent with our observations in chapters 5 and 6, which showed that opportunity factors varied somewhat less over time than did measures of social disorganization. Perhaps in this context, the relatively stronger impacts of social disorganization in understanding change are influenced by the relatively greater variability observed in social disorganization measures in our sample. But clearly, the most important finding drawn from our models of crime waves and crime drops is the salience of social disorganization theory. Once again, our work provides strong support for the inclusion of the social disorganization perspective in theorizing about the criminology of place.

Conclusions

In this chapter, we brought together a broad range of variables reflecting social disorganization and opportunity theories into a single statistical model of developmental trajectories of crime at place. As we noted in previous chapters, our reliance on retrospective data sources meant that we could not identify many key variables in these perspectives, and we were often limited in the time periods we could observe. Nonetheless, our analyses provide the most comprehensive examination of the factors predicting crime at place that has been published to date.

The most important single finding here is that both opportunity and social disorganization perspectives have considerable salience in understanding crime at place, and that together they allow us to develop a very strong level of prediction of crime. While opportunity variables appear to provide stronger consistency with crime patterns at places than the social disorganization perspective, the social disorganization perspective also accounts for a large proportion of variability in our model. Crime at street segments is highly predictable. This is a key finding of our work and provides strong reinforcement for the idea of the tight coupling of crime at place that we introduced in chapter 1. This chapter illustrates that crime is coupled to place because places evidence specific characteristics that inhibit or encourage crime. Differences of crime opportunities across street segments are related to differences in crime patterns, and differences in social disorganization across the micro communities of street segments are also related to the crime patterns we observe.

We have focused in on two main questions in examining the importance of specific variables on developmental crime patterns: Which variables explain membership in the chronic-crime pattern (as opposed to the crime-free pattern), and how do changes in opportunity and social disorganization influence changes in crime patterns? The former analysis showed that a wide array of measures were related to being in a chronic-crime pattern street segment. The most important influences represented the dimension of suitable targets of the opportunity perspective. But other dimensions of both opportunity and social disorganization also had strong influences. Importantly, the impacts of these perspectives on crime hot spots were overall consistent with that predicted by theory.

In examining crime waves and crime drops, we were very limited in the measurement of variables that represented change in opportunity and social disorganization over time. But the measures that could be examined in this way again were associated with crime patterns in the direction that would be expected. In these analyses we found a particularly strong impact of measures of social disorganization. We argued that one explanation for this might be the fact that situational opportunities at places in a natural context often do not vary greatly in a 16-year time frame. Of course, this does not mean that social control agents or governmental agencies cannot create such changes quickly, for example through the increase of guardianship in hot spots policing programs (Braga and Weisburd, 2010) or changes in the opportunity structure of places through situational prevention strategies (Clarke, 1992).

Overall, our findings indicate that crime at place is very predictable. Even though we are at a relatively early stage in the development of research in the criminology of place, our models provide strong explanation for the crime problems we observe. This suggests that the criminology of place may have particularly strong policy relevance, a point that we will examine in more detail in the next chapter.

{ 8 }

Conclusions

When scholars and practitioners have thought about the crime problem, they have generally begun with a fundamental assumption that has focused their interests and their investigations. That assumption is simply that crime is a product of human agency, and because of that, the key unit of the study of crime and its control must be people. Criminologists accordingly have focused on the factors that cause individuals to become involved in crime or that lead them to desist from criminal behavior. Similarly, crime prevention practitioners have looked to develop crime prevention policies that would rehabilitate and change offenders or that would deter them from future criminal behavior. What is common to these approaches is the focus on people as the key unit of analysis for understanding and doing something about the crime problem.

In this book, we have taken a very different approach to the crime problem. We recognize at the outset the importance of human agency. Crimes are committed by people, and individuals are an integral part of the crime equation. But the human agency that is involved in choosing to commit crimes is carried out in the context of particular environments. Our approach has been to see how our understanding of the crime problem can be enhanced by focusing our interests on where crime occurs. We have not ignored people in this context. The people who live, work, and visit places are an important part of our efforts to understand crime at place, as we have seen in prior chapters. Rather, we began our investigation by putting places at the center of the crime equation, and then asking how people and other characteristics of places influence the likelihood of crime. A key finding of our study is that crime is "tightly coupled" to place. In this context, crime should not be seen as a serendipitous occurrence at place, a random event that can move with ease across places in the city. Rather, our work emphasizes that there are characteristics of places that strongly link crime to small areas of geography like street segments.

Our emphasis on putting places at the center of the crime equation represents a new way of thinking about the crime problem. In this concluding chapter, we want to focus on how this approach has added to our knowledge about crime and crime prevention. Does the criminology of place offer new insights into our understanding of crime? Does it provide new opportunities for doing something about the crime problem? We begin by reviewing the major findings of our study and their implications for our understanding of crime and crime prevention. We focus on five specific contributions that we noted in our introductory chapter:

1) Crime is tightly concentrated at crime hot spots, suggesting that we can identify and deal with a large proportion of crime problems by focusing on a very small number of places.
2) These crime hot spots evidence very strong stability over time, and thus present a particularly promising focus for crime prevention efforts.
3) Crime at places evidences strong variability at micro levels of geography, suggesting that an exclusive focus on higher geographic units, like communities or neighborhoods, will lead to a loss of important information about crime and the inefficient focus of crime prevention resources.
4) It is not only crime that varies across very small units of geography, but also the social and contextual characteristics of places. The criminology of place in this context identifies and emphasizes the importance of micro units of geography as social systems relevant to the crime problem.
5) Crime at place is very predictable, and therefore it is possible to not only understand why crime is concentrated at place but also to develop effective crime prevention strategies to ameliorate crime problems at places.

After summarizing the main research findings of our study, we consider the broad policy implications of our work. We argue that crime prevention policy, and not just theoretical criminology, must begin to focus interest on crime at place. The criminology of place provides new and important insights into how society should deal with the crime problem. Finally, before concluding, we discuss specific limitations of our study and how future research can improve our understanding of the criminology of place. In concluding, we argue that places should form a central concern of criminologists, policy makers, and practitioners in the twenty-first century.

The Law of Concentrations of Crime at Place

A key requirement for a science of the criminology of place and the adoption of place-based crime prevention is that crime is heavily concentrated in what have been termed "crime hot spots" (Sherman, Gartin, and Buerger, 1989;

Sherman and Weisburd, 1995; Weisburd and Green, 1995). The tight coupling of crime and place would predict a consistency and stability in the concentration of crime at place, reflecting the fact that there are specific processes that bring crime to concentrate at specific places.

In contrast, if crime were only weakly coupled to place, we would not expect strong crime concentrations in the city. Crime in this context would be distributed randomly across places in the city, as there would be little binding crime to specific places. If crime is concentrated in crime hot spots, then it is natural to ask what accounts for that concentration. What leads crime to be coupled to specific places? In turn, a concentration of crime at place suggests that there may be an opportunity to more efficiently allocate crime prevention resources by focusing them at specific places, rather than spreading them widely across places in the city.

As we have noted in our introductory chapter, a number of studies beginning in the late 1980s suggest that significant clustering of crime at place exists at micro levels of geography, regardless of the specific unit of analysis defined (see Brantingham and Brantingham, 1999; Pierce, Spaar, and Briggs, 1988; Roncek, 2000; Sherman, Gartin, and Buerger, 1989; Weisburd and Green, 1994; Weisburd, Maher, and Sherman, 1992, Weisburd et al., 2004; Weisburd, Morris, and Groff, 2009). Sherman, Gartin, and Buerger's (1989) seminal analysis of emergency calls to street addresses over a single year in Minneapolis, Minnesota, found that only 3.5 percent of the addresses in the city produced 50 percent of all crime calls to the police. They regarded these results as so startling that they called for a new area of study, which they termed the "criminology of place."

Other studies produced similar evidence of the concentration of crime in crime hot spots. Weisburd and Mazerolle (2000), for example, found that approximately 20 percent of all disorder crimes and 14 percent of crimes against persons were concentrated in just 56 drug-crime hot spots in Jersey City, New Jersey, an area that comprised only 4.4 percent of street segments and intersections in the city. Similarly, Eck, Gersh, and Taylor (2000) found that the most active 10 percent of places (in terms of crime) in the Bronx and Baltimore accounted for approximately 32 percent of a combination of robberies, assaults, burglaries, grand larcenies, and auto thefts.

Our study includes the longest time series of data ever used to examine the concentration of crime at place. Our findings confirm earlier studies and document once again the tremendous concentration of crime at micro levels of geography in a city. Using 16 years of data for street segments, we find that about 50 percent of crime is found at just 5 to 6 percent of street segments. More than 20 percent of crime incidents in Seattle were found at just 1 percent of the street segments.

But our data go beyond prior studies by not only identifying strong concentrations of crime at micro levels of geography, but also identifying a stability of crime at place over a long time series (see also Weisburd et al., 2004). For each of the 16 years we observe crime at street segments in Seattle, we find a very similar level of concentration. This stability of crime concentrations across time was well illustrated in figure 3.2. It is in some sense startling that over 16 years, about the same number of street segments produce about the same proportion of crime, especially when we consider that there were important changes in the level of crime in Seattle during this period. Despite a more than 20 percent decline of crime at street segments, the number of street segments that account for 50 percent of crime each year remained very stable.

In chapter 3, we raised the question of whether this stability could be termed a "law of crime concentrations." Our finding, as we noted there, is particularly interesting in light of Emile Durkheim's classic proposition that the level of crime is stable in society, or rather that there was a "normal level" of crime in society (Durkheim, 1895 [1964]). For Durkheim, this meant that crime was not necessarily an indication of an illness or pathology in society, but rather that healthy societies would inevitably have some normal level of crime. Crime waves and crime drops in this context can be seen as the result of some "abnormality" in society that results from crisis or dramatic social change.

Underlying Durkheim's proposition is his understanding of crime as a product of social definition. Kai Erikson (1966) was to build upon this idea in his classic study *Wayward Puritans*, where he sought to show that the definition of crime has a social function. By defining others as deviant, society can help draw the boundaries between acceptable and unacceptable conduct (see also Adler and Adler, 2009; Becker, 1963). Defining people as criminal in this sense serves a function in defining the moral boundaries of society. We can know the boundaries of acceptable behavior by observing "deviants" who are sanctioned for violating societal norms.

Crime rates over the last few decades would seem to strongly contradict Durkheim's conception of normal levels of crime in society. Between 1973 and 1990, violent crime doubled (Reiss and Roth, 1993), and in the 1990s the United States experienced a well-documented "crime drop" (Blumstein and Wallman, 2000). In the 1970s, Alfred Blumstein and colleagues (Blumstein and Cohen, 1973; Blumstein and Moitra, 1979; Blumstein, Cohen, and Nagin, 1977) hypothesized that Durkheim's proposition could be applied to punishment in America, where imprisonment rates had remained static for a long period of time (see also Tremblay, 1986). But recent dramatic increases in U.S. incarcerations in the 1980s and 1990s would seem inconsistent with the normal crime, or "normal punishment" (Blumstein and Cohen, 1973) hypothesis, unless of course we were to postulate that these are periods of dramatic social change.

While Durkheim's proposition regarding a normal level of crime in society does not seem to fit recent experience and is seldom discussed by criminologists today, our data suggest that there is indeed a "normal level of crime" in cities, but one that relates to the concentration of crime at place and not to the overall rate of crime. We think in this context that a different proposition from

Durkheim's can be raised at this juncture and should be examined in future studies. There appears to be a "law of concentrations" of crime at place. Despite changes in crime rates, the concentration of crime follows a consistent pattern across time in Seattle. This is an intriguing finding that places Durkheim's theorizing in a new light.

At the outset, it is important to note that there are as well strong similarities in levels of concentrations observed across cities. Sherman, Gartin, and Buerger (1989) found that 3 to 4 percent of addresses produced 50 percent of emergency calls to the police in Minneapolis. Pierce, Spaar, and Briggs (1988) found an almost identical distribution of crime calls at addresses in Boston. Our data in Seattle find only a slightly lower level of concentration, which could easily be explained by the differences in unit of analysis (addresses versus street segments) or the nature of the data used. Our study, for example, excluded a number of street segments that were officially part of the street grid, but did not fulfill our requirements as possible behavior settings.[1] Using a similar unit of analysis, Weisburd and Amram (forthcoming) found that 5 percent of the street segments in Tel Aviv were responsible for 50 percent of the crime incidents, a statistic remarkably similar to the results in Seattle.

Can we use Durkheim's initial insights to consider possible reasons for this law of concentrations of crime at place? If we follow Durkheim and other theorists that built on his work, we would look to the role of crime at place in defining normative boundaries in society. In this case, we might argue that a certain number of places in the city with severe crime problems serve as lessons for the city more generally. This would fit well with our finding, discussed in chapter 4, that crime hot spots are found throughout the city. Accordingly, we all have direct visceral experiences with the "bad places" in the city, and perhaps that serves to define for the rest of us the "moral boundaries" of place. The normal level of crime concentrations in this context would relate to the proportion of problem places that are needed to bring the lessons of moral boundaries to the city's residents.

Another possible explanation for a law of concentrations comes from our identification in chapters 5 and 6 of the concentration of other characteristics of places in the city. For example, we noted in chapter 5 that the concentration of bus stops or number of public facilities stayed relatively constant across time as did the concentration of crime. Perhaps the law of concentrations of crime is related to the overall distribution of social and environmental characteristics of places in cities. Does the stability of patterns of business and employment in a city, for example, reflect more general patterns of concentration that are related to the growth and development of urban areas? Certainly cities regulate such concentrations, by defining commercial, business, and industrial use of property. Perhaps the normal concentrations of crime are simply a reflection of the normal concentrations of other social activities in the city. Our data suggest that there are hot spots of crime opportunities and social disorganization and that those characteristics evidence relative stability in concentrations at place (see chapters 5 and 6). The law of concentrations of crime at place may simply be a reflection of a more general law of the stability of concentrations of specific aspects of social and economic life in the city. Indeed, this is consistent with Juran's (1951) identification of the Pareto Principle, which he argued could be applied widely across social and physical phenomena.

But this brings us back to Durkheim, because crime is a social phenomenon and its tolerance is a social construct. Is society willing to tolerate crime in only a certain proportion of the landscape of a city? Is the law of concentrations a result of the boundaries of crime at place that citizens are willing to tolerate? Will people become worried and call for action when crime hot spots increase beyond a specific proportion of places in the city, and will they become more lax when the concentrations are below that level?

We think that these are intriguing questions and that our work has uncovered an important social law that needs to be examined in more detail in other studies, drawing upon other sources of data about the organization of city life. But irrespective of our search for a broader understanding of the law of concentrations of crime, our data provide strong reinforcement for the idea that crime is not randomly spread across the city but is concentrated at specific places often termed crime hot spots. This concentration of crime at place is consistent with an assumption of the tight coupling of crime at place. It also suggests that there may be strong opportunities for crime prevention by focusing resources at the places where crime is concentrated.

Stability and Variability of Crime at Place

Concentration itself does not necessarily provide a solid empirical basis for either refocusing crime prevention resources or calling for significant theorizing about why crime is concentrated at place. The law of concentrations shows that crime concentrations are similar across place over time. It does not confirm that crime patterns at specific places are consistent over time. For example, it could be that 5 or 6 percent of street segments in Seattle include 50 percent of crime each year, but that those streets change year to year. If that were the case, then the underlying assumption that crime is tightly coupled to place would be brought into question. It would also be true that the opportunities for creating more efficient crime prevention by focusing on hot spots would be challenged. A crime prevention policy focused on hot places would simply be chasing crime around the city.

Our data do not support a model of shifting high crime places. Indeed, our work has strongly reinforced the idea of strong bonds between crime and place. In chapter 3, we examined the developmental trends of crime at street segments in Seattle over a 16-year period. We identified a group of different patterns. One clear pattern of chronic or hot spot crime places emerged, including about 1 percent of Seattle street segments. This pattern began our observation period as the most serious hot spots in Seattle, and remained hot spots throughout the time period observed. Though just 1 percent of the city landscape, they accounted for more than 20 percent of crime in the study period. The relative intensity of crime at these places, and the stability over time of this developmental pattern in our data, suggests that there are specific characteristics of these places that generate or attract crime. In studies of individual behavior these are often termed "risk factors" for crime (Farrington, 1997; Green et al., 2008; Hawkins et al., 1998; Nagin, 1999; Nagin and Tremblay, 2001), a concept we return to later in the chapter.

The persistence of these high crime places, and the fact that they include so much crime, reinforces our earlier observation regarding the opportunities of place-based prevention. These data suggest not only that a large proportion of the crime problem can be addressed at a relatively small number of places, but also that without intervention, those places would continue to be hot spots of crime. They represent a set of stable targets for crime prevention that will provide substantial crime prevention benefit if programs or policies succeed.

Reflecting a similar underlying structure of tight coupling between crime and place are the more than 80 percent of the street segments in the city which had very little or no crime throughout the study period. Here, there would seem to be factors that help places resist or discourage crime. Again, drawing from studies of individual criminality, we might term these "protective factors" (see Brennan et al., 1997; Farrington and West, 1993; Wikström and Loeber, 2000). The tight coupling of crime at place would not only predict that some places have characteristics that create risks of crime, but also that other places may have characteristics that act as protective factors against crime.

We also observe markedly increasing and decreasing crime trends, though this was true for a relatively fewer numbers of street segments. About 12 percent of the street segments in Seattle evidenced strongly decreasing trends during the study period. Interestingly, as we described in chapter 3, these street segments had a crime decline almost equivalent to the overall crime drop in Seattle during this period. This led us to suggest that traditional approaches that speak about crime patterns across large geographic areas were likely to miss important variation within the city. For example, in our study the vast majority of street segments changed little during a period when Seattle overall experienced a more than 20 percent decline in crime at street segments. The crime decline was concentrated in Seattle at a relatively small number of places as we expect it was in most other cities.

Importantly, during the crime decline some street segments in Seattle experienced crime waves. Almost 5 percent of street segments had sharply increasing developmental trends during a period of large crime declines across the city. Indeed, these street segments evidenced an average increase in crime of about

95 percent during this period. Clearly, by focusing on citywide or large area trends, we will miss important variation within the city. Only a small proportion of Seattle street segments experienced a crime decline in the 16 years we studied, and a not insignificant group of street segments (about 1,124) experienced "crime waves" during this period. This suggests the importance of the criminology of place for thinking about the crime problem more generally.

The Importance of Studying Crime at Micro Units of Geography

Our analyses of the geography of developmental patterns of crime at street segments provided important insights into our understanding of the processes that generate crime. Perhaps the key objection to our work would be that we have unnecessarily rarified our geographic analysis, and that our choice of a micro-place unit for studying crime provides no benefit over the study of higher order geographic processes. Are crime hot spots at a micro geographic level just proxies for larger hot spot communities? Is study of place in the micro context, as we have defined it, really necessary for understanding crime in urban areas? Or is it simply cutting up the pie in additional pieces without adding new information about the crime problem? These questions are key to our understanding of the criminology of place. We have argued that crime is tightly coupled to *micro units* of geography. In chapter 4, we subjected this proposition to direct empirical analysis.

Our study provides unambiguous answers to these questions. We do not find evidence suggesting that the processes explaining crime patterns at street segments come primarily from higher geographic influences such as communities. There are indications of the influence of higher order trends in our data, for example in the fact that higher crime street segments are not distributed at random and are more likely to be closer to each other than would be predicted simply by chance. But these indications of macro geographic influences are much outweighed in our data by evidence of the importance of looking at crime at the micro level (i.e., street segments in our study). There is strong street-to-street variability in crime patterns in our data, and such variability emphasizes the importance of studying crime at place at a micro unit of analysis.

We do find cases in our data where several adjacent street segments, one after another, evidence similar developmental trends of crime. Nonetheless, the evidence of heterogeneity of street segments, even in areas where specific patterns are more common (for example the southeastern sections of Seattle), points to the critical importance of understanding how characteristics of places at the street segment level influence crime, as do our observations that crime hot spots are spread throughout the city landscape. More general evidence of spatial heterogeneity found in statistical analyses of the geography of street segments in our study further reinforces this.

Indeed, when we looked at spatial attraction and repulsion of different developmental patterns, we did not find a single example of significant spatial repulsion at any of the distances we examined. This is a particularly intriguing finding, because it suggests that even when the spatial patterns are radically different from street to street, they are not consistently governed by forces pushing them away from each other. If crime patterns at place were simply the result of higher order forces, then we might expect just such an outcome. Area trends would be determinate of local trends, and accordingly there would be spatial repulsion of specific trends, for example hot spots in "good neighborhoods" and cool spots in "bad neighborhoods." Our findings do not support such a model of crime patterns in the city in which the presence of, for example, chronic hot street segments means that crime-free street segments are not to be found in the same area. Though there are area-wide trends, for example residential areas with larger numbers of crime-free or low-crime-pattern street segments, higher crime patterns are often interspersed in these areas as well.

An intriguing question raised by the variability of crime across street segments relates to potential impacts of displacement of crime (see Reppetto, 1976; Weisburd et al., 2006). One possible explanation for the tremendous street-by-street variability that we observe is that crime is constantly shifting from place to place. While it is impossible in our data to fully understand the role of displacement in understanding crime problems at micro geographic levels, the stability of crime at place we discussed earlier certainly suggests that displacement is not a major cause of the street-by-street variability in crime that we observe. Indeed, while we observe a good deal of street-by-street variability in crime patterns, there is as we described in chapter 3 tremendous stability of crime at the street segment level. Such stability is inconsistent with the displacement hypothesis. Moreover, as we will argue later when we focus directly on policy recommendations of our work, recent studies show that displacement is not an inevitable outcome of crime prevention at hot spots, and indeed is an unlikely occurrence (Braga, 2005; Guerette and Bowers, 2009; Weisburd et al., 2006). We suspect that displacement is not a critical feature for understanding street-by-street variability in crime.

At the same time, there are certainly forces pushing down on the street segments that we study. These may come from communities and the specific social and economic changes that they experience. It may also come from higher levels of geography, for example, national social or economic processes. But our data illustrate clearly that much is lost if we simply examine crime trends at the geographic levels that have traditionally interested criminologists. Much of the action of crime comes from very small geographic units such as street segments. We think our findings suggest that it is time to move the geographic cone of criminological interests and crime prevention to the criminology of place.

Hot Spots of Opportunity and Social Disorganization

If crime is tightly coupled to place, then we should be able to identify the specific characteristics of places that lead to specific crime patterns of crime at place. For example, we should be able to identify the risk factors that lead to higher crime at place, or the protective factors that seem to insulate places from crime. But for such characteristics to have salience for our understanding of the criminology of place, they must vary at the same geographic level as crime. For example, if a specific characteristic that leads to higher risk of crime is found across a community, it may help us to understand why there are more crime hot spots in that area overall, but it would not help us to understand why there is variability within that community. Such variability has been the main focus of the criminology of place.

Do characteristics that have been assumed to influence crime at place vary at a micro level of geography? Are there hot spots of characteristics that increase risks of crime, or hot spots of characteristics that would be expected to discourage crime at place? These questions have not been raised systematically in earlier studies, but are key to advancing our knowledge of why crime is concentrated and stable at micro levels of geography.

OPPORTUNITY THEORIES AND THE CRIMINOLOGY OF PLACE

The importance of opportunity theories for understanding crime at small units of geography is well established (Brantingham and Brantingham, 1981, 1984; Clarke, 1983, 1992, 1995; Cohen and Felson, 1979; Cornish and Clarke, 1986). Indeed, the major theorists in this area have seen crime opportunities as the key variables in understanding the concentrations of specific crimes at specific places (Brantingham and Brantingham, 1981, 1984; Clarke, 1983, 1992, 1995; Cohen and Felson, 1979; Cornish and Clarke, 1986; Eck and Weisburd, 1995; Weisburd et al., 2004). This reliance on opportunity theories is easy to understand when we consider that these scholars have generally focused on crimes rather than criminals. A focus on crime naturally leads scholars to specific places or situations, and the opportunities that situations and places provide for crime. We expected at the outset that measures reflecting opportunity perspectives would vary at the street segment level. However, we wanted to examine whether this assumption would be strongly supported by empirical data.

We examined four main dimensions of opportunity theory: (1) motivated offenders; (2) suitable targets; (3) guardianship; and (4) accessibility/urban form. Opportunity measures are, as we expected, concentrated and evidence strong variability across places. For example, 50 percent of high-risk juveniles (a proxy in our work for "motivated offenders") are consistently found on between 3 and 4 percent of the total number of Seattle street segments. In turn, half of all the employees (a proxy for "suitable targets") in the city were located on less than 1 percent of Seattle street segments. In routine activity theory, both of these characteristics would be expected to increase the risk of crime at place (Brantingham and Brantingham, 1995; Weisburd, Groff, and Morris, 2009). In chapter 5, we showed that there are hot spots of motivated offenders, suitable targets, and capable guardians. This was not suprising given prior theorizing, but our data are among the first to illustrate this fact.

We also find that opportunity characteristics of places evidence much spatial heterogeneity. As with crime, we observed a great deal of street-by-street variability in the nature of crime opportunities. In statistical terms, there is a significant amount of negative spatial autocorrelation evident in the variables we examined. In this sense, while there are hot spots of crime opportunities, such hot spots are not clustered only in specific neighborhoods. Our results suggest that characteristics reflecting opportunity theories are indeed associated with specific street segments and are not simply reflecting larger area trends. At the same time, for many of the traits identified here, we also saw concentrations in larger areas, suggesting as we had seen with the distribution of crime at street segments that larger area effects are also at play in influencing larger concentrations of certain opportunity characteristics in specific areas of the city.

One intriguing finding in chapter 5 is that many of the opportunity characteristics of place we examined stayed relatively stable over the periods for which we had data available. Of course, as we noted in chapter 5, we could not measure some elements of opportunity theory directly, and perhaps if we could have, we would have observed more variability in opportunity characteristics of place over time. However, the stability of opportunity characteristics of places over time is not surprising. We would not expect land usage to change day to day or even year to year. Residential blocks are likely to remain so, as are commercial streets. While businesses may hire or fire employees or go out of business, dramatic changes are likely to take long periods of time. Facilities that may increase suitable targets, such as libraries, parks, or community centers, are even less likely to change over time because of the cost to the community to alter infrastructure. Even when facilities are added or closed, there is little change in the overall pattern of the facilities. The impact of any changes is highly localized to the streets nearby (Groff, 2011). These are all components of opportunity theories and suggest a natural stability in characteristics of opportunity at place.

It certainly seems reasonable to postulate that such stability in characteristics of place is a key reason why crime at place is relatively stable over time. If opportunities for crime are indeed related to developmental crime patterns at places (as was illustrated in chapter 7), then if those characteristics evidence relative stability over time, we would expect relative stability in crime patterns as well.

SOCIAL DISORGANIZATION AND THE CRIMINOLOGY OF PLACE

We noted in chapter 6 that social disorganization theories have been used primarily to understand the concentration of crime at higher levels of geography. They have been linked strongly to concepts of neighborhoods and communities (Bursik and Grasmick, 1993; Sampson and Groves, 1989; Sampson, Raudenbush, and Earls, 1997; Shaw and McKay, 1942 [1969]), and have rarely been used to understand micro-geographic processes (for exceptions see Rice and Smith, 2002; Taylor, 1996). For criminologists who have placed emphasis on social disorganization theory, social processes occur in relatively larger areas where social and economic forces influence the ability of communities to regulate and enforce norms on their members.

We believe that neglect of social disorganization theory in the criminology of place has hindered the development of theory and empirical analysis, and that the inclusion of social disorganization perspectives in our work is one of the most important contributions of our study. The founders of the social disorganization perspective sought to bring into our understanding of crime the important social dynamics that occur within communities in urban areas. They were concerned with the face-to-face interaction of community members and the ways in which communities differed in their abilities to control misbehavior. Social disorganization theory places emphasis on the social processes that occur in social systems, emphasizing that the ecological nature of community is key to understanding the crime problem.

Routine activity theory (Cohen and Felson, 1979), situational crime prevention theory (Clarke, 1980, 1983), and crime pattern theory (Brantingham and Brantingham, 1993a) are the key sources for the opportunity perspectives we have described in this book. While their focus on the context and situation of criminal events naturally makes these important perspectives in the criminology of place, they have often ignored the fact that places have a social context that may reflect not situational opportunities but underlying social processes that impact upon crime. Such social processes have been seen as the province of more traditional theorizing and sometimes have been neglected because they seem unlikely to be influenced by crime prevention. Opportunity theorists do not doubt the importance of social forces such as poverty or illiteracy in crime, but they believe that these, like the influence of the weather on crime, do not provide direct solutions to crime problems (Birkbeck and LaFree, 1993; Clarke, 1995). It is interesting in this regard that theorists associated with the social disorganization perspective have taken the opposite view, suggesting that opportunity-based crime prevention may work in the short run, but social interventions broadly focused will be needed to have long term effects on crime (Sampson, Raudenbush, and Earls, 1997).

We think that the idea of behavior settings, which we have used in defining the street segment as a key unit of analysis in the criminology of place, is consistent in many ways with the concept of community as presented in the social disorganization perspective (Barker, 1968; Wicker, 1987; Taylor 1997, 1998). It also offers, as we discuss in more detail when we focus on policy implications of our work, an opportunity for directing social interventions at a scale that is within reach of crime prevention practitioners in cities. Behavior settings are micro communities, or "small scale social systems" (Wicker, 1987: 614), evidencing many of the characteristics that defined neighborhoods and communities for the Chicago School or later theorists in this area.

For example, as we noted in Chapter 1 (drawing from Taylor 1997, 1998), people who frequent a street segment get to know one another and become familiar with each other's routines. Residents develop certain roles they play in the life of the street segment. There is the person who is always there to help neighbors, the busybody, the organizer, and even the person that seems to disregard everyone else by having a noisy dog or teenage children who play loud music late Saturday night. On many streets, there is at least one neighbor who will accept packages for other residents when they are not at home. Norms about acceptable behavior develop and are generally shared. Shared norms develop from interactions with other residents and observations of behaviors that take place on the block without being challenged. Street segments are likely to have standing patterns of behavior that are temporally specific. The mail carrier delivers at a certain time of day, the corner resident is always home by 5 PM, another neighbor always mows his lawn on Saturday.

Our point is that the street segment is a type of community, which may not include all elements that are traditionally attached to this concept, but certainly is likely to include many. It is at the very least a first building block of community, and in that context, street segments are likely to function as a key unit for informal social control at a micro-ecological level. We think that street segments provide a unit of analysis that "fits" with both ecological theories and opportunity theories, which led us to explore whether characteristics of social disorganization varied at a micro level of geography.

Our findings regarding the distribution of characteristics of social disorganization across places are striking. There is tremendous concentration and variation in most of the measures that we examined. Looking both at structural and mediating variables of social disorganization, we found that there are hot spots of social disorganization at the street segment level. For example, we collected data on public housing and Section 8 vouchers at street segments in Seattle, finding that there are public housing assistance hot spots. Indeed, 50% of housing assistance is consistently found on about 0.4% of the street segments in Seattle. Fully 50 percent of truant students (a mediating variable used as a proxy for "unsupervised teens") were consistently found to live on between 2 and 3.5 percent of the total street segments during the study period. And these hot spots were not simply part of contiguous hot spots at larger geographic levels. They are not found only in specific neighborhoods; rather, they are distributed across the city landscape.

We found strong evidence of spatial heterogeneity of social disorganization at street segments. While there are sometimes clusters of street segments with specific traits in what may be termed communities or neighborhoods, there is also significant street-by-street variation in such concentrations. This is an extremely important finding, since it suggests that a perspective that has generally been seen as relevant at higher levels of geography shows concentration and variability at the street segment level. The fact that there are hot spots of social disorganization at this level raises the intriguing question of whether such hot spots are related to hot spots of crime (see later). But irrespective of that relationship, our work is the first to establish that social disorganization variables are concentrated at micro levels of geography and vary significantly at that level.

Hot Spots of Crime Are Predictable

Having established that crime is tightly coupled to place at a very micro level of geography, it was natural to turn to the factors that appeared to bind crime to street segments. In chapters 5 and 6, we showed that characteristics of social disorganization and opportunity were concentrated at places and that they evidenced strong geographic heterogeneity. In chapter 7, we turned to the relationship between these theoretical perspectives and variability in developmental patterns of crime at place. Are hot spots of social disorganization and crime opportunities related to crime at street segments? Are key theoretical dimensions of crime opportunities and social disorganization related to developmental crime patterns at places?

Our findings from a multinomial regression analysis were unambiguous. We observed a very high degree of statistical fit between theories of opportunity and social disorganization and crime at street segments. Using a Pseudo R^2 measure suggested by Nagelkerke, we gain a value of explanation in our model of 0.68. To put this in context, in chapter 7 we compared this result to a study conducted by Weisburd and Piquero (2008) that assessed model fit in tests of criminological theory more generally. They found that the median value for R^2 in studies they reviewed was only 0.36, and a quarter of the studies examined had values of less than 0.20. The average R^2 value for person-based studies in that study was about 0.30.

The very high model fit statistics we observed reinforce the conclusion that crime is bound tightly to place by specific characteristics of places. We find that much of the variation in developmental patterns of crime at place can be explained, and indeed that the level of explanation is considerably higher than that found in more traditional studies of criminality and crime. Crime at place in this sense is systematically related to the specific characteristics of opportunity and social disorganization that we have focused upon in our study. While the criminology of place is a relatively new area of study in criminology, we already can explain a good deal of the variability of crime at place. This suggests, in turn, that we have strong tools to ameliorate crime problems at places. We will focus on this more directly in the next section, but at this juncture we think it important to note that crime at place is very predictable. Such predictability is consistent with our position that crime is tightly coupled to place by specific characteristics that vary at a micro level of geography.

Given the reliance of crime and place scholars on opportunity theories for understanding the causal mechanisms that underlie crime at place and the general neglect of social disorganization perspectives in this area, we also sought to compare the strength of each perspective in predicting crime patterns at places. One conclusion is clear from our analyses: variables representing both theoretical perspectives have relevance for understanding developmental crime patterns of street segments. In an overall model test, nearly all of our measures of opportunity and social disorganization are found to be significantly related to developmental patterns of crime at place. Our findings that opportunity measures have salience for understanding variation in crime patterns at places are important, but not surprising given the key role of opportunity theories in early research in the criminology of place. The fact that measures of socioeconomic status, physical disorder, unsupervised juveniles, and collective efficacy also have significant relationships to developmental crime patterns at street segments stakes out new territory, suggesting that it is time to bring the social disorganization perspective to the criminology of place.

But what if we want to compare directly the specific explanatory power of each perspective? Are opportunity perspectives as represented in our study more salient for understanding the criminology of place than social disorganization perspectives? We used a direct method for making this comparison, one that examined how well each theory independently fit the variation in developmental crime patterns we observed. Using this approach, both perspectives provided a strong fit to developmental patterns of crime at place. The opportunity perspective provided a value of explained variance (Pseudo R^2) of 0.66 versus 0.51 for the social disorganization measures. This suggests that a model exclusively concerned with opportunities for crime (as we measure them) is likely to provide a higher level of prediction of developmental patterns of crime at place. However, the differences were not as large as we might have expected given the theoretical predominance of opportunity perspectives in this area.

We think that our data support an "integrated theoretical approach" (Bernard and Snipes, 1996) to the criminology of place. Both opportunity measures and social disorganization measures provide important information for understanding variation in developmental patterns of crime at place. An exclusive theoretical approach focusing on either one or the other theory strikes us as inconsistent with the empirical data we examined. It is time to include both opportunity and social disorganization in our understanding of the criminology of place (see also Rice and Smith, 2002; Smith, Frazee, & Davison, 2000; and Maimon and Browning, 2010 for examples of systematic theory integration at the micro level).

We recognize in taking this approach that social disorganization theory has been assumed to influence crime only at much higher geographic levels. It is traditionally thought of as a theory of communities and neighborhoods. But social disorganization, as we have argued throughout this work, is as meaningful a concept at the street segment level as it is at the larger community level. This is something that most people who live in a city will recognize. The immediate social context of city life is the people on one's block. These are the people that one sees each day, and those who have most immediacy when we are concerned with problems or seek help.

The Chinese folk saying that we quoted in chapter 1 that "(n)eighbors next door are more important than relatives far away," strikes us as particularly salient for understanding our data. Neighbors close by play a key part in modern urban life, and they are the key context in which our daily lives are located. In some ways, it seems quite natural that social disorganization perspectives should be salient on street segments as well as in larger communities. The sense of belonging to a community of residents does not necessarily follow the boundaries of a politically defined community. Our first encounter with social life each day is likely to come when we walk out on our street. It is its look and feel that provides a visceral sense of the order of our immediate world. We suspect in this context that community social controls begin with the social order of our streets. The larger community is built up one by one from those streets, but it does not take away from the fact that the idea of community is relevant at the street segment level. What our study illustrates is that there is tremendous variation from street to street in such elements of community life, and these variations are strongly related to developmental patterns of crime at place.

WHAT DIFFERENTIATES CRIME HOT SPOTS FROM CRIME-FREE STREET SEGMENTS

While we presented an overall analysis of developmental crime patterns, we focused particular attention on comparing hot spot street segments (i.e., the chronic-crime pattern) with street segments that were found to be generally crime free in our study. This comparison provided the greatest contrasts in our data and allowed us to focus in directly on why some places become hot spots of crime while others seem to discourage crime events.

The two most important predictors of crime hot spots are drawn from the opportunity perspective. Both relate to the suitability of places as crime targets. The larger the residential population of a street segment, the more likely it is to be a crime hot spot. Similarly, when there are more employees on a street segment, it is much more likely to be a hot spot of crime. These findings reinforce a more general conclusion of the opportunity perspective. The factors that increase the risks of crime relate directly to the situational opportunities that places present. When more people live on a block, there is more potential for crime because there are more potential victims (and perhaps higher numbers of motivated offenders as well). When more employees work on the block, they increase the amount of crime on that street, because, as we discussed in chapter 7, they are likely to increase the volume of targets on the street.

Another indicator of crime opportunities, arterial roads, also increases the risks of crime on street segments markedly in our data. Arterial roads are much more likely to be crime hot spots. Again, the component of situational opportunities is reflected strongly in our data. Arterial roads are more likely to bring together motivated offenders and suitable targets, because they are easily accessible. They again increase the volume of routine activities at places.

But opportunity measures are not the only key variables in our analysis. Three variables that reflect the social disorganization perspective also have very large impacts on the likelihood of a street segment being a crime hot spot. The higher the level of physical disorder on a street segment, the greater the likelihood of it being a high-crime street segment. This is very much consistent with the idea that an inability of these small social systems to control disorderly behavior will increase the risk of crime.[2] High socioeconomic status, in contrast, acts as a protective factor for crime, with crime hot spots much less likely to be found at places with wealthier residents (as reflected in higher property values) who presumably are able to bring into play both formal and informal social controls more effectively.[3] Perhaps most interesting is the very strong impact of collective efficacy in our study, as reflected in voter participation. Collective efficacy seems to act as a strong protective factor for crime at place. Accordingly, the direct situational opportunities that increase crime risk are one part of the crime equation at places, but social factors that act to insulate places from crime risks are another.

UNDERSTANDING CRIME WAVES AND CRIME DROPS

While we were limited in the time frames that could be examined, we also focused our analysis on how changes in opportunity and social disorganization variables over time were related to increasing and decreasing developmental patterns of crime. One complication in developing this analysis is that many of the opportunity measures simply did not evidence significant change in the study period. This is one reason we argued earlier for the overall stability of crime trends at places that we observe in our study. While factors such as the presence of an arterial road increases dramatically the risk of a street segment being a crime hot spot, the road network is stable over time, and accordingly, change will not be predictive of crime waves and crime drops during the study period. Similarly, other measures of situational opportunities such as bus stops or public facilities are also very stable across the study period, though they also significantly increase the risk of crime at place. Importantly, the fact that many of these measures do not vary strongly across a 16-year period does not indicate that they would not vary across much longer time periods.

Accordingly, it is not surprising that the social disorganization variables that evidence overall greater variability in the time frame examined are found in our analyses to be particularly salient in distinguishing places that have distinct increasing versus decreasing crime trends in the 16 years we observed. Structural measures of social disorganization, such as increasing physical disorder and decreasing socioeconomic indicators at street segments, are strongly related to increasing crime trends. But mediating variables of social disorganization also are important in distinguishing crime waves from crime drops. Street segments are much more likely to have crime waves if the number of unsupervised teens (as represented by truant juveniles) increases, and much more likely to have crime drops if this number decreases. Similarly, increasing levels of collective efficacy (as measured by percent of active voters on a street) are likely to decrease the risk of crime waves and increase the likelihood of crime drops. These findings again point to the relevance of social disorganization at the street segment level and the importance of including social disorganization perspectives in our understanding of the criminology of place.

While opportunity variables did not figure as prominently in understanding crime waves and crime drops, two indicators that did show significant change at street segments over time remained significant in these analyses. Residential population and number of employees, which were the single most important variables in our general model of developmental crime trends at places, continued to be significant in our understanding of the contrast between increasing and decreasing trajectory patterns. As expected, increasing residential population and increasing employment were found to be risk factors for crime waves.

Recognizing the Tight Coupling of Crime to Place: Policy Implications

We have shown so far that our findings have important implications for our understanding of crime. However, we also think that our study has direct implications for crime prevention policy. Our work reinforces a growing trend in crime prevention that seeks to focus efforts on the context of crime (Brantingham and Brantingham, 1993a; Clarke, 1995; Weisburd, 2002). Specifically, our findings point to the importance of focusing crime prevention efforts on places within communities, and the fact that criminologists and crime prevention practitioners can identify and address particular characteristics of places that are related to developmental crime patterns. Our work suggests that a program of crime prevention at place would have tremendous "efficiency" for police and other crime prevention practitioners (see also Weisburd and Telep, 2010). Efficiency is important because crime prevention resources are limited.

While the efficiency of crime prevention approaches can be defined in a number of different ways, we think it reasonable to begin with a definition of efficiency that suggests that strategies are more efficient to the extent that they offer the same crime prevention value with a smaller number of targets. To the extent that crime is concentrated among a small number of potential targets, the efficiency of crime prevention can be maximized. We find that 5 to 6 percent of street segments each year include half of all crime incidents. One percent of the street segments in the chronic-crime pattern are responsible for more than a fifth of all crime incidents in the city. This means that crime prevention practitioners can focus their resources on relatively few high crime places and deal with a large proportion of the crime problem.

Of course, crime is also concentrated among offenders, a fact pointed out in research by Marvin Wolfgang, Robert M. Figlio and colleagues (1972) four decades ago. Looking at a cohort of almost 10,000 boys from Philadelphia in the 1940s and following them through 1963, they found a remarkably similar statistic of crime concentrations for people to that observed in our study of places. Chronic offenders making up just 6 percent of their sample were responsible for 51.9 percent of offenses committed by the cohort. However, a crime prevention focus on six percent of a large population such as that in a city like Seattle, would lead to the focus on many thousands of people in any specific population cohort.

Moreover, places unlike people are not "moving targets." The American Housing Survey from the U.S. Census Bureau shows that on average Americans move once every seven years (American Housing Survey Branch, 2005). It is reasonable to assume that offenders move even more often than this. Studies have often noted the difficulty of tracking offenders for survey research (Laub and Sampson, 2003; Wolfgang, Thornberry, and Figlio, 1987), and it is a common experience of the police to look for an offender and find that he or she no longer lives at the last known address. Place-based crime prevention provides a target that "stays in the same place." This is not an insignificant issue when considering the investment of crime prevention resources.

Evidence of the stability of crime patterns at places in our work also suggests the possible efficiency of place-based approaches. If there is instability of crime across time at a unit of analysis, then crime prevention strategies will be less efficient. For example, let us say that criminals vary in offending greatly over time with a very high peak in one time period and very low activity in subsequent periods. Investment of resources in incarceration of such offenders may have little real crime prevention benefit, though of course it may satisfy important considerations of just punishments for criminals.

There is perhaps no more established fact in criminology than the variability and instability of offending across the life course (Bushway, Thornberry, and Krohn, 2003; Laub and Sampson, 2003; Nagin, 1999; Robins, 1966). This may be contrasted with the findings in our study. In chapter 3, we show not only that about the same number of street segments were responsible for 50 percent of the crime each year, but also that developmental patterns of street segments were overall relatively stable across the study period. This stability suggests that place-based crime prevention will not only be more efficient in terms of the number of targets, but also in the application of interventions to specific targets. A strategy that is focused on chronic-crime pattern street segments is not likely to be focusing on places that will naturally become cool a year later. The stability of crime at place across time makes crime places a particularly salient focus for investment of crime prevention resources.

THE THREAT OF CRIME DISPLACEMENT?

But won't the focus on specific hot spots of crime simply displace crime to other places (Reppetto, 1976)? We have argued in this book that a finding of tight coupling of crime to place, and especially of a relative stability of crime patterns over time, argues against the idea that crime will easily move from place to place. But there is also strong empirical evidence that displacement is not an inevitable outcome of place-based crime prevention and that it is in fact less common than what Clarke and Weisburd (1994) have termed a "diffusion of crime control benefits." It is in this context more likely that place-based prevention will lead to areas nearby improving as a result of focused crime prevention than such areas becoming worse due to displacement of crime.

Since 1990, there have been five main reviews of empirical studies that report on displacement: Barr and Pease (1990); Eck (1993); Hesseling (1994); Guerette and Bowers (2009); and Bowers et al. (2011). All five reviews arrive at the same basic conclusions: there is little evidence that crime prevention strategies lead to displacement, and if displacement does occur it is usually offset by the amount of crime prevented. Guerette and Bowers (2009), examining situational crime prevention strategies, found that 37 percent of the observations showed evidence of spatial diffusion of benefits while only 23 percent showed evidence of spatial displacement. Bowers and colleagues (2011), focusing specifically on geographically focused police interventions, also found that a diffusion of crime control benefits is a more likely outcome of such initiatives than spatial crime displacement.

One area where the evidence regarding displacement is particularly strong and consistent is spatial displacement as an outcome of hot spots policing. A Campbell systematic review on hot spots conducted by Braga, Papachristos, and Hureau (forthcoming; see also Braga, 2001, 2005, 2007) used meta-analysis to examine displacement data for 13 tests, finding an overall small but significant diffusion of crime control benefits across studies. Only one study (Ratcliffe et al., 2011) found evidence of significant crime displacement, and even here the amount of displacement was far less than the main crime prevention benefit of the intervention.

Only one of the studies reviewed was developed directly as a test for displacement and not as an overall assessment of crime prevention at crime hot spots. Weisburd and colleagues (2006) designed their study to examine possible displacement and diffusion of crime in police interventions directed at prostitution, violence and drug activity at two crime hot spots in Jersey City, New Jersey. Accordingly, their measures were particularly sensitive to possible displacement and diffusion outcomes. To assess displacement and diffusion they conducted more than 6,000 20-minute social observations at the research sites, supplemented by interviews with arrestees from the target areas and ethnographic field observations. The study found little evidence supporting the displacement hypothesis and strong and significant diffusion of crime prevention benefits to nearby areas.

These findings are not surprising in the context of our study of developmental patterns of crime at place in Seattle. Our findings emphasize that there are strong links between the characteristics of places and crime at place. In this context, it is easy to understand resistance to displacement. Crime does not easily move from place to place because crime is tightly coupled to place.[4]

THE IMPORTANCE OF FOCUSING ON "MICRO" PLACES

Our work also reinforces the importance of focusing in on "micro" places rather than larger geographic units such as communities or police precincts. Our data suggest that crime prevention at larger geographic units is likely to suffer an "ecological fallacy" in which crime prevention resources are spread thinly across large numbers of street segments when the problems that need to be addressed are concentrated only on some of the street segments in that area. Criminologists and crime prevention practitioners need to recognize that definitions of neighborhoods as "bad" or problematic are likely to miss the fact that many places in such areas have little or no crime. In turn, crime prevention resources should be focused on the hot spots of crime within both "good" and "bad" neighborhoods.

Such an approach might also offset public concerns about the fairness of the allocation of crime prevention resources. In many cities today, progressive police chiefs are focusing police services in the poor and disadvantaged neighborhoods where crime problems are of most concern. This strategy, while recognizing that crime is not spread evenly across neighborhoods, is often politically risky, because citizens in wealthier and more socially organized areas will object to police services being moved from their neighborhoods. Our data suggest that a "neighborhood" focus does not recognize that crime hot spots are indeed spread throughout the city, and therefore the police may miss important crime problems if they are focused on "bad communities" rather than "bad places."

Inevitably, greater investment is likely to be made in specific parts of a city where there are somewhat greater concentrations of problem places (for example, the southeastern part of Seattle), but even better neighborhoods in the city are not likely to be ignored using an approach that puts micro conceptions of place at the center of crime prevention. The fact that crime hot spots can be found in "good" as well as "bad" neighborhoods suggests that a focus on the specific places where crime problems are concentrated will lead to tremendous diffusion of crime prevention resources across a city. At a policy level, our research reinforces the importance of initiatives like hot spots policing, which address specific streets or areas within larger communities (Braga, 2001; Braga and Weisburd, 2010; Sherman and Weisburd, 1995; Weisburd and Green, 1995). If police become better at recognizing the "good streets" in the more disadvantaged areas and the "bad streets" in the better off communities, they can more efficiently allocate police resources to the specific places that need them the most.

THE IMPORTANCE OF RECOGNIZING RISK AND PROTECTIVE FACTORS OF PLACES

Our data also illustrate that criminologists, police, and crime prevention practitioners can identify key characteristics of places that are correlated with crime. We have documented that crime is tightly coupled to place by specific opportunity and social disorganization characteristics of street segments.

The importance of suitable targets and motivated offenders in understanding developmental crime trends at places emphasizes the potential for reducing crime by increasing guardianship. For example, in areas where there are large numbers of employees or larger residential populations, it would seem prudent to also increase police presence. The same is true of streets that are arterial roads and streets with transportation nodes. But our data suggest not only that places with these characteristics are likely to have crime problems, but that the introduction of such risk factors may turn a low crime street into a high crime street. When new businesses or factories are opened on streets, or when new residential buildings including large numbers of residents are built, and when new bus or train stops are introduced, the community and the police should prepare to prevent crime problems before they emerge.

Deterrence through increased police presence or private security is clearly one way to reduce the risks of crime at place. The very strong evidence regarding the effectiveness of hot spots policing programs reinforces this assumption since increased guardianship is a critical component of such interventions (Braga and Weisburd, 2010). Durlauf and Nagin (2011) emphasize this point in their recent comparisons of the effectiveness of public investment in policing as contrasted with corrections. They argue that there is very strong evidence that deterrence through policing does work and can provide strong crime prevention outcomes. Indeed, the effectiveness of deterrence of crime at place is a major factor in their conclusion that there should be a shift in criminal justice investment from corrections to policing.

But crime prevention through deterrence is not enough. Police officers must be given the support and training to allow a problem-solving orientation to develop (Braga and Weisburd, 2010). Our results indicate the importance of both the social and the physical environment in understanding why some street segments and not their neighbors suffer from high crime rates. These findings provide evidence that police should take a more holistic approach to addressing crime problems. For example, using this information, they can more precisely target community building, order maintenance, and more traditional law enforcement operations to maximize efficiency and effectiveness. More broadly, they can work with other city agencies to change the physical and social environments of problem places (Johnson, Lab, and Bowers, 2008). Alterations to the built environment that improve surveillance, control access, and increase the capacity for territoriality among legitimate users can reduce crime (Lab, 2007).

Importantly, a discussion of crime prevention opportunities to increase guardianship should not be limited to the police. Programs aimed at making employees of businesses better place managers have the potential to reduce crime (Eck, 1995b; Madensen and Eck, 2008, 2012). Place managers such as store employees, parking lot attendants, and bartenders can control specific elements of the environment which increase the risks or reduce the rewards of criminal activities.

A key finding of our work is that social disorganization is also important risk factor for crime hot spots. This suggests that formal social controls, such as law enforcement, may not be enough for effectively altering trajectories of crime at places in the long term (see also Earls, 1991). It may be critical to also consider how the police and other crime prevention agents can influence the social and structural features of hot spots of crime. In this sense, the police and other crime prevention practitioners can try to enhance protective factors that discourage crime on street segments, such as increasing collective efficacy or improving social and economic conditions. In some ways, criminologists have long been concerned with how to alter community dynamics in the long-term pursuit of crime reductions. For example, advocates of the "broken windows" perspective have long argued this point, noting that a key role of the police is to reduce fear in communities and through this to empower citizens to reestablish community social control and community norms (Hinkle and Weisburd, 2008; Kelling and Coles, 1996; Wilson and Kelling, 1982). Our work suggests that the role of the police as "watchmen" in local communities should be focused not broadly in communities but specifically at places that evidence serious crime problems.

But if important mechanisms underlying developmental patterns of crime at place can be found in factors such as economic deprivation or collective efficacy, as indicated by our work, then a much broader set of social interventions may also be required to change the trajectories of crime at crime hot spots. Is that set of interventions too remote from crime prevention to have relevance for criminal justice and the criminology of place?

The focus on the specific places where crime problems are found provides an opportunity to "lower the scale" of social interventions, and accordingly to make such interventions relevant to crime prevention practitioners. It is one thing to attempt change in the social conditions of an entire neighborhood or city. It is another to try to ameliorate problems on specific blocks. One indication that this is possible comes from Redlands, California, where the police department was able to manage housing and social service resources so that they were focused on specific census tracts where crime problems were most serious (Weisburd, Morris, and Ready, 2008).[5] The California example suggests that a focus on even smaller geographic units, such as street segments, is possible. Perhaps the criminology of place provides a scale of intervention that can rekindle interest in the importance of social and structural interventions in doing something about crime.

It may be necessary to focus social interventions more carefully, providing, for example, economic support to problematic street blocks and not to neighborhoods overall. And here we return to one of the early reasons why situational crime prevention and opportunity perspective theorists have sometimes ignored broader social aspects of crime prevention. Like the weather, which has also been found to influence crime, social processes such as poverty and social disorganization more generally were seen to be outside the control of crime prevention practitioners (Clarke, 1995). These were problems that could not be directly impacted by crime prevention, and therefore were thought to be better left as factors we know influence crime but which do not contribute to the immediate amelioration of crime problems. But the fact that such processes operate on a very micro geographic level offers opportunity for much more targeted efforts to change the social context of places. Crime prevention agents may be able to influence change on specific street blocks, as opposed to cities or neighborhoods more generally.

Given the close relationship between place, crime, and health (Fitzpatrick and LaGory, 2010), it is equally likely that health-related prevention activities might be more effectively implemented at street segments. Promising prevention programs often fail upon general implementation because they are employed in places that are less risky and more heterogeneous (Welsh, Sullivan, and Olds, 2010). Focusing on hot spots means programs are addressing the riskiest of micro-level places and ones with predominantly homogeneous populations. It is also plausible that core elements of successful neighborhood-level programs such as identifying and mobilizing key leaders, increasing social cohesion, measuring risk and protective factors, and developing interventions (Loeber and Farrington, 1998) can all be used to greater effect when applied at the street segment level.

Our work suggests the importance of focusing crime prevention, whether it is at the level of local police agents or in terms of the development of social programs for hot spots of crime. This idea has also been suggested in recent studies of prisoner reentry. Scholars have identified "million dollar blocks" that include large numbers of people who are in jail or prisons (Cadora, Swartz, and Gordon, 2003). They argue that more could be gained by focusing resources on the street blocks where these prisoners come from, rather than on their incarceration (Clear, 2008). Whatever the approach that is taken, it is time to recognize the need to focus crime prevention resources at micro places such as street segments.

Limitations

While we think our work has contributed a good deal to our knowledge of the criminology of place, we want to note before concluding some specific limitations of our data and suggest promising areas for future research. Perhaps most significant is the fact that by necessity we were limited to retrospective data collection. We think we have accessed a wide array of data from a large number of data sources. Indeed, we were surprised at the breadth and depth of information that we were able to collect retrospectively. In this context, our study includes, to our knowledge, the most comprehensive longitudinal database ever compiled for a study of places at a very small geographic level.

But having noted that we were able to provide a more in-depth view of crime at place than any prior study we know of, we think it important to recognize that retrospective data collection is by its nature limited. As we noted in chapters 5 and 6, many of our measures are proxies for variables we would have liked to collect but were unable to identify. For example, we used school and voter information to estimate population statistics at street segments. Sometimes, as we noted earlier, our difficulty in collecting such social data retrospectively developed from the fact that confidentiality requirements prohibit the U.S. Census from allowing access to data at micro levels of geography, such as the street segment. Our study suggests that it is critical to find solutions to this problem of confidentiality, given the importance of micro geographic units in the development of the crime problem.

More generally, there is much we would want to know about street segments that we could not learn simply from collecting official information. For example, people commit crime, and their role in the crime equation is a central one.

Certainly, to learn more about the causes of crime at place we would want to know more than we could retrospectively about the people who live, visit, or work on street segments, and the people that offend there. Data on people at places and narratives of their experiences are certainly necessary to develop a clearer picture of the developmental patterns of crime at place.

We noted earlier the absence of what is a key indicator of guardianship at places—police presence. It is in some sense surprising, given the growing evidence of the importance of place in crime, that Seattle and other large cities have had little ability to know specifically where the police are. Recent innovations suggest that this situation is likely to change. For example, as we noted in chapter 5, a few police departments in the United States are now using automated vehicle locator systems (AVL) to keep track of where police patrol is concentrated. But such data were not available in Seattle, nor in other cities, for the time span we examine.

These limitations regarding data available for our study suggest the importance of a prospective longitudinal study of crime at place that would capture at specific times both the characteristics of places and people (see Weisburd, Lawton, and Ready, 2012). Prospective longitudinal studies are common in studies of human development more generally (e.g., see Browning, Thornberry, and Porter, 1999; Elliott, Huizinga, and Ageton, 1985; Loeber et al., 2001; Moffitt, Lynam, and Silva, 1994), though they are expensive to conduct and take patience and a long-term perspective on knowledge by funders. However, our data suggest the importance of such studies. What we have learned already implies that crime places should be an important focus for future prospective longitudinal study.

FOCUSING ON DIFFERENT TIME PERIODS AND SPECIFIC TYPES OF CRIME

Another limitation of our study is that we emphasize long-term crime trends and do not examine trends within more limited time periods. While others have shown strong variability in crime across a daily cycle (e.g., see Bromley and Nelson, 2002; Felson and Poulsen, 2003; Gottfredson, Gottfredson, and Weisman, 2001), our concern has been with the variability of crime across a 16-year period. In this regard, our study does not examine crime trends within years and is thus not sensitive to the seasonal variation in crime that some scholars have observed (e.g., see Ceccato, 2005; Cohn and Rotton, 2000; Farrell and Pease, 1994; Hipp et al., 2004). Our neglect of these questions does not reflect a conclusion that such variation of crime across the day or across seasons is not important. Rather, in looking to yearly trends in crime we did not focus our lens on these questions.

A similar limitation develops from our decision to focus on crime as a general phenomenon at street segments. A number of other scholars have begun to consider the specific trends of specific crimes at place (Braga, Papachristos, and Hureau, 2010; Weisburd, Morris, and Groff, 2009; Yang, 2010). Such trends are important, but given the very small unit of analysis we have chosen, analyses of very specific crime patterns would have been limited. Our concern was with the overall trends in crime across street segments over a 16-year period. We recognize the importance of specific inquiries for specific crimes, but such analyses were beyond the scope of our research.

LIMITATIONS IN DRAWING CAUSAL INFERENCES

While we examine the correlates of developmental crime patterns at places, we cannot make unambiguous statements about the causal patterns underlying our data. For example, reports of physical disorder are very strongly correlated with street segment presence in more serious or chronic-crime trajectory patterns. But our data do not allow us to establish that physical disorder leads to more serious crime problems. Even though we find that changes in physical disorder and changes in crime are related, it may be that a third cause unmeasured in our analysis is in fact the ultimate cause of the relationships observed (Yang, 2010). This limitation is not unique to our study, but one that affects observational studies more generally (Shadish, Cook, and Campbell, 2002).

Prospective longitudinal studies would allow researchers to develop more careful analyses of causal patterns across time. We have already noted the importance of such prospective longitudinal research. But we also think that our work suggests the importance of experimental studies of crime and place. Randomized experiments are generally most useful when there are strong basic research findings suggesting underlying causal relationships (Lipsey et al., 2006; Weisburd and Hinkle, 2012). Randomized experiments are not efficient tools for identifying possible patterns, but rather for testing them. When implemented properly, they are the clearest method for establishing cause and effect (Cook and Campbell, 1979; Farrington, 2003; Weisburd, 2003). Our work has raised a number of propositions regarding the relationship between opportunity and social disorganization, and developmental crime trends. We would hope that future researchers when developing prospective studies would also build into their designs experimental manipulations based on what is already known about crime at place (for a similar suggestion regarding studies of individual criminality, see Farrington, Ohlin, and Wilson, 1986).

Linked to this concern with the internal validity of our causal findings is the question of whether we can make generalizations beyond Seattle. Is there reason to believe that our findings would be restricted to the city of Seattle? The overall trends of concentration of crime would suggest that they are not, since studies in a number of jurisdictions have shown similar concentrations of crime, at least using cross-sectional data (e.g., see Eck, Gersh, and Taylor, 2000; Sherman, Gartin, and Buerger, 1989; Pierce, Spaar, and Briggs, 1988;

Spelman, 1995; Weisburd and Mazerolle, 2000; Weisburd and Amram, forth-coming). But absent other studies that look at developmental crime patterns at places, we cannot make any certain statement about the generalizability of our data. Again, we encourage other researchers to replicate our work in other jurisdictions. This is essential if we are to build a science of the criminology of place.

Conclusions

For most of the last century, criminologists and crime prevention practitioners have tried to understand why people become involved in crime and what programs can be developed to discourage criminality. Our work suggests that it is time to consider another approach to the crime problem, one that begins not with the people who commit crime but the places where crimes are committed. Our work shows that street segments in the city of Seattle represent a key unit for understanding the crime problem. This is not the geographic unit of communities, neighborhoods, precincts, or police beats that have generally been the focus of criminologists or crime prevention practitioners, but our study shows that our understanding of crime and our ability to ameliorate crime problems should be strongly linked to such micro crime places.

Crime varies greatly at a very small geographic level, as do the opportunities for crime and social factors related to crime. Crime places, often as small as street segments, are small social systems, and in this sense a key building block in understanding the crime problem. We have shown that crime is tightly coupled to place. That tight coupling in turn provides an opportunity for the development of successful crime prevention programs. It is time to place greater emphasis in crime prevention on the importance of "neighbors next door" and the ways in which the opportunities for crime at place and the social fabric of places jointly produce crime in cities.

Trajectory Analysis Model Selection
and Diagnostic Statistics

There are various decisions to be made before determining the final model: type of the model (Zero Inflated Poisson [ZIP], Censored Normal [CNORM], or Poisson), order of the model, and number of groups. Since our data have a significant proportion of streets with no crime throughout the 16 years, a Zero Inflated Poisson (ZIP) was chosen to take into account intermittency. To determine the order of the model, we tested all the models as linear, quadratic, and cubic forms to examine which worked the best to suit our data. The results show that the quadratic model form fits best.

A key decision in these analyses is choosing the number of trajectory groups. We followed the exhaustive approach detailed in Nagin (2005). That is, we tested for all possible combinations of number of groups and polynomial order of each trajectory. Specifically, we began our modeling exercise by fitting the data to a three trajectory-group intercept-only model. We then fit the data to four trajectories and compared this fit with the three-group solution. When the four-group model proved better than the three-group model, we then estimated the five-group model and compared it to the four-group solution. We continued adding groups, each time finding improvement on the Bayesian Information Criterion (BIC), until we arrived at 24 groups. The same process was repeated for linear, quadratic, and cubic models. When we went beyond 22 groups, the model became extremely unstable and thus, we did not think adding more groups would provide any valuable information.

The decision-making process of determining the final trajectory model includes choices that are not determined by any absolute criteria. We first evaluated the trajectory results using the BIC to determine the optimal number of groups in the analysis: $BIC = \log(L) - 0.5\,k\,{*}\log(N)$; where L is the value of the model's maximized likelihood estimates, N is the sample size, and k is the number of parameters estimated in the given model. Because more complex models will generally improve the fit of a given analysis, the BIC encourages a parsimonious solution by penalizing models that increase the number of groups unless they substantially improve fit. The final model selected is the quadratic ZIP model with 22 trajectory groups (BIC = −688289.00).

In addition to the Bayesian Information Criterion (BIC), trajectory analysis requires researchers to also consider posterior probabilities of group assignment, odds of correct classification, estimated group probabilities, and whether meaningful groups are revealed (Nagin, 2005). In this study, the minimum average within-group posterior probability in the model is 0.774 (for trajectory group 6) and the majority of groups have average posterior probabilities above 0.90. In terms of the odds of correct classification (OCC), the following table shows that the lowest value is 32.780 and the majority have OCC values over 100 (table A1.1). Nagin (2005: 88) suggests that when average posterior probabilities are higher than 0.7 and OCC values are higher than 5, the group assignments represent a high level of accuracy. Judging by these standards, the 22-group model performs satisfactorily in classifying the 24,023 street segments into separate trajectories.

TABLE A1.1 Odds of Correct Classification by Trajectory

Trajectory Group	# of Streets	% of Total Streets	Average Posterior Probability	Odds Correct Classification
1	51	0.212	0.992	59999.310
2	3804	15.835	0.922	62.792
3	423	1.761	0.826	265.470
4	2543	10.586	0.795	32.780
5	3903	16.247	0.879	37.496
6	1648	6.860	0.774	46.390
7	2182	9.083	0.832	49.725
8	2916	12.138	0.823	33.625
9	164	0.683	0.952	2865.251
10	877	3.651	0.836	134.422
11	953	3.967	0.862	150.790
12	1103	4.591	0.847	114.683
13	567	2.360	0.920	475.293
14	316	1.315	0.934	1055.523
15	292	1.216	0.961	1996.018
16	920	3.830	0.879	182.935
17	372	1.549	0.920	726.563
18	125	0.520	0.979	8772.120
19	307	1.278	0.950	1460.133
20	170	0.708	0.979	6540.415
21	247	1.028	0.988	8071.106
22	140	0.583	0.975	6790.917

{ APPENDIX 2 }

Ripley's *K* Function

The incorporation of spatial methods into criminological research has increased rapidly since the 1990s (Messner and Anselin, 2004). Researchers have taken seriously the error introduced by failing to account for spatial effects when analyzing inherently spatial data and have responded by incorporating a range of spatial data analysis techniques.[1] This research continues that trend by using spatial statistics to describe geographic patterns of crime trajectories across street segments. By quantifying the patterns in the data, we can further our understanding of the "underlying process that generated the points" (Fotheringham, Brundson, and Charlton, 2000: 131). Here we use a Ripley's *K* to describe the degree to which street segments of the same trajectory pattern are found near one another. It is especially useful because it identifies not only whether the data are significantly clustered, but also at what geographic distances.

A Ripley's *K* is often used to describe the local spatial dependence in point patterns. To use the statistic, we represented each street segment using its midpoint. The Ripley's *K* allows us to test whether the street segments of the same trajectory pattern are significantly more clustered, dispersed, or random than would be expected under an assumption of complete spatial randomness (CSR) (Bailey and Gatrell, 1995). The statistic reported from Ripley's *K* is the L value. All Ripley's *K* statistics were calculated in CrimeStat 3.0 (Levine, 2005). This is a rescaled Ripley's *K* where CSR is represented by a horizontal zero line. In order to provide a measure of significance, 100 permutations in a Monte Carlo simulation were used to develop an envelope of the minimum and maximum values under CSR. The odds of getting a result outside the envelope were one in 100 (or 0.01).

To accomplish this comparison, the Ripley's *K* is calculated and then compared to the reference line representing CSR. If $K(h) > \pi d^2$ then clustering is present (Bailey and Gatrell, 1995: 90–95; Kaluzny et al., 1997: 162–163). In the

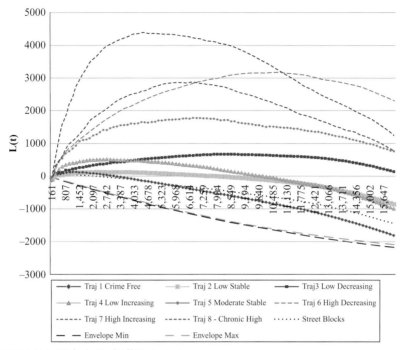

FIGURE A2.1 *Ripley's K of All Trajectories*

equation, *h* = the radius of the distance band and d_{ij} = the distance between an event *i* and an event *j*. The presence of the L-value line for any trajectory pattern above and outside the CSR envelope or values (see Envelope Min and Envelope Max in figure A2.1) representing a 95 percent confidence interval indicates that the members of the trajectory pattern are closer together than would be expected under an assumption that the street segments in that group were spread randomly across the map. See chapter 4 for a detailed interpretation of the figure.

{ APPENDIX 3 }

Cross-*K* Function

We continue the commitment to more rigorous description of spatial patterns begun in appendix 2 here in appendix 3. Here we explain the use of spatial statistics to describe geographic patterns of crime trajectory pattern membership across street segments. This assists with our understanding of underlying processes. We use the cross-*K* statistic with the SPlancs[©] library in R to answer the question of whether the members of one temporal trajectory pattern are found near the members of another temporal trajectory pattern (e.g., are chronic-crime street segments consistently found near moderate-stable street segments?). Each street segment is represented by a dot (i.e., a point) on the map.

A cross-*K* function is used to test for attraction,[1] repulsion, or independence between two patterns. This statistical technique determines whether the pattern of street segments belonging to one trajectory is significantly different from the pattern of street segments in another trajectory (Bailey and Gatrell, 1995; Rowlingson and Diggle, 1993). As described by Rowlingson and Diggle (1993) and applied here, the cross-*K* function expresses the expected number of street segments of a particular trajectory pattern (e.g., low-decreasing) within a specified distance of an arbitrary point of a second type of street segment (e.g., low-increasing), divided by the overall density of low-increasing street segments.

The statistic makes use of a series of random toroidal shifts on one set of points and compares the cross-*K* function of the shifted points with another fixed set (Rowlingson and Diggle, 1993).[2] This creates a distribution against which the actual patterns can be compared. To create the envelopes, 1,000 simulations were run of each pairwise comparison. Thus, there is a one in 1,000 possibility the results were obtained by chance. The null hypothesis of the cross-*K* test is independence between the two spatial distribution patterns (i.e., the spatial pattern of one trajectory group pattern is unrelated to the pattern of the other pattern being compared).

We conducted a series of pairwise comparisons to evaluate the spatial distribution of each trajectory pattern as compared to those of every other trajectory pattern. Specifically, using pattern 1 as an example we compared pattern 1 to pattern 2, pattern 1 to pattern 3…pattern 1 to pattern n until pattern 1 had been compared to all other patterns. We then repeated that series for pattern 2 as compared to all other patterns and so on. In total, this yielded 28 sets of comparisons.

We now discuss in greater detail how the output of the cross-K informs our question of whether there are specific pairs of temporal trajectory patterns that are also physically proximal. The application of a cross-K analysis allows us to systematically compare the distances between pairs of street segments from two different trajectory patterns. For example, a finding of attraction in the configuration of two trajectory patterns can be interpreted as a situation in which street segments of one trajectory pattern are found near street segments of the comparison trajectory pattern. Since the patterns "hang" together, it can be assumed that a common underlying process or processes are driving both patterns. A finding of independence in the comparison can be interpreted as showing no relationship between the locations of street segments in the two patterns. Thus, it is likely that unrelated processes are driving the observed patterns. A finding of repulsion also indicates that different processes are at work and that those processes do not occur at the same places. The observed relationships between pairs of trajectory patterns provide evidence regarding the scales at which the processes producing them are operating.

Data Collection

We began the data collection effort with a list of constructs important under opportunity theories and social disorganization theories that we wanted to represent for each street segment in Seattle. Related to opportunity theories, we wanted data to describe the number of motivated offenders, suitable targets, and informal guardians on a street segment as well as place characteristics such as accessibility. For social disorganization theories, we wanted to represent economic deprivation, racial heterogeneity, social ties, collective efficacy, informal social control, and physical deterioration. Using the experience of one of the coauthors (Groff) in identifying and collecting data about micro-level places, we identified likely data sources to represent the constructs just listed.

As we note in the main text, there were some types of information that we were unable to collect. For example, related to opportunity theory, we could not obtain data on automobile parking for all streets in Seattle. This would have been a good indicator of potential targets for auto theft. As discussed in chapter 5, census geographic definitions are not consistent with the street segment unit of our study, and thus census data were not available to us. Limitations of historical land use data made it impossible to accurately distinguish multi-family land use, renter-occupied housing, and real estate sales. For example, without accurate demographic information available at the street level, we had to rely on data collected from public school students to create a proxy to represent population heterogeneity. Such information would have allowed us to better represent informal social control stemming from residential stability and lower housing density. Lack of information collected from residents over time also affected our ability to quantify or to track changes in the strength of social ties and mutual trust among residents. Finally, we were not able to get information on the health of the residents at the individual street segment level. While these omissions were less than ideal, we were prepared to encounter difficulties in collecting data at the micro level and were still able to obtain a wide variety of information.

Characteristics of Street Segments: Opportunity Perspectives

Based on the opportunity theory perspective, we collected data on 16 characteristics for each street segment in Seattle (table A4.1). These characteristics were then aggregated to create the final 10 characteristics we focused on for the analysis (table A4.2). The 16 source characteristics are discussed next.

Overall, the geocoding rate for data sets was very good. It varied from a low of 87 percent for the business data to a high of 100 percent for some of the public facilities.[1] Vacant land is one non-geocoded data set that contained the highest level of missing data.[2] Retrospective data collection was the single most challenging aspect of the research effort.

A) PUBLIC SCHOOL STUDENTS

Data about public school students was obtained from Seattle Public Schools. It included all public school students from grades 3–12. The total number of public school students ranged from a low of 35,857 in 1992 to a high of 37,433 in 2004. The number of juveniles was relatively stable over the study period, with 37,029 registered in 2004. Three analysis variables were developed for use in the study: (1) total number of public school students who resided on each street segment, (2) the total number of students who were considered truant (10 or more absences in a school year) and (3) the total number of students who were considered to be low academic achievers.[3]

The number of students classified as low academic achieving (LAA) was typically three times that of truant students in any given year (mean of 14,366 versus 4,634). The year with the lowest number of LAA students was 2004 (25.11 percent) and the year with the highest number was 1997 when there were 13,563 (38.2 percent) LAA students identified. That was also the year with the highest proportion of students classified as LAA. The lowest number of truant students was in 2004 when there were 3,581 (9.85 percent). The highest number occurred in 1994 when there were 6,489 (18.4 percent) truant students. That was also the year with the highest proportion of students classified as truant.

For our final analysis, we created a variable defined as "high-risk juveniles," which represented the total number of students who were considered either truant (i.e., they had 10 or more unexcused absences) or were categorized as low academic achievers. The number of high-risk juveniles fluctuated from 14,524 in 1992 to a high of 15,908 in 1997 before falling to its lowest level in 2004 (n = 11,230).

TABLE A4.1 Roots of Characteristics Used in the Model

Variable	Geocoding Hit Rate	Data Source	Contributes to:
Total public school students with 10 or more unexcused absences and/or flagged as low academic achievers	97.1%	Seattle Public Schools	High-Risk Juveniles
Total number of employees at businesses located on the block	87.8%[1]	InfoUSA database of all businesses in Seattle	Employment
Total number of public school students	97.1%	Seattle Public Schools	Residents
Total number of registered voters	99.7%	Labels & Lists Inc.	Residents
Total retail business sales on the block	86.9%	InfoUSA database of all businesses in Seattle	Business Crime Attractors/Crime Generators—Total Sales
Community centers	100%	Fleets and Facilities Department, City of Seattle	Public Crime Attractors/Crime Generators
Hospitals	100%	Yellow pages	Public Crime Attractors/Crime Generators
Libraries	100%	Seattle Public Libraries	Public Crime Attractors/Crime Generators
Parks	97.9%	Fleets and Facilities Department, City of Seattle	Public Crime Attractors/Crime Generators
Middle and high schools	100%	Seattle Public Schools	Public Crime Attractors/Crime Generators
Street type	N/A	Seattle GIS	Type of street (arterial vs. residential), Static across all years
Total number of bus stops	Came as shapefile	Department of Transportation (Metro Transit Division)	Bus Stops
Percentage of vacant land parcels	N/A[2]	Developed from Historic Assessor's Data (Seattle Planning Department) and parcel boundaries (King County GIS)	Vacant Land

(Continued)

TABLE A4.1 Continued

Variable	Geocoding Hit Rate	Data Source	Contributes to:
Total number of police stations within 1,320 feet of a street block	100%	Fleets and Facilities Department of the city of Seattle—location source, variable calculated by researchers	Fire and Police Stations
Total number of fire stations within 1,320 feet of a street block	100%	Fleets and Facilities Department, City of Seattle—location source, variable calculated by researchers	Fire and Police Stations
Total amount of watts per street segment	Came as shape file	Seattle Public Utilities	Street Lighting

[1] Since this data set was pulled by zip code there are quite a few records that are outside the city of Seattle but still have Seattle addresses. In addition, some address fields are blank and others have P.O. Boxes and not street addresses.
[2] Getting the historical information joined to the shape file of parcels required several steps and resulted in an average of 81 percent of the parcels having land use information.

Note: The geocoding rate listed represents an average across all years.

B) BUSINESSES

After trying unsuccessfully to obtain business license data, we finally purchased data from InfoUSA. While they had data available from 1998 to 2004, the data were expensive so we purchased every other year (i.e., 1998, 2000, 2002, and 2004). The vendor could only pull data by zip code, which meant we obtained quite a few records from outside of Seattle that still had Seattle addresses.[4] We believe the relatively low geocoding rate of 87.8 percent reflects the influence of businesses that were located outside Seattle and thus unmatchable. Unfortunately, it was impossible to distinguish between those records that were unmatched because they were outside of Seattle and those that were genuinely unmatched but inside Seattle. Thus, the inability to identify records outside of Seattle artificially lowered our match rate; the true rate was in all likelihood much higher. The total number of businesses per year ranged from a low of 32,517 in 1998 to 37,916 in 2000 before dropping again to 34,547 in 2004. The average number of businesses per year was 35,573. We aggregated the geocoded records to street segments and calculated the total number of employees.

Because of the important relationship between retail establishments and crime levels, we isolated all businesses that were primarily retail focused and used total retail sales as the measurement of the intensity of retail on a street.[5] Roughly 10 percent of all businesses were retail businesses. The number of retail businesses declined over the time period. The highest number was 3,333 in 2000 followed by 3,331 in 2002. The earliest and latest years were both lower with 3,251 in 1998 and 3,160 in 2004. We then aggregated the total amount of sales for each retail business to the street segment on which it was located.

C) REGISTERED VOTERS

Our figures related to voting behavior also were purchased from a vendor, Labels & Lists Inc. (table A4.1). These data were originally collected by the Elections Department for King County, but they do not keep historical records. Thus, we turned to Labels & Lists Inc., which kept historical records of Elections Department data back to 1999. The total number of registered voters increased from 383,216 in 1999 to the highest number of 418,665 in 2002, and then declined to 345,664 in 2004. From these records we developed a variable that contains the total number of registered voters for each year. This information was used later to help estimate adult residential population.

D) PUBLIC FACILITIES

The data on the locations of facilities were primarily obtained from the city departments that run them (table A4.1). Seattle Fleets and Facilities Department was helpful with the police facilities, fire facilities, parks, and community centers. Obtaining the current locations was very straightforward. As mentioned earlier, the challenge came when we tried to establish which facilities had opened, closed (even temporarily), or changed location during our study period.

As it turned out, the number of each type of public facilities was relatively small and very stable. There were 26 community centers from 1989 to 2003. Two were added in 2004 for a total of 28 community centers at the end of the study period. There were 13 hospitals in Seattle over the entire study period. There were 17 libraries in 1989 and 21 in 2004. Middle and high schools had some minor fluctuations over the years (e.g., closing for remodeling) but in general they showed an increase from 28 facilities in 1989 to 30 in 2004. Except for hospitals, public facilities were distributed evenly across Seattle.

To represent the crime-generating effect of public and quasi-public facilities on nearby street segments, we calculated a spatial variable using a geographic information system (GIS). This variable represents the number of public and quasi-public facilities (i.e., community centers, hospitals, libraries, parks, and middle and high schools) within a 1,320-foot distance (i.e., a quarter mile) of each street segment. Distance was measured along the street network using the ArcGIS™ Network Analyst extension. Using street network distance was especially important in a city like Seattle, which is trisected by waterways. Since these waterways must be crossed using bridges, they represent significant physical barriers to travel.

Police and fire stations were considered separately because they represent the potential guardianship effect of police and fire personnel on the street segment and on nearby street segments (table A4.1). From 1989 to 2001, there were four police stations. Another station was added in 2002 to increase the number to five stations. There were 33 fire stations throughout the time period. To capture the effect of police and fire stations on nearby street segments, we used the same methodology as for public facilities: we calculated a spatial variable using a GIS. This variable captured the number of police and fire stations within a 1,320-foot distance (i.e., a quarter mile) of each street segment. Once again, distance was measured along the street network using the ArcGIS™ Network Analyst extension.

E) BUS STOPS

The data describing bus stops were obtained from the Metro Transit Division of the Department of Transportation (table A4.1). The number of bus stops in Seattle decreased over the study period (mean = 4,160). The highest number existed in 1998 (n = 4,287), and by 2004 there were 4,053 bus stops. While this was a relatively minor drop, it is mirrored in the number of street segments with a bus stop, which had also fallen from 3,106 in 2008 to 2,989 in 2004. About one-third of those streets experienced a change over the time period (some gained or lost service completely).

F) VACANT LAND

Assembling vacant land information required two separate data sources (table A4.1). Historical data related to land use codes and value from 1989–1999 came from the Planning Department. More recent data was obtained from the King County Tax Assessor's web site (2000–2004). From these data, we calculated the percentage of the total number of parcels on each street that were vacant land.

Relatively few streets in Seattle contained vacant land. Between 1989 and 2004, only about 5 to 8 percent of street segments per year had any vacant parcels. The percentage of streets with at least one vacant parcel declined over the time period, reaching a low of 4.7 percent in 2004.

G) STREET LIGHTING

Information on street lighting was supplied by Seattle Public Utilities and was used to create a total number of watts per street value for 1997–2004 (table A4.1).[6] The number of street poles and their associated lights increased steadily over the time period (from 68,725 in 1997 to 83,709 in 2004). This overall increase was in contrast to variability at the individual street segment level, where there was change in both directions. The street lighting wattage decreased on 540 streets (413 were residential and 127 were arterial). Almost all these streets were concentrated in one suspiciously rectangular area in the northeast part of the city. The utility department had no explanation for this "dark" area. Wattage increased on 5,420 streets (4,059 were residential and 1,361 were arterial). Street segments with decreasing lighting were spread throughout the city with the exception of west Seattle in which there were no increasing streets.

H) STREET TYPE

We obtained street type information as part of the street centerline file (table A4.1).[7] Seattle GIS provided their 2006 street centerline file, which we used to develop the units of analysis and to obtain information on street type. We considered two types of streets in the study: arterial and residential (which includes walkways/stairs). Arterial streets are higher traffic streets that have higher speed limits.[8] They collect traffic flowing from residential streets and provide for movement within areas of the city while still enabling access to abutting land uses. Residential streets also provide access to land uses, but they have lower speed limits and are designed to carry less traffic.

I) FINAL CHARACTERISTICS FOR ANALYSIS

These characteristics were then used to create the final characteristics for analyses reported in chapters 5 and 7 (table A4.2). Each of the final 10 characteristics represents one of four constructs: motivated offenders, suitable targets, guardianship, or accessibility/urban form. All the final data sets have a geographic extent that includes the entire city of Seattle. However, their temporal extent varies. We were able to get only the crime data and the public facilities data over the entire study period. The temporal period of the other characteristics range from four years of coverage to 13 years of coverage.

Characteristics of Street Segments: Social Disorganization

Based on social disorganization theories, we collected nine characteristics for each street segment in Seattle at the address level of analysis (table A4.3). These characteristics were then aggregated to create the final eight characteristics we focused on for the analysis (table A4.4). The geocoding rate varied from a low of 93.3 percent for the physical disorder incidents to a high of 100

TABLE A4.2 Sources and Extents of Opportunity Theory Variables and Means and Standard Deviations for Starting Values

Variable	Definition	Source	Temporal Extent	Years	Starting Mean (S.D.)
High Risk Juveniles	Total number of public school students with 10 or more unexcused absences and/or flagged as low academic achievers	Seattle Public Schools	13 years	1992–2004	0.615 (2.102)
Employment	Total number of employees at businesses located on the street segment	InfoUSA database of all businesses in Seattle	4 years over a 7-year period	1998, 2000, 2002, 2004	14.914 (127.245)
Residents	Composite variable combining the total number of public school students and the total number of registered voters	Seattle Public Schools (public school students), Labels & Lists Inc. (voter registration)	6 years	1999–2004	17.787 (27.213)
Business Crime Attractors/Crime Generators	Total retail business sales on the street segment	InfoUSA database of all businesses in Seattle	4 years over a 7-year period	1998, 2000, 2002, 2004	1.750 (27.670)
Public Crime Attractors/Crime Generators	Calculated variable capturing the total number of Public Facilities within 1,320 feet of a street street segment	Fleets and Facilities Department, City of Seattle (Community centers), Seattle Public Libraries, Seattle School District	16 years	1989–2004	0.534 (0.845)
Street type	Type of street (arterial vs. residential), Static across all years	Seattle GIS	Static	2006	0.270 (0.442)

Bus Stops	Total number of bus stops	Department of Transportation (Metro Transit Division)	8 years	1997–2004	0.176 (0.510)
Vacant Land	Percentage of vacant land parcels	Developed from Historic Assessor's Data (Seattle Planning Department) and parcel boundaries (King County GIS).	6 years over a 14 years	1991, 1993, 1995, 1997, 1998, 2004	0.019 (0.103)
Fire and Police Stations	Calculated variable capturing the total number of police or fire stations within 1,320 feet of a street segment	Fleets and Facilities Department	16 years	1989–2004	0.068 (0.260)
Street Lighting	Total amount of watts	Seattle Public Utilities	8 years	1997–2004	3.952 (6.937)

percent for the public housing units. One notable deficiency in the data representing characteristics of parcels was related to the relatively lower join rate (about 80 percent) for the data regarding residential property values and type of land use.

A) RESIDENTIAL PROPERTY VALUE

Assembling residential property values for Seattle required two separate data sources (table A4.3). Historical data related to land and building values for 1989–1999 came from the Planning Department, and more recent data was obtained from the King County Tax Assessor's web site (2000–2004). From these two data sets, we calculated a weighted index variable to represent the

TABLE A4.3 Roots of Characteristics Used in the Model

Variable	Geocoding Hit Rate	Data Source	Contributes to:
Residential property value	N/A[1]	Developed from Historic Assessor's Data (Seattle Planning Department) and parcel boundaries (King County GIS).	Socioeconomic Status (as represented by residential property value)
Type of land use	N/A[1]	Developed from Historic Assessor's Data (Seattle Planning Department) and parcel boundaries (King County GIS).	Mixed Land Use
Total number of illegal dumping and litter incidents	93.3%	Seattle Public Utilities	Physical Disorder
Total number of public housing units	100%	Seattle Housing Authority	Housing Assistance
Total number of Section 8 housing vouchers	99.7%	Seattle Housing Authority	Housing Assistance
Total number of public school students with 10 or more unexcused absences	97.1%	Seattle Public Schools (public school students)	Truant Juveniles
Racial Heterogeneity of public school students	97.1%	Seattle Public Schools (public school students)	Racial Heterogeneity
Percent of active voters represented on each street	99.7%	Labels & Lists Inc. (voter registration)	Percent of Active Voters
Distance from geographic center of Seattle	N/A[2]	Seattle GIS	Urbanization

[1] Getting the historical information joined to the shape file of parcels required several steps and resulted in an average of 81 percent of the parcels having land use information.

[2] No street centerline file was available for 1989, so we used the same one throughout the study period.

ranked property value on each street segment. To create this variable, we first ranked all the property values in the city from 1 to 10, with 10 being the highest value. In order to separate the single-family housing from multifamily dwellings, we ranked these two groups separately. Then we combined the ranks of single-family housing (SF) and multifamily housing (MF) into a final number that represents the property value of a street. We also weighted the ranks by percentage of housing type in the given street so the composite score also reflects the proportion of the type of property. The index ranges from 0 to 10, with zero representing a street with no residential property. This variable contributed to our measure of the socioeconomic status of each street (table A4.4).

B) LAND USE TYPE

Similarly, assembling land use information required two separate data sources (table A4.3). Historical data related to land use codes from 1989–1999 came from the Planning Department. No historical data related to land use was available from the King County Tax Assessor's web site; 2004 data were available, however, and those were used. From these two data sources we calculated the percentage of the total of each type of land use on each street segment. Finally, we created a dichotomous variable representing those streets with percent residential land use between 25 percent and 75 percent that also have nonresidential land uses present (e.g., commercial, institutional, industrial, but not solely water or vacant land). Streets meeting this criterion were coded as mixed land use. This variable contributed to Mixed Land Use (table A4.4).

C) PHYSICAL DISORDER

Data documenting physical disorder incidents were collected from Seattle Public Utilities (tables A4.3 and A4.4). The incidents in this database were generated from problems noticed by inspectors (self-initiated), reports from other agencies, and from citizens calling the hot line or emailing the agency to report physical disorder problems. The physical disorder measure includes: illegal dumping, litter, graffiti, weeds, vacant buildings, inoperable cars on the street, junk storage, exterior abatement, substandard housing, and minor property damage. The types of dumping and litter items recorded in the database consist of things like tires, appliances, yard waste, mattresses, and freezers, to list just a few. This database covers the time period from 1992–2004, but the information was not consistently gathered for 1992. Therefore, this study only uses information from 1993 to 2004. There were 42,331 incidents in the original database and 93.3 percent of them were successfully geocoded.

D) PUBLIC HOUSING

The locations of public housing communities and the total number of units in each community were collected from the Seattle Housing Authority (table A4.3). Several of the large communities reported one total number of units for the entire complex (High Point, New Holly, and Rainier Vista). For these, we divided the total number of units by the number of street segments that participated in the development and allocated the resulting number of units to each street in the development. There were 5,857 public housing units from 1989–1997. In 1997, the number dropped to 5,299 units and stayed there until 2002, when it dropped again to 4,218. Two subsequent changes occurred in the last two years of the study period: first a reduction to 3,838 units in 2003 and then a slight increase to 3,896 units in 2004. This variable contributed to the composite variable of Housing Assistance (table A4.4).

E) SECTION 8 VOUCHERS

We obtained information on the allocation of Section 8 vouchers in Seattle from the Seattle Housing Authority (table A4.3). Section 8 housing vouchers can be used to rent any apartment for which the management will accept the vouchers. Vouchers allow individuals to rent market-rate apartments for a reduced cost, with the voucher bridging the gap between what the individual can pay and market-rate rent. The number of vouchers increased 34.4 percent from 1,674 to 2,250 between 1998 and 2004. The minimum number of vouchers on a given street was zero across all years, while the maximum ranged from a low of 125 in 2003 to a high of 152 in 1999. This variable contributed to the composite variable of Housing Assistance (table A4.4). The presence of public housing units and Section 8 voucher holders show where the disadvantaged populations are located.

F) HOUSING ASSISTANCE

The variable called Housing Assistance consists of the total number of public housing units plus the total number of Section 8 vouchers in use on a street segment. We created this variable to capture the total number of housing units on each street segment receiving some type of housing assistance (table A4.4).

G) TRUANT JUVENILES

Data about truant juveniles were obtained from Seattle Public Schools as part of the public school's student database (tables A4.3 and A4.4). Truant juveniles were defined as the total number of students with 10 or more unexcused absences in a school year (see earlier section on public school data for more information). The lowest number of truant students in any given year was 3,581 (9.85 percent) in 2004. The highest number occurred in 1994 when there were 6,489 (18.4 percent) truant students. That was also the year with the highest proportion of students classified as truant.

H) RACIAL HETEROGENEITY

Racial heterogeneity was estimated using information that was part of the Seattle Public Schools' student database (tables A4.3 and A4.4). The data contain racial identification of all students enrolled in Seattle's public schools from 1992 to 2004. Four racial groups were identified in this study: white, black, Asian, and Hispanic. The probabilities of each racial group encountering another out-group member were then computed and averaged to form an overall racial heterogeneity index. The detailed computation process of the variable is described in chapter 6.

I) PERCENT OF ACTIVE VOTERS

The variable Percent Active Voters was drawn from the voting database (tables A4.3 and A4.4). The data include not only the registered voters' voting behaviors (whether they voted or not in the given year) for the current year but also their past voting frequency dating back to 1990. To differentiate active voters from the rest, we compared each registered voter's short-term average voting behavior to the population's short-term voting average in the most recent two years. In any given year, if a person had an average short-term voting behavior greater than the mean of Seattle's registered voters, then we assigned this person an active voter status. On each street, the number of active voters is divided by the number of total registered voters to get the percentage of active voters. This value is used as a proxy of residents' willingness to participate in public affairs.

J) DISTANCE FROM CITY CENTER

The distance from the city center was calculated from each street segment to the geographic center of Seattle (tables A4.3 and A4.4).[9] This measure represents the degree of urbanization of each street. The geographic center of Seattle was located at 331 Minor Avenue N.[10] Distance was measured along the street network using the ArcGIS™ Network Analyst extension. Using street network distance was especially important in a city like Seattle, which is trisected by waterways. Since these waterways must be crossed using bridges, they represent significant physical barriers to travel.

K) FINAL CHARACTERISTICS FOR ANALYSIS

The preceding characteristics were then used to create the final characteristics for analyses reported in later chapters (table A4.4). Each of the final eight characteristics represents one of two theoretical dimensions. The structural dimension includes socioeconomic status, mixed land use, urbanization, housing assistance, physical disorder, and racial heterogeneity. The intermediary dimensions of the effects of structural factors on crime include unsupervised teens and willingness to intervene in public affairs.

TABLE A4.4 Sources and Extents of Social Disorganization Variables and Means and Standard Deviations for Starting Values

Variable	Definition	Temporal Extent	Years	Starting Mean (S.D.)
Socioeconomic Status (as represented by residential property value)	To create this variable, we first ranked all the property in the city from 1 to 10, with 10 being the highest value. In order to separate the single-family (SF) housing from multifamily (MF) dwellings, we ranked these two groups separately. Then we combined the ranks of SF and MF into a final value that represents the property value of a street. We also weight the ranks by percentage of housing type on the given street so the composite score of SES also reflects the proportion of the type of property.	6 years over a 14-year period.	1991, 1993, 1995, 1997, 1998, 2004	4.491 (3.608)
Mixed Land Use	Dichotomous variable representing those streets with nonresidential land use (e.g., commercial, institutional, industrial, but not solely water or vacant land) and between 25% and 75% residential land use	6 years over a 14-year period.	1991, 1993, 1995, 1997, 1998, 2004	0.04 (.207)
Physical Disorder (count)	Total number of reported physical disorder incidents	12 years	1993–2004	0.112 (0.379)
Housing Assistance	Composite variable of the total number of public housing units and the total number of Section 8 vouchers in use.	7 years	1998–2004	0.375 (4.615)
Truant Juveniles	Total number of public school students with 10 or more unexcused absences	13 years	1992–2004	0.244 (0.834)

Variable	Definition	Temporal Extent	Years	Starting Mean (S.D.)
Racial Heterogeneity (students)	The probabilities of each racial group to encounter another out-group member	13 years	1992–2004	0.017 (0.038)
Percent of Active Voters	Percent of active voters represented on each street	6 years	1999–2004	0.375 (0.317)
Urbanization	Distance from geographic center of Seattle	Static	2006	255.712 (117.415)

The spatial and temporal extent of each characteristic as well as its definition is included in table A4.4. All the final data sets have a geographic extent that includes the entire city of Seattle. However, their temporal extent varies. We were not able to obtain any of these characteristics for the entire study period. The temporal coverage of other characteristics ranged from a low of six years of coverage for percent of active voters to a high of 13 years for physical disorder.

{ APPENDIX 5 }

Additional Statistical Models

TABLE A5.1 Full Multinomial Regression Model Including Odds Ratios and Significance Levels (Crime-Free Pattern is the Reference Group)

Variable	Low-Stable	Low-Decreasing	Low-Increasing	Moderate-Stable	High-Decreasing	High-Increasing	Chronic
Social Disorganization							
Property Value (B)	0.930‡	0.939‡	0.878‡	0.825‡	0.758‡	0.815‡	0.704‡
Housing Assistance (B)	1.021	1.054†	1.076‡	1.085‡	1.070†	1.094‡	1.104‡
Physical Disorder (B)	7.335‡	6.022‡	8.236‡	17.286‡	15.302‡	19.014‡	25.634‡
Truant Juveniles (B)	1.653†	1.719†	2.296‡	2.518‡	1.993†	3.330‡	2.585‡
Racial Heterogeneity(B)	1.199	2.526	0.095	0.894	0.069	0.047	0.010
% Active Voters (B)	0.704‡	0.816	0.279‡	0.077‡	0.188‡	0.044‡	0.041‡
Urbanization	0.998‡	0.994‡	0.999†	0.996‡	0.995‡	0.997‡	1.000
Mixed Land Use	1.119	1.142	1.220	1.152	1.267	1.233	1.565
Physical Disorder (C)	3.025‡	2.417‡	3.810‡	4.888‡	3.662‡	5.045‡	6.169‡
Truant Juveniles (C)	1.358*	1.284	2.089‡	1.843‡	1.505†	2.497‡	1.969‡
Racial Heterogeneity(C)	0.160*	0.153	0.187	0.982	0.019*	5.362	0.009
Opportunity							
High-Risk Juveniles (B)	1.860‡	1.737‡	1.903‡	2.034‡	2.292‡	2.009‡	2.218‡
Employees (B)	1.065‡	1.067‡	1.071‡	1.074‡	1.073‡	1.074‡	1.075‡
Bus Stops (B)	1.288‡	1.253‡	1.439‡	1.631‡	1.636‡	1.777‡	1.831‡
% Vacant Land (B)	2.204‡	2.033*	4.486‡	1.384	1.311	4.300*	1.482
Street Lighting (B)	1.045‡	1.037‡	1.070‡	1.070‡	1.070‡	1.079‡	1.089‡
Residents (B)	1.196‡	1.187‡	1.221‡	1.237‡	1.229‡	1.239‡	1.241‡
Police/Fire Stations	1.131	1.207	1.250	0.913	1.446*	1.046	1.555*
Public Facilities	1.079†	1.148‡	1.024	1.282†	1.446‡	0.992	1.237*
Arterial Roads	1.812‡	1.938‡	1.976‡	5.435‡	4.255‡	6.494‡	10.870‡

(Continued)

TABLE A5.1 Continued

Variable	Low-Stable	Low-Decreasing	Low-Increasing	Moderate-Stable	High-Decreasing	High-Increasing	Chronic
Total Retail Sales (B)	1.005	1.006	1.007	1.007	1.006	1.008	1.007
High-Risk Juveniles (C)	1.229‡	1.126*	1.259‡	1.226†	1.254‡	1.205†	1.242†
Employees (C)	1.026‡	1.026‡	1.031‡	1.031‡	1.031‡	1.032‡	1.031‡
% Vacant Land (C)	2.848‡	2.734*	2.485	4.988*	4.900†	4.155	5.803
Residents (C)	1.052‡	1.043‡	1.078‡	1.067‡	1.050‡	1.062‡	1.055‡
Other Variables							
Segment Length	1.035†	1.144‡	0.973	1.042	1.050*	1.036	1.021
Spatial Lag (B)	1.109‡	1.050‡	1.171‡	1.153‡	1.124‡	1.210‡	1.224‡
Spatial Lag (C)	1.069‡	0.878‡	1.224‡	1.104†	0.998	1.270‡	1.170‡

n = 24,023; B = beginning value; C = change variable;

* p < .05,

† p < .01,

‡ p < .01.

Cox and Snell Pseudo R² = .632; Nagelkerke Pseudo R² = .684.

TABLE A5.2 Comparison of Low-Increasing Trajectory Pattern vs. Low-Decreasing Pattern

Variable	b	Standard Error	Odds Ratio
Social Disorganization			
Property Value (B)	−0.057	0.020	0.945†
Housing Assistance (B)	0.173	0.049	1.189‡
Physical Disorder (B)	0.329	0.150	1.389*
Truant Juveniles (B)	0.431	0.175	1.539*
Racial Heterogeneity (B)	−3.154	1.669	0.043
% Active Voters (B)	−0.917	0.273	0.400†
Urbanization	0.004	0.000	1.004‡
Mixed Land Use (B)	0.007	0.226	1.007
Segment Length	−0.162	0.026	0.850‡
Property Value (C)	−0.117	0.042	0.890†
Housing Assistance (C)	0.366	0.076	1.442‡
Physical Disorder (C)	0.510	0.127	1.666‡
Truant Juveniles (C)	0.616	0.123	1.851‡
Racial Heterogeneity (C)	0.140	1.361	1.151
% Active Voters (C)	−0.600	0.291	0.549*
Mixed Land Use (C)	0.000	0.437	1.000
Opportunity			
High-Risk Juveniles (B)	−0.005	0.074	0.995
Employees (B)	0.003	0.001	1.003‡
Bus Stops (B)	0.107	0.086	1.113
% Vacant Land (B)	1.056	0.538	2.875*
Street Lighting (B)	0.029	0.007	1.029‡
Residents (B)	0.028	0.003	1.028‡
Total Retail Sales (B)	0.001	0.002	1.001
Police/Fire Stations	0.256	0.162	1.292
Public Facilities	−0.106	0.060	0.900
Arterial Roads	−0.014	0.128	0.986
High-Risk Juveniles (C)	0.072	0.050	1.074
Employees (C)	0.003	0.001	1.003†
Bus Stops (C)	−0.121	0.221	0.886
% Vacant Land (C)	−0.222	0.604	0.801
Street Lighting (C)	0.000	0.000	1.000
Residents (C)	0.038	0.007	1.039‡
Total Retail Sales (C)	0.000	0.000	1.000
Spatial Lag (B)	0.095	0.011	1.100‡
Spatial Lag (C)	0.309	0.028	1.362‡
Constant	−1.767	0.291	0.171‡

n = 3,105; B = beginning value; C = change variable;
* $p < .05$,
† $p < .01$,
‡ $p < .001$.
Cox and Snell Pseudo R^2 = .246; Nagelkerke Pseudo R^2 = .352.

TABLE A5.3 Comparison of High-Increasing Trajectory Pattern vs. High-Decreasing Pattern

Variable	b	Standard Error	Odds Ratio
Social Disorganization			
Property Value (B)	0.054	0.038	1.056
Housing Assistance (B)	0.032	0.012	1.032†
Physical Disorder (B)	0.405	0.163	1.500*
Truant Juveniles (B)	0.457	0.173	1.579†
Racial Heterogeneity (B)	0.153	2.891	1.165
% Active Voters (B)	−2.496	0.653	0.082‡
Urbanization	0.001	0.001	1.001
Mixed Land Use (B)	0.060	0.459	1.062
Segment Length	0.024	0.031	1.024
Property Value (C)	−.043	0.093	0.958
Housing Assistance (C)	0.035	0.041	1.036
Physical Disorder (C)	0.451	0.160	1.570†
Truant Juveniles (C)	0.472	0.144	1.603†
Racial Heterogeneity (C)	6.912	2.845	1.005E3*[1]
% Active Voters (C)	−2.192	0.698	0.112†
Mixed Land Use (C)	1.102	0.728	3.010
Opportunity			
High-Risk Juveniles (B)	−0.114	0.057	0.893*
Employees (B)	0.001	0.000	1.001
Bus Stops (B)	0.036	0.119	1.037
% Vacant Land (B)	1.128	0.931	3.090
Street Lighting (B)	0.005	0.008	1.005
Residents (B)	0.009	0.002	1.009‡
Total Retail Sales (B)	0.003	0.002	1.003
Police/Fire Stations	−0.371	0.260	0.690
Public Facilities	−0.337	0.101	0.714†
Arterial Roads	−0.377	0.259	0.686
High-Risk Juveniles (C)	−0.066	0.052	0.936
Employees (C)	0.001	0.001	1.001*
Bus Stops (C)	−0.116	0.288	0.891
% Vacant Land (C)	0.318	0.912	1.375
Street Lighting (C)	0.000	0.000	1.000
Residents (C)	0.010	0.007	1.010
Total Retail Sales (C)	0.000	0.000	1.000

Variable	b	Standard Error	Odds Ratio
Spatial Lag (B)	0.073	0.016	1.075‡
Spatial Lag (C)	0.229	0.037	1.258‡
Constant	−1.911	0.557	0.148‡

n = 793; B = beginning value; C = change variable;
* p < .05,
† p < .01,
‡ p < .001.
Cox and Snell Pseudo R^2 = .225; Nagelkerke Pseudo R^2 = .325.

[1] The very large odds ratio for this measure results in good part from the distribution of the variable (0–.1825) relative to the unit measurement of change in the odds ratio (0–1). Rescaling the measure, for example, from 0 to 182.5 produces an odds ratio of 1.007.

{NOTES}

Chapter 1

1. There is no single accepted definition of a hot spot although hot spots are commonly understood to be "[a]reas of concentrated crime" (Eck et al., 2005: 2; see also Harries, 1999). Early efforts to identify hot spots examined the distribution of crime events and used statistical techniques to identify clusters that represented the smallest areas with the highest crime. The first software developed to examine crime hot spots was the Spatial and Temporal Analysis of Crime (STAC) developed by the Illinois Criminal Justice Information Authority in 1988 (see http://www.icjia.state.il.us/public/index.cfm?metasection=Data&metapage=St acFacts). Over the last 20 years, the term hot spot has been applied to crime occurring at different size places such as addresses (Eck and Weisburd, 1995; Eck, Gersh, and Taylor, 2000; Sherman, Gartin, and Buerger, 1989), street blocks (Groff, Weisburd, and Yang, 2010; Taylor, Gottfredson, and Brower, 1984; Weisburd and Green, 1994; Weisburd et al., 2004; Weisburd, Morris, and Groff, 2009), and areas (i.e., clusters of addresses or blocks) (Block and Block, 1995). It is critical to note that empirical tools to analyze spatial patterns require theoretical underpinnings in order to understand spatial patterns (Eck and Weisburd, 1995; Eck et al., 2005; Maltz, Gordon, and Friedman, 1990 [2000]; Roncek and Maier, 1991). Here we apply the term to individual street segments with high amounts of crime over the entire study period.

2. Weisburd and Piquero (2008), for example, found that studies that sought to predict crime were more likely to focus on individuals than any other units of analysis. Examining articles in the journal *Criminology* that tried to model crime, they found that 94 of 169 articles (55.6 percent) published between 1968 and 2005 used the individual as the unit of analysis. Other units commonly found in the study included cities or counties (14 percent) and neighborhoods (9 percent). More recently, Eck and Eck (2012) reviewed all of the research papers in *Criminology and Public Policy* since its inception and found that none addressed crime at place.

3. For a notable example of an early approach which did place emphasis on the "micro" idea of place as discussed here, see Shaw (1929).

4. The existence of repeat victimization provides another example of the tight coupling of crime and place. Recent studies show that if a target is victimized once, it is much more likely to be victimized a second time (Farrell and Pease, 1993; Pease, 1998). It is also the case that potential targets nearby are also more likely to become victims, which is generally termed "near repeat victimization" (Johnson and Bowers, 2004; Johnson, Bowers, and Hirschfield, 1997; Morgan, 2001; Ratcliffe and Rengert, 2008; Townsley, Homel, and Chaseling, 2003).

5. See Johnson, Lab, and Bowers (2008) for an examination of crime stability at a different temporal and spatial scale than discussed here.

6. Our work in this area is also described in Groff, Weisburd, and Morris (2009) and Groff, Weisburd, and Yang (2010).

7. Work examining the links between place characteristics and crime is also being conducted by the Institute for Canadian Urban Research Studies (see http://www.icurs.ca) at Simon Fraser University led by Paul and Patricia Brantingham.

8. For a description of the process of identification of the sites, see Weisburd, Lum, and Yang (2004).

9. In discussing the history of Seattle, we draw heavily from Seattle's official website at: http://www.seattle.gov/CityArchives/Facts/history.htm.

10. The following types of features in the street centerline were excluded: freeways and freeway ramps (ST_CODE = 4), transit only (ST_CODE = 9), railroads (ST_CODE = 50), trails (ST_CODE = 22) and administrative street designations (ST_CODE = 70 and ST_CODE = 71). When processing the remaining features, we used a set of decision rules to create the units of analysis so they would be consistent across the entire city. Street segment intersections were created under the following circumstances: (1) when a street crossed beyond Seattle city limits; (2) at a "T" intersection; (3) when a street changed names or switched from public to private concomitant with a physical change of direction; and (4) when the street length would be over 2,400 feet (except for private streets and park streets). The average length of a street segment in Seattle is 387 feet. The majority of the streets (roughly 64 percent) are between 200 and 600 feet. Using our decision rules, very few streets (less than 2 percent) ended up longer than 1,000 feet.

11. While it is possible to randomly assign the events at intersections to the street segments involved for the purposes of statistical analysis, this strategy has its drawbacks. For example, it could artificially inflate the crime rate for low-crime street segments attached to a high-crime intersection, especially in a situation where the crime is "flowing" from other participating segments to the intersection but is mostly unrelated to the low-crime segment.

12. Another set of places excluded from our data were all street segments on the University of Washington campus. After 2001, the University of Washington Police Department began collecting and reporting their own data and no longer funneled their data through the Seattle Police Department. Given the relatively small number of street segments involved, and the absence of data in the latter part of our time series, we decided to exclude these street segments altogether.

Chapter 2

1. This section of our chapter draws heavily from a paper by Weisburd, Bruinsma, and Bernasco (2009). We are especially indebted to Gerben Bruinsma for his insights and comments on the historical development of crime and place.

2. In France and England, the Reform Movement focused its policy on public health and education for the poor.

3. In those days, parts of Belgium and Luxembourg were also included in the Netherlands.

4. The real estate agent had discovered zones in the city of Chicago when he made up an inventory of price changes of houses and real estate. He contacted Burgess regarding his findings, which led to the now famous geographic model of crime and social problems in the urban context.

5. It might be argued in this regard that our work is vulnerable to the concerns of ecological fallacy raised by Robinson (1950). However, we think that street segments are much less likely to include the broad variability in traits that led to Robinson's original conceptualization. We recognize that there will be variability within street segments, but we think that such variability is limited enough, as we noted earlier, to avoid many types of averaging errors (see Smith, Frazee, and Davison, 2000 for a similar argument). Moreover, we do not try to make inferences from places to people in our work. Our primary purpose is to describe and explain crime at street segments.

Chapter 3

1. See Ratcliffe (2005) for a discussion of temporal variation of point patterns (i.e., individual crime locations) within areas.

2. We were not able to distinguish for "traffic" and "unknown" cases whether incidents were crime related because the incident report database does not include details of the events recorded. According to the Seattle Police Department, traffic incident reports were most likely not traffic citations, but rather hit-and-run crimes, drunk driving, and accidents involving injuries. In cases where events were clearly not crime related, such as reports of assistance or administrative activities of police, we excluded them.

3. It is difficult to compare our data to general crime statistics in part because overall crime incidents are not available in the Uniform Crime Report (UCR), which reports on crime incidents in the nation more generally for the earlier period of our data collection. Moreover, our data include only crime incidents at street segments, making a more general comparison difficult. Looking only at Part I crimes in our data and in other cities, the crime drop we observe is 24.97 percent which is slightly larger than that reported nationally between 1990 and 2004 (18 percent; see UCR, 2005). But it is smaller than that found in that period in such cities as New York (69 percent decline in Part I crime between 1990 and 2001; see New York Police Department, 2010) and Washington, DC (51 percent decline in Part I crime between 1993 and 2004; see Metropolitan Police Department, 2010).

4. Our results here differ slightly from those reported in Weisburd et al. (2004) where 4 to 5 percent of street segments included 50 percent of crime incidents for 14 years (1989–2002). These differences develop primarily from our direct definition of street segments as contrasted with "hundred blocks," and subsequent deletion of hundred blocks that were not seen as relevant to our interest in street segments as "behavior settings" (see chapter 1).

5. Wilcox and Eck (2011) argue for an "iron law of troublesome places" in regard to facilities that have high crime. Citing a study by Eck, Clarke, and Guerette (2007), which examined 37 studies from four countries of 16 different types of facilities, they note that a small proportion of facilities in all studies produced a large proportion of the crime.

6. The lack of homogeneity in the groups is the explicit trade-off for the relaxation of the parametric assumptions about the random effects in the linear models (Bushway, Thornberry, and Krohn, 2003).

7. In terms of the debate surrounding the latent groups identified by the trajectory analysis (see Eggleston, Laub, and Sampson, 2004; Sampson, Laub, and Eggleston, 2004; Laub, 2006), Nagin (2005: 173) points out that the trajectory groups are not immutable or "real." They should be used as an approximation of complex underlying reality or to reveal population heterogeneity. Our use of trajectory analysis follows this approach.

8. We used a Zero Inflated Poisson (ZIP) method for this analysis as it performed better in terms of convergence than the standard Poisson model. The ZIP model builds on a standard Poisson model by accommodating more crime-free segments in any given period than predicted by the standard Poisson distribution. This is especially important in our analyses because of the large number of crime-free segments in our data. The substantive differences in outcomes of the two types of analyses are not large. Additionally, we found that the quadratic form was uniformly a better fit than the linear model, and that the cubic model did not improve the fit over the quadratic model in the case of a small number of groups.

9. BIC = $\log(L) - .5k * \log(N)$; where L is the value of the model's maximized likelihood estimates, N is the sample size, and k is the number of parameters estimated in a given model. Because models including more trajectories almost always improve the fit of a given analysis, the BIC criteria encourages a parsimonious solution by penalizing models that increase the number of trajectories unless they substantially improve the fit of the model.

10. See appendix 1 for more diagnostic statistics related to the trajectory analysis.

Chapter 4

1. Readers should note slight scale changes among figures 4.1, 4.2, and 4.3. These were necessary to provide maximum enlargement of the three sections of Seattle.

2. Since the trajectory pattern membership is nominal data, we conducted a series of comparisons (see Griffiths and Chavez, 2004). In each comparison, one trajectory group pattern was coded as "1" and the rest of the patterns were coded "0." The local Moran's I value is calculated for each observation taking into account the values of its neighbors. Then each observation is classified by its statistical relationship to its neighbors as well as to a random distribution. The Moran's I can be used to identify positive spatial autocorrelation (high values surrounded by high values and low values surrounded by low values) as well as negative spatial autocorrelation (low values surrounded by high values or vice versa). Positive spatial autocorrelation occurs when an observation's Moran's I value is correlated with the weighted average of Moran's I values for neighboring observations in the same direction. Relationships among observations can also be classified as low-high and high-low representing negative spatial autocorrelation. In these cases, an observation's Moran's I is significantly different from the weighted average of the neighboring Moran's I values. Statistically significant relationships are identified by comparing the observed distribution to a distribution representing complete spatial randomness. The mapped observations represent the cores of spatial clusters (Anselin, 2003).

3. All LISA analyses were done in GeoDa 9.5i©. We used a Monte Carlo simulation with 999 permutations in the significance tests (Anselin, 2003).

4. We ran the analysis at a distance of 2,800 feet using 400-feet bins. This distance allowed us to more closely inspect the variations in the cross-K statistic at short distances using a confidence envelope. To create the envelopes, 1,000 simulations were run of each pair comparison. Thus, there is a one in 1,000 possibility the results were obtained by chance. The null hypothesis of the cross-K test is independence (i.e., the spatial pattern of one trajectory group is unrelated to the pattern of the other group being compared). When $K(i,j)$ is consistently above the line of independence but falls within the significance simulation envelope, the pattern of street segments in the two temporal trajectories being compared is independent at all distances. For distances at which the $K(i,j)$ line is above the

simulation envelope, the two patterns display attraction. In other words, they are dependent upon one another, and the form of the dependence is attraction (rather than repulsion which would be the finding if the $K(i,j)$ line was below the simulation envelope). When the $K(i,j)$ line falls on the upper bound of the simulation envelope, the interpretation is one of weak attraction in the two patterns. The analysis produced 28 graphs. Space constraints do not allow the inclusion of the graphs in the book; however, they are available from the authors. For more detail on the statistical approach used here, see appendix 3.

Chapter 5

1. Only general population characteristics are provided at the census block level. Block-level data come from the short form questionnaire, which everyone received in the 1990 and 2000 decennial Census of population and housing.

2. Low academic achievers were flagged by the Seattle Public Schools. They used a variety of standardized assessment data (e.g., WASL, ITBS, ITED, TAP, CAT, CTBS). If a student met any of the following criteria across two years, they were flagged as low achieving: (1) CAT/CTBS instrument—any student with an NCE less than 36 in either reading *or* math; (2) ITBS/ITED/TAP—any student with an NCE less than 36 in either reading *or* math; and (3) WASL—any student with a level of 1 in either reading *or* math.

3. More detail on other years of analysis can be found in Weisburd, Groff, and Yang (2010), or by request to the authors.

4. Another dimension that we were unable to include has to do with the role of individual behavior in creating suitable targets (Averdijk, 2010, 2011).

5. We included libraries in this measure since they tend to attract a wide cross-section of residents, some of whom are vulnerable targets such as young children and the elderly.

6. Parks and schools present an analytical challenge in that they often are bounded by more than one street segment. This issue is not addressed in the study. Parks and schools are allocated to the street segment on which their street address is located. We recognize this as a deficiency, but given the relatively small numbers of parks and schools, we believe the effects on the results are minimal.

7. The distribution of the average total number of public facilities within one-quarter of a mile of a place was computed as follows: The total number of public facilities within a quarter-mile drive of each street segment is computed for each year. Then we take an average of the first three years to represent the beginning of the study period.

8. We recognize that this relationship can be very complex. For example, Decker, Shichor, and O'Brien (1982) show that increases in population density are associated with increases in robbery and assault, small increases in motor vehicle theft, but decreases in burglary and household larceny.

9. When we compare our data to the U.S. Census estimates overall for Seattle we gain, not surprisingly, population estimates that are about a quarter lower than reported in the census. Our measure produced a population estimate of 437,612 in 2001, which decreased to 381,815 by 2004. The census reports a population of 563,374 in 2000 (U.S. Census Bureau, 2000) and 536,946 in 2005 (U.S. Census Bureau, 2005).

10. To obtain this estimate, we aggregated the residential population for street segments to the block group in which the street segment falls. However, street segments can be shared among multiple block groups. In these cases, we adjusted the amount of population

allocated to each block group depending on the extent to which the street segment was shared among block groups. In the simple case of a street segment that falls in two block groups, half the population was allocated to each of the two block groups. In Seattle, approximately 60 percent of all street segments belong to a single block group and 40 percent are shared among multiple block groups. Of the street segments shared by multiple block groups, about 98 percent are shared by two block groups. Overall the estimate produced by the aggregation of the street segment residential population is correlated strongly (0.70) and highly significantly ($p < 0.01$) with the census block group counts for residential population five years of age and older.

11. There have been a variety of studies which have identified a positive relationship between commercial areas (Beavon, Brantingham, and Brantingham, 1994; Crewe, 2001; Duffala, 1976; LaVigne, 1994), nonresidential land use, and crime (Kurtz et al., 1998; Perkins et al., 1993; Taylor et al., 1995), as well as studies too numerous to cite that have looked at the relationship between various types of businesses and crime (see Bernasco and Block, 2011).

12. The earliest year with available data was 1998, and cost precluded purchasing every year. We thought changes were unlikely to be substantial each year, which is borne out by the distributions of the data we examined.

13. Hillier and colleagues (Hillier, 1999, 2004; Hillier and Shu, 2000; Hillier and Sahbaz, 2005; Hillier et al., 1976) have pioneered a sophisticated theory of accessibility called "space syntax." However, the software that allows construction of space syntax measures cannot accommodate a network of as many links as Seattle has. In order to use space syntax, we would have had to simplify the network, which meant getting rid of many street segments. Since we wanted to model each street segment in Seattle, we could not use space syntax to analyze our data.

14. We recognize there is a large body of work examining accessibility at higher levels of geography but are restricting our discussion to street segment level studies (see for example studies such as Bernasco and Luykx, 2003; Grannis, 1998; Greenberg, Rohe, and Williams, 1982; Reynald et al., 2008).

15. Limited access highways are excluded from the study since they do not fit our definition of a place; see chapter 1.

16. We recognize that this relationship can be complex. It is not just the street type but the overall accessibility of the street that has been found to be important in understanding residential burglary rates. More permeable neighborhoods tend to have higher residential burglary rates (Bevis and Nutter, 1977; White, 1990). Permeability is calculated as the number of streets connecting to arterials as they run through the neighborhood. The theory is that the arterial roads bring potential offenders into the area, and then the attractiveness of easy ingress and egress leads them to search for potential targets in the area. Another study found that street segments along moderate-volume roads experienced higher rates of residential burglary because they have enough traffic to expose them to potential offenders but not enough to make for effective surveillance (Brantingham and Brantingham, 1982). But yet another study found that the higher rates of residential burglary were on residential (low volume) roads and very-high-volume residential roads (Rengert and Wasilchick, 2000). These mixed findings may be related to a lack of surveillance on residential roads and the anonymity that comes with very busy residential streets. To add to the mixed findings, dead-end streets have been shown to be less likely to be victimized by residential burglars

(Frisbie et al., 1978; Hakim, Rengert, and Shachamurove, 2000; Maguire, 1982) but only certain types of non-through roads (Johnson and Bowers, 2010). Still other studies find that the accessibility of a place is directly related to crime more generally (Beavon, Brantingham, and Brantingham, 1994; Greenberg, Rohe , and Williams, 1982) and to the attractiveness of a street for street robbery (Wright and Decker, 1997).

17. We considered trying to obtain street centerline files for the previous years in the study, but concluded it was unnecessary because of the maturity of the street network in Seattle. We checked with the Planning Department of the City of Seattle to identify the number of changes in the street network that had occurred within Seattle over the time period. They reported only one change that they knew of which would have changed the street network. In addition, the completeness and accuracy of the address ranges had been gradually improved over the time period. Using an earlier version of the street centerline file would have just reduced the accuracy of our geocoding effort.

18. For example, Dallas, Texas, has been working with the Police Foundation to develop measures of police patrol in specific parts of the city through a National Institute of Justice grant. While AVL has been employed in many cities for a number of years, it is only recently that all cars have come to be equipped with AVL in individual jurisdictions. Moreover, in many jurisdictions there is strong resistance on the part of unions to the use of AVL to track police presence. The systems are generally used only for emergencies, for example, to track missing cars.

19. The only measure of police presence we could obtain was for 2001–2004, and it was based on calls for service. In other words, the data represented an aggregate measure of the amount of time spent (time between arrival and departure) on each street segment. The measure included answering a call for service, taking a crime report, and making an arrest. Since much of that time was spent taking crime reports, the measure was highly correlated with the crime data.

20. We considered analyzing police and fire stations separately, but decided not to because the numbers of police stations in any given year are too small (n = 4 in most years).

21. The distribution of the average total number of fire and police stations within one-quarter of a mile of a place was computed as follows: We examined two time points, the beginning (1989–1991) and the end (2002–2004) of the study period. The total number of fire and police stations within a quarter mile drive of each street segment was computed for each year. Then we took an average of the first three years to represent the beginning of the study period and an average of the last three years to represent the end.

22. This information was calculated using a multistep process. First, we located all the light poles along the streets included in the study. Information from Seattle Public Utilities was then used to identify the number and illumination of each light on a pole. Second, the total amount of light being provided by each pole was summed. Third, all the poles on each street were added to arrive at the total light (in watts) on a street segment. This multistep procedure enabled us to examine the amount of street lighting on each street.

Chapter 6

1. These were the only years for which we were able to obtain data from the Seattle Planning Department.

2. To achieve this, we separately rank averaged property values for single-family housing and multifamily housing, assigning each street a rank between 1 and 10 based on the average values of properties. For example, streets with the highest 10 percent of single-family-building values received a rank of 10 while streets with the lowest values received a rank of 1. The same procedure was repeated for multifamily housing. Finally, the ranks of each street on the single-family property value and multifamily property value were then weighted by the percentages of the type of housing of a given street and then combined to create a property value index to represent the SES of a street. The index ranges from 0 to 10, with zero representing a street with no residential property.

3. The mean property value for all street segments increased every year between 1989 and 2004.

4. More detail on other years of analysis can be found in Weisburd, Groff, and Yang (2010), or by request to the authors.

5. See the U.S. Department of Housing and Urban Development's website http://portal. hud.gov/portal/page/portal/HUD/topics/rental_assistance/phprog for a description of public housing at the federal level.

6. Some of the public housing developments report individual addresses, while others report only one aggregate figure, even when the development stretches across several streets. If we try to analyze the individual unit reports, then the housing data will be intrinsically clustered. Using a typical spatial statistic would not produce meaningful results. Another issue is the problem of a large development that reports on one total number of units even though the development stretches across several street segments. We decided that for each large development in the study period, we would allocate a number of units to each street by dividing the total number of units by the number of streets in each development. This is the reason why there are fractional numbers in the data describing the characteristic.

7. We recognize that there are discrepancies between the statistics presented on residential property and land use in this chapter (e.g., between estimates of property values and land usage) and chapter 5 (examining residential population). These discrepancies are due to the different databases that are employed to gain information, as well as the different time periods examined.

8. We relied on the same databases for this measure as property values. As noted in endnote 1, such data were available only for specific years.

9. Racial heterogeneity is calculated by multiplying the percentage of whites by the percentage of non-whites to indicate the probability that two randomly selected individuals from an area will be members of different racial groups. To take into account the multiracial character of Seattle, we use the same formula mentioned above but further modify the approach to incorporate the racial dynamics in Seattle. Four racial groups were identified in this study, including white, black, Asian, and Hispanic. The probabilities of each racial group encountering another out-group member were then computed and averaged to form an overall racial heterogeneity index. The racial heterogeneity index was created based on the following equation:

$$HETEROGENITY_j = \{(\%WHITE_j * \%NONWHITE_j) + (\%BLACK_j * \%NONBLACK_j) + (\%ASIAN_j * \%NONASIAN_j) + (\%HISPANIC_j * \%NONHISPANIC_j)\}/4$$

(where j denotes year of information).

10. We used 331 Minor Avenue N as the city center. We then measured the distance from each street segment to the city center, along the street network. Using the street network

provides a more realistic estimate of travel distance between two places than does Euclidean (i.e., "as the crow flies") distance.

11. Sampson, Raudenbush, and Earls (1997: 919) defined informal social control with a five-item Likert scale, with one item that refers to children "skipping school and hanging around the corner...."

12. We recognize that this measure will be highly correlated with our measure of "high-risk juveniles" in the opportunity perspective. Nonetheless, the two indicators are not measuring the same concept. The opportunity measure in this case is based on information not only on truancy, but also on poor educational performance. Nonetheless, the correlation of the two measures is 0.91. We discuss the possible impacts of this high correlation on our modeling of trajectory patterns in chapter 7.

13. Our finding here is consistent with Sampson's (2009: 264) observation that at different higher units of geography, traits of social disorganization cluster: "...concentrated poverty and other correlates and disadvantage coincide with the geographic isolation of racial minority and immigrant groups. Moreover, these patterns are not unique to any one city and extend across multiple ecological units of analysis ranging from census tracts to metropolitan areas and even states."

Chapter 7

1. Moreover, if we take this approach, then each of our comparisons would be based on different size samples, and those samples would have varied a good deal because our trajectory patterns range in size from about 200 to 12,000 street segments. The statistical problem here is that the varying sample sizes would then result in incorrect tests of levels of statistical significance (see Weisburd and Britt, 2007, chapter 19).

2. For static variables (like number of facilities or arterial roads; see chapter 5), only the beginning values are used in the model—as measuring changes would not be meaningful. For dynamic variables, we used a step-wise process to examine the impact of each change variable after all the basic variables are taken into account. It is important to note that the inclusion of baseline measures and change measures creates the potential for multicollinearity in these models. Our model already includes a large number of correlated independent variables, and it was important to reduce additional variables that might contribute to multicollinearity and thus model instability. Thus, if a change variable was not significant using the likelihood ratio test in the multinomial model, it was not included in the final model. Using these criteria, change measures were not included for arterial road, police/fire station, public facilities, urbanization, and length of the street because these were static variables. Additionally, change measures were not included for property values, housing assistance, percentage of active voters, total retail sales, number of bus stops, and watts of street lighting because they did not meet our likelihood ratio test criterion. After the exclusion of the above variables, only seven change variables were included in the final model (eight if we count the spatial lag of crime difference as one of them).

3. The value of each neighboring street segment within one-quarter mile is multiplied by the spatial weight (i.e., distance) and then the products are averaged.

4. One concern with such a large number of independent variables in a model is that there will be substantial multicollinearity. Multicollinearity can impact regressions by creating model instability. We ran a series of multicollinearity diagnostic tests and did not find

evidence of serious problems in our data, except for two variables, number of employees and total business sales. For this reason we decided to use total retail sales rather than total business sales in the final models. We also were concerned about possible collinearity between high-risk juveniles and unsupervised teens. As we noted in endnote 12 in chapter 6, the bivariate correlation between these measures was very high (r = 0.91). The initial inspection of VIF shows some concerns of potential collinearity on both high-risk juveniles and unsupervised teens, but examining the corresponding condition indices and variance proportions of these two variables the diagnostics suggested their inclusion would not seriously impact the overall models (Tabachnick and Fidell, 2001). Additional diagnostics suggested that this was correct. We ran the models with each of these measures included separately and included together. The effects of other measures were not significantly impacted by the inclusions of the two measures. In turn, both had strong and significant impacts in the models. This suggested to us that the measures were not creating model instability, and given their theoretical distinction, we decided to include both indicators in the final models.

As a diagnostic for multicollinearity more generally, we also ran sensitivity tests to examine whether the results changed greatly under different specifications and inclusion of different groups of variables. We found overall that the models were stable.

5. It is important to note that there is much debate regarding the development of appropriate measures of variance explained for nonlinear models (e.g.,see Anderson-Sprecher, 1994; Kvålseth, 1985). This is particularly the case when the outcome measures examined deal with problems that are not based on interval-level distributions, and thus in some sense have no real measure of variance. Nonetheless, we still think that a broad statement regarding the strength of the models is important, and that the limitations do not outweigh the potential for adding insights to our understanding of the criminology of place.

6. We noted in chapter 6 that we used a conservative definition for mixed land use. We also included mixed land use in the model defined as any mixed land used. The variable was also not statistically significant under this assumption.

7. A closer look at the table in appendix 5 shows that the basic relationships described in this chapter are replicated generally in the overall model. In general, larger effects are found in the chronic-crime pattern comparison.

8. The standardized logistic regression coefficient is calculated by multiplying the parameter estimate times the standard deviation of the measure. While there is considerable controversy regarding the interpretation of these standardized coefficients (e.g., see Kaufman, 1996), we think they provide a very general sense for comparing the strength of variable impacts across a model.

9. At the same time, Averdijk (2010, 2011) found that victimization does not have a significant effect on routine activities and thus on exposure to risk.

10. We urge some caution in interpreting the odds ratio statistic in this case and others where odds ratios are very large. In such cases, a general interpretation of coefficient effects as very large should be used rather than a specific odds ratio outcome.

11. Accordingly, there are very few crime-free street segments with physical disorder problems, and their large number combined with the relatively large number of high crime street segments with these problems likely inflates the estimates in the model.

12. As we noted in chapter 6 (see note 12), there is a strong correlation between our measure of truant juveniles and that of high-risk juveniles (see also note 5 in this chapter). The fact that both indicators are strong and significant in these models suggests that they are

indeed capturing different dimensions of variability in developmental crime patterns at street segments.

13. Following the approach we used for the main model, we excluded measures that did not evidence variability over time in these analyses. At the same time, we did not use a selection process (based on significant change) as described in note 2, in good part because change is the critical dimension in these analyses. We examined the models for instability and multicollinearity, and overall model stability was high. There is some evidence of multicollinearity in the low crime model for high-risk juveniles and residential population, and for the high crime model for high-risk juveniles and truant juveniles. In both cases, high-risk juveniles are not found to be significant in the models including the second variable, but are significant when the variable is not included. Given the fact that overall model stability is not impacted by the inclusion or exclusion of these measures, we decided that including them was the correct modeling decision. Overall, it would seem that the measurement of high-risk juveniles in these cases is not as important as that of residential population or truant juveniles.

14. We do not report odds ratios or standardized coefficients because of the varying time periods examined in the change measures. However, the odds ratios are included in appendix 5 for the information of the interested reader.

15. It might also be that changes in opportunity are more directly linked to specific types of crime rather than crime in general. An increase in vacant land, for example, might spark increased disorder-related crimes rather than increases in aggravated or simple assault. But neither of those increases might be enough to notice if the outcome measure is total crime.

Chapter 8

1. See chapter 1 for a discussion of behavior settings.

2. Of course, as noted in chapter 6, some scholars argue that both disorder and crime are products of other social forces (see also our discussion of limitations later in the chapter). While we recognize that the relationship here may not be causal, there is a strong correlation in our data between physical disorder and crime. This relationship is consistent with traditional conceptions of social disorganization theory.

3. In correspondence with Marcus Felson, he argued that this mechanism, as well as other social disorganization processes, may in the end reflect routine activity mechanisms. For example, SES may be a proxy for likely offenders and potential targets. More housing assistance and public housing in this context may simply be measuring the fact that there are more opportunities for crime (perhaps because of larger numbers of potential offenders) in poorer areas. While we recognize that concepts in the theoretical perspectives we examine may overlap, the fact that SES continues to have salience in our models after controlling for a series of opportunity measures indicates that it stands as an independent correlate of crime at place.

4. For a more detailed discussion of the relationship between the tight coupling of crime and place and displacement, see Weisburd and Telep (2012). Additionally, see recent work by Brantingham and Brantingham (2003) as well as Eck and Madensen (2009) on how we can use the characteristics of crime events and places to identify areas where displacement is more likely to occur.

5. It is interesting in this regard that an evaluation of the Redlands program (Weisburd, Morris, and Ready, 2008) suggested that a reason for failure of the intervention was the relatively larger areas that were the focus of police interventions. Our work suggests that such socially based interventions would be better focused on street segments than census block groups.

Appendix 2

1. The volume of research explicitly examining spatial dependence or spatial error in their models is far too large to detail here. The following studies are provided as examples: Baller et al. (2001); Chakravorty and Pelfrey (2000); Cohen and Tita (1999); Cork (1999); Jefferis (2004); Morenoff and Sampson (1997); Roman (2002). In addition, see Bernasco and Elffers (2009) for an overview of spatial methods.

Appendix 3

1. Since street segments are stationary, attraction in this context refers to a tendency for street segments of one trajectory pattern to be found in closer proximity to street segments of another trajectory pattern than would be expected under independence (i.e., their patterns are similar).

2. A toroidal shift provides a simulation of potential outcomes under the assumption of independence. This is accomplished by repeatedly and randomly shifting the locations for one type of street segment and calculating the cross-K function for that iteration. The outcomes are used to create test statistics in the form of an upper and lower envelope. One thousand iterations were used for each simulation, except the generation of the test statistic for the crime-free trajectory pattern for which we used 100 iterations because of the large number of street segments.

Appendix 4

1. These were above the commonly accepted minimum acceptable geocoding rate of 85 percent (Ratcliffe, 2004).

2. The historical data related to real property (i.e., value and land use type) was the most problematic to assemble. The final data set had about 20 percent missing data.

3. Data describing the number of public schools students were provided at the hundred-block level and geocoded by the researchers to the street segment. The data were for academic years. We refer to each academic year by its earlier calendar year (e.g., data for 1989–1990 are used to represent 1989).

4. The following zip codes were used to define Seattle: 98101, 98102, 98103, 98104, 98105, 98106, 98107, 98108, 98109, 98112, 98115, 98116, 98117, 98118, 98119, 98121, 98122, 98125, 98126, 98133, 98134, 98136, 98144, 98146, 98168, 98177, 98178, 98195, and 98199.

5. The following North American Industrial Classification (NAIC) codes were used to identify retail businesses: 441–Motor Vehicle and Parts Dealers; 442–Furniture and Home Furnishings Stores; 443–Electronics and Appliance Stores; 444–Building Material and Garden Equipment and Supplies Dealers; 44612–Cosmetics, Beauty Supplies, and Perfume

Stores; 44613–Optical Goods Stores; 44619–Other Health and Personal Care Stores; 448–Clothing and Clothing Accessories Stores (Retail); 451–Sporting Goods; Hobby, Book, and Music Stores (Retail); 452–General Merchandise Stores (Retail); 453–Miscellaneous Store Retailers (Retail).

6. When representing lighting related to a street, we only included light poles that were within 90 feet of the street centerline for residential roads and within 300 feet for arterial roads. The two different thresholds were used because of the difference in the average width of an arterial street and a residential street. After establishing the street poles with light that might reach the edge of the street, we then found the total wattage for the street lights associated with each pole and aggregated the total watts by street segment.

7. We used the 2006 centerline file since the Seattle Planning Department and Seattle GIS department verified there had been no significant changes in the street configuration, nor had there been any annexations during the study period.

8. Information on street classifications was retrieved from the King County Department of Transportation web site at http://www.kingcounty.gov/transportation/kcdot/Roads/TransportationPlanning/ArterialClassificationSystem.aspx. Briefly, arterial streets are those that carry larger volumes of traffic. Residential streets run through neighborhoods and are designed to carry lower volumes of local travel at slower speeds. Walkways are non-vehicular paths or stairways that typically connect two residential streets.

9. We also considered using the cultural center of Seattle, but we could find no documentation regarding a cultural center. The librarians at the Seattle Public Library identified the Westlake Center (4th Avenue and Pine Street), which opened in 1988, as the cultural center (personal conversation, 2008). Since the two addresses are only 3,650 feet (a little less than three-quarters of a mile) apart as the crow flies, we went with the geographic center, which was verifiable.

10. The geographic center of Seattle is located at N 47° 37.271 W 122° 19.986, which translates to 331 Minor Avenue N (see http://www.waymarking.com/waymarks/WM29A8).

{ REFERENCES }

Abbott, A. (1997). Of time and space: The contemporary relevance of the Chicago school. *Social Forces, 75*(4), 1149–82.

Adler, P. A., & Adler, P. (2009). *Constructions of deviance: Social power, context, and interaction.* 6th ed. Belmont, CA: Wadsworth Publishing.

Agnew, R. (1992). Foundation for a general strain theory of crime and delinquency. *Criminology, 30*(1), 47–87.

Agnew, R. (1999). A general strain theory of community differences in crime rates. *Journal of Research in Crime and Delinquency, 36*(2), 123–55.

Agresti, A. (1996). *An introduction to categorical data analysis.* New York: Wiley.

Akers, R. L. (1973). *Deviant behavior: A social learning approach.* Belmont, CA: Wadsworth.

Albrecht, H. J., & Moitra, S. (1988). Escalation and specialization—A comparative analysis of patterns in criminal careers. In G. Kaiser & I. Geissler (eds.), *From crime and criminal justice: Criminological research in the 2nd decade at the Max Planck Institute in Freiburg* (pp. 115–36). Freiburg, Germany: Max Planck Institute.

Amazon.com, Inc. (2010). Amazon.com announces fourth quarter sales up 42% to $9.5 billion. Press release accessed November 6, 2011, at: http://phx.corporate-ir.net/phoenix.zhtml?c=97664&p=irol-newsarticle&id=1380452.

American Housing Survey Branch. (2005). *American Housing Survey for the United States: 2005.* Washington, DC: Housing and Household Economic Statistics Division, U.S. Census Bureau.

Anderson-Sprecher, R. (1994). Model comparisons and R^2. *American Statistician, 48*(2), 113–17.

Andrews, D. A., Zinger, I., Hoge, R. D., Bonta, J., Gendreau, P., & Cullen, F. T. (1990). Does correctional treatment work? A clinically relevant and psychologically informed meta-analysis. *Criminology, 28*(3), 369–404.

Anselin, L. (1988). *Spatial econometrics: Methods and models.* Boston: Kluwer Academic Publishers.

Anselin, L. (2003). *GeoDa 0.9 user's guide.* Urbana: Spatial Analysis Laboratory, University of Illinois.

Anselin, L., Cohen, J., Cook, D., Gorr, W., & Tita, G. (2000). Spatial analysis of crime. In D. Duffee (ed.), *Criminal Justice 2000, Measurement and analysis of crime and justice,* vol. 4 (pp. 213–62). Washington, DC: National Institute of Justice, U.S. Department of Justice.

Appleyard, D. (1981). *Livable streets.* Berkeley: University of California Press.

Auerhahn, K. (1999). Selective incapacitation and the problem of prediction. *Criminology, 37*(4), 703–34.

Averdijk, M. (2010). *Individuals' victimization patterns over time.* Amsterdam: Vrije University.

Averdijk, M. (2011). Reciprocal effects of victimization and routine activities. *Journal of Quantitative Criminology, 27*(2), 127–49.

Bagley, C. (1916). *History of Seattle from the earliest settlement to the present time*, vol. 1. Chicago: S.J. Clarke Publishing Company.

Bailey, T. C., & Gatrell, A. C. (1995). *Interactive spatial data analysis*. Essex: Longman Group Limited.

Bak, P. (1994). Self-organized criticality: A holistic view of nature. In G. Cowan, D. Pines, & D. E. Meltzer (eds.), *Complexity: Metaphors, models, and reality* (pp. 477–95). Reading, MA: Addison-Wesley.

Balbi, A., & Guerry, A-M. (1829). *Statistique comparée de l'état de l'instruction et du nombre des crimes dans les divers arrondissements des Académies et des Cours Royales de France.* Paris: Everat.

Baldwin, J., & Bottoms, A. E. (1976). *The urban criminal*. London: Tavistock.

Baller, R. D., Anselin, L., Messner, S. F., Deane, G., & Hawkins, D. F. (2001). Structural covariates of U.S. county homicide rates: Incorporating spatial effects. *Criminology, 39*(3), 561–90.

Barker, R. G. (1968). *Ecological psychology: Concepts and methods for studying the environment of human behavior*. Stanford, CA: Stanford University Press.

Barnett, A., & Lofaso, A. J. (1985). Selective incapacitation and the Philadelphia birth cohort. *Journal of Quantitative Criminology, 1*(1), 3–36.

Barr, R., & Pease, K. (1990). Crime placement, displacement, and deflection. In M. Tonry & N. Morris (eds.), *Crime and Justice: A Review of Research*, vol. 12 (pp. 277–318). Chicago: University of Chicago Press.

Baumer, E. P., Lauritsen, J. L., Rosenfeld, R., & Wright, R. (1998). The influence of crack cocaine on robbery, burglary, and homicide rates: A cross-city, longitudinal analysis. *Journal of Research in Crime and Delinquency, 35*(3), 316–40.

Beavon, D. J. K., Brantingham, P. L., & Brantingham, P. J. (1994). The influence of street networks on the patterning of property offenses. In R. V. Clarke (ed.), *Crime Prevention Studies*, vol. 2 (pp. 115–48). Monsey, NY: Criminal Justice Press.

Becker, H. S. (1963). *Outsiders: Studies in the sociology of deviance*. Glencoe, IL: Free Press of Glencoe.

Begg, C. B., & Gray, R. (1984). Calculation of polychotomous logistic regression parameters using individualized regressions. *Biometrika, 71*(1), 11–18.

Beirne, P. (1987). Adolphe Quetelet and the origins of positivist criminology. *American Journal of Sociology, 92*(5), 1140–69.

Beirne, P., & Messerschmidt, J. (1991). *Criminology*. San Diego: Harcourt Brace Jovanovich.

Bellair, P. E. (1997). Social interaction and community crime: The importance of neighbor networks. *Criminology, 35*(4), 677–704.

Bernard, T. J. (2001). Integrating theories in criminology. In R. Paternoster & R. Bachman (eds.), *Explaining criminals and crime* (pp. 335–46). Los Angeles: Roxbury.

Bernard, T. J., & Snipes, J. B. (1996). Theoretical integration in criminology. In M. Tonry (ed.), *Crime and Justice: A Review of Research*, vol. 20 (pp. 301–48). Chicago: University of Chicago Press.

Bernasco, W., & Luykx, F. (2003). Effects of attractiveness, opportunity and accessibility to burglars on residential burglary rates of urban neighborhoods. *Criminology, 41*(3), 981–1001.

Bernasco, W., & Nieuwbeerta, P. (2005). How do residential burglars select target areas? *British Journal of Criminology, 45*(3), 296–315.

Bernasco, W., & Elffers, H. (2009). Statistical analysis of spatial crime data. In A. Piquero & D. Weisburd (eds.), *Handbook of quantitative criminology* (pp. 699–724). New York: Springer.

Bernasco, W., & Block, R. (2011). Robberies in Chicago: A block-level analysis of the influence of crime generators, crime attractors, and offender anchor points. *Journal of Research in Crime and Delinquency, 48*(1), 33–57.

Bersani, B. A., Nieuwbeerta, P., & Laub, J. H. (2009). Predicting trajectories of offending over the life course: Findings from a Dutch conviction cohort. *Journal of Research in Crime and Delinquency, 46*(4), 468–94.

Bevis, C., & Nutter, J. B. (1977). Changing street layouts to reduce residential burglary. Paper presented at the meeting of the American Society of Criminology, Atlanta, GA.

Bick, J. (2005). The Microsoft millionaires come of age. *New York Times*, May 29.

Birkbeck, C., & LaFree, G. (1993). The situational analysis of crime and deviance. *Annual Review of Sociology, 19,* 113–37.

Black, D. (1970). Production of crime rates. *American Sociological Review, 35*(4), 733–48.

Blau, J. R., & Blau, P. M. (1982). The cost of inequality: Metropolitan structure and violent crime. *American Sociological Review, 47*(1), 114–29.

Block, C. R. (1997). The GeoArchive: An information foundation for community policing. In D. Weisburd & T. McEwen (eds.), *Crime mapping and crime prevention. Crime Prevention Studies*, vol. 8 (pp. 27–81). Monsey, NY: Criminal Justice Press.

Block, R. L., & Block, C. R. (1995). Space, place and crime: Hot spot areas and hot places of liquor-related crime. In J. E. Eck & D. Weisburd (eds.), *Crime and place. Crime Prevention Studies*, vol. 4 (pp. 145–83). Monsey, NY: Willow Tree Press.

Block, C., Dabdoub, M., & Fregly, S. (eds.). (1995). *Crime analysis through computer mapping.* Washington, DC: Police Executive Research Forum.

Blokland, A. A. J., Nagin, D. S., & Nieuwbeerta, P. (2005). Life span offending trajectories of a Dutch conviction cohort. *Criminology 43*(4), 919–54.

Blumstein, A., & Cohen, J. (1973). A theory of the stability of punishment. *Journal of Criminal Law and Criminology, 64*(2), 198–207.

Blumstein, A., & Cohen, J. (1979). Estimation of individual crime rates from arrest records. *Journal of Criminal Law and Criminology, 70*(4), 561–85.

Blumstein, A., & Moitra, S. (1979). An analysis of the time series of the imprisonment rate in the states of the United States: A further test of the stability of punishment hypothesis. *Journal of Criminal Law and Criminology, 70*(3), 376–90.

Blumstein, A., & Wallman, J. (eds.). (2000). *The crime drop in America*. Cambridge: Cambridge University Press.

Blumstein, A., Cohen, J., & Nagin, D. (1977). The dynamics of a homeostatic punishment process. *Journal of Criminal Law and Criminology, 67*(3), 317–34.

Boeing Corporation (n.d.). History: Heritage of innovation. Accessed November 6, 2011, at: http://www.boeing.com/history/index.html.

Boggs, S. L. (1965). Urban crime patterns. *American Sociological Review, 30*(6), 899–908.

Bottoms, A. E., Claytor, A., & Wiles, P. (1992). Housing markets and residential community crime careers: A case study from Sheffield. In D. J. Evans, N. R. Fyfe, & D. T. Herbert (eds.), *Crime, policing and place: Essays in environmental criminology* (pp. 118–44). London: Routledge.

Bowers, K., Johnson, S., Guerette, R. T., Summers, L., & Poynton, S. (2011). Spatial displacement and diffusion of benefits among geographically focused policing interventions. Campbell Collaboration systematic review, accessed November 7, 2011, at: http://www.campbellcollaboration.org/lib/download/1171/.

Braga, A. A. (2001). The effects of hot spots policing on crime. *Annals of the American Academy of Political and Social Science, 578*, 104–25.

Braga, A. A. (2003). Serious youth gun offenders and the epidemic of youth violence in Boston. *Journal of Quantitative Criminology, 19*(1), 33–54.

Braga, A. A. (2005). Hot spots policing and crime prevention: A systematic review of randomized controlled trials. *Journal of Experimental Criminology, 1*(3), 317–42.

Braga, A. A. (2007). *Effects of hot spots policing on crime.* Campbell Collaboration systematic review, accessed November 7, 2011, at: http://www.campbellcollaboration.org/lib/download/118/.

Braga, A. A., & Bond, B. J. (2008). Policing crime and disorder hot spots: A randomized controlled trial. *Criminology, 46*, 577–608.

Braga, A. A., & Weisburd, D. L. (2010). *Policing problem places: Crime hot spots and effective prevention.* New York: Oxford University Press.

Braga, A. A., Papachristos, A. V., & Hureau, D. M. (2010). The concentration and stability of gun violence at micro places in Boston, 1980–2008. *Journal of Quantitative Criminology, 26*(1), 33–53.

Braga, A. A., Papachristos, A. V., & Hureau, D. M. (Forthcoming). The effects of hot spots policing on crime: An updated systematic review and meta-analysis. *Justice Quarterly*.

Braga A. A., Weisburd, D., Waring E. J., Mazerolle, L. G., Spelman, W., & Gajewski, F. (1999). Problem-oriented policing in violent crime places: A randomized controlled experiment. *Criminology, 37*(3), 541–80.

Braga, A. A., Kennedy, D. M., Waring, E. J., & Piehl, A. M. (2001). Problem-oriented policing, deterrence, and youth violence: An evaluation of Boston's Operation Ceasefire *Journal of Research in Crime and Delinquency, 38*(3), 195–225.

Brantingham, P. J., & Brantingham, P. L. (1977). Housing patterns and burglary in a medium-sized American city. In J. Scott & S. Dinitz (eds.), *Criminal justice planning* (pp. 63–74). New York: Praeger.

Brantingham, P. J., & Brantingham, P. L. (eds.). (1981). *Environmental criminology.* Beverly Hills, CA: Sage Publications.

Brantingham, P. J., & Brantingham, P. L. (1984). *Patterns in crime.* New York: Macmillan.

Brantingham, P. J., & Brantingham, P. L. (1990). Situational crime prevention in practice. *Canadian Journal of Criminology, 32*(1), 17–40.

Brantingham, P. J., & Brantingham, P. L. (2003). Anticipating the displacement of crime using the principles of environmental criminology. In M. Smith & D. Cornish (eds.), *Theory for practice in situational crime prevention. Crime Prevention Studies*, vol. 16 (pp. 119–48). Monsey, NY: Criminal Justice Press.

Brantingham, P. L., & Brantingham, P. J. (1975). Residential burglary and urban form. *Urban Studies, 12*, 104–25.

Brantingham, P. L., & Brantingham, P. J. (1982). Mobility, notoriety, and crime: A study of crime patterns in urban nodal points. *Journal of Environmental Systems, 11*(1), 89–99.

Brantingham, P. L., & Brantingham, P. J. (1993a). Environment, routine, and situation: Toward a pattern theory of crime. In R. V. Clarke & M. Felson (eds.), *Routine activity and rational choice. Advances in Criminological Theory*, vol. 5 (pp. 259–94). New Brunswick, NJ: Transaction Publishers.

Brantingham, P. L., & Brantingham, P. J. (1993b). Nodes, paths and edges: Considerations on the complexity of crime and the physical environment. *Journal of Environmental Psychology, 13*(1), 3–28.

Brantingham, P. L., & Brantingham, P. J. (1995). Criminality of place: Crime generators and crime attractors. *European Journal on Criminal Policy and Research, 3*(3), 5–26.

Brantingham, P. L., & Brantingham, P. J. (1999). Theoretical model of crime hot spot generation. *Studies on Crime and Crime Prevention, 8*(1), 7–26.

Brantingham, P. L., Brantingham, P. J., Vajihollahi, M., & Wuschke, K. (2009). Crime analysis at multiple scales of aggregation: A topological approach. In D. Weisburd, W. Bernasco, & G. J. N. Bruinsma (eds.), *Putting crime in its place: Units of analysis in geographic criminology* (pp. 87–122). New York: Springer.

Bratton, W., & Kelling. G. (2006). There are no cracks in the broken windows. *National Review* (online), February 28.

Brennan, P. A., Raine, A., Schulsinger, F., Kirkegaard-Sorensen, L., Knop, J., Hutchings, B., Rosenberg, R., & Mednick, S. A. (1997). Psychophysiological protective factors for male subjects at high risk for criminal behavior. *American Journal of Psychiatry, 154*(6), 853–55.

Bromley, R. D. F., & Nelson, A. L. (2002). Alcohol-related crime and disorder across urban space and time: Evidence from a British city. *Geoforum, 33*(2), 239–54.

Brower, S. (1980). Territory in urban settings. In I. Altman & C. M. Werner (eds.), *Human behavior and environment: Current theory and research*, vol. 4. New York: Plenun.

Browning, K., Thornberry, T. P., & Porter, P. K. (1999). *Highlights of findings from the Rochester Youth Development Study*. OJJDP Fact Sheet. Washington, DC: Office of Juvenile Justice and Delinquency Prevention.

Bryk, A. S., & Raudenbush, S. W. (1987). Application of hierarchical linear models to assessing change. *Psychological Bulletin, 101*(1), 147–58.

Bryk, A. S., & Raudenbush, S. W. (1992). *Hierarchical linear models: Applications and data analysis methods*. Thousand Oaks, CA: Sage Publications.

Bulmer, M. (1984). *The Chicago School of sociology. Institutionalization, diversity, and the rise of sociological research*. Chicago: University of Chicago Press.

Burgess, E. W. (1925 [1967]). The growth of the city. An introduction to a research project. In R. E. Park & E. W. Burgess (eds.), *The city: Suggestions for the investigation of human behaviour in the urban environment*. Chicago: University of Chicago Press.

Burgess, E. W., & Bogue, D. J. (1964a). Research in urban society: A long view. In E. W. Burgess & D. J. Bogue (eds.), *Contributions to urban sociology* (pp. 1–14). Chicago: University of Chicago Press.

Burgess, E. W., & Bogue, D. J. (1964b). The delinquency research of Clifford R. Shaw and Henry D. McKay and associates. In E. W. Burgess & D. J. Bogue (eds.), *Contributions to urban sociology* (pp. 591–615). Chicago: University of Chicago Press.

Bursik, R. J., Jr. (1984). Urban dynamics and ecological studies of delinquency. *Social Forces, 63*(2), 393–413.

Bursik, R. J., Jr. (1986). Ecological stability and the dynamics of delinquency. In A. J. Reiss Jr. & M. Tonry (eds.), *Communities and crime. Crime and Justice: A Review of Research*, vol. 8 (pp. 35–66). Chicago: University of Chicago Press.

Bursik, R. J., Jr. (1988). Social disorganization and theories of crime and delinquency: Problems and prospects. *Criminology, 26*(4), 519–51.

Bursik, R. J., Jr. (1989). Political decisionmaking and ecological models of delinquency: Conflict and consensus. In S. F. Messner, M. D. Krohn, & A. E. Liska (eds.), *Theoretical integration in the study of deviance and crime* (pp. 105–17). Albany: State University of New York Press.

Bursik, R. J., Jr., & Webb, J. (1982). Community change and patterns of delinquency. *American Journal of Sociology, 88*(1), 24–42.

Bursik, R. J., Jr., & Grasmick, H. G. (1993). *Neighborhoods and crime: The dimensions of effective community control.* New York: Lexington Books.

Bushway, S. D., Thornberry, T. P., & Krohn, M. D. (2003). Desistance as a developmental process: A comparison of static and dynamic approaches. *Journal of Quantitative Criminology, 19*(2), 129–53.

Bushway, S. D., Sweeten, G., & Nieuwbeerta, P. (2009). Measuring long term individual trajectories of offending using multiple methods. *Journal of Quantitative Criminology, 25*(3), 259–86.

Butts, J. A. (2000). *Youth crime drop.* Washington, DC: Urban Institute.

Byrne, J. M., & Sampson, R. J., (eds.). (1986). *Social ecology of crime.* New York: Springer-Verlag.

Cadora, E., Swartz, C., & Gordon, M. (2003). Criminal justice and human services: An exploration of overlapping needs, resources and interests in Brooklyn neighborhoods. In J. Travis & M. Waul (eds.), *Prisoners once removed: The impact of incarceration and reentry on children, families, and communities* (pp. 285–311). Washington, DC: Urban Institute Press.

Catalano, F. R., Arthur, M. W., Hawkins, J. D., Berglund, L., & Olson, J. J. (1998). Comprehensive community- and school-based interventions to prevent antisocial behavior. In R. Loeber & D. Farrington (eds.), *Serious and violent juvenile offenders: Risk factors and successful interventions* (pp. 248–83). Thousand Oaks, CA: Sage Publications.

Ceccato, V. (2005). Homicide in São Paulo, Brazil: Assessing spatio-temporal and weather variations. *Journal of Environmental Psychology, 25*(3), 307–21.

Chakravorty, S., & Pelfrey, W. V. J. (2000). Exploratory data analysis of crime patterns: Preliminary findings from the Bronx. In V. Goldsmith, P. McGuire, G. J. H. Mollenkopf, & T. A. Ross (eds.), *Analyzing crime patterns: Frontiers of practice* (pp. 65–76). Thousand Oaks, CA: Sage Publications.

Chilton, R. J. (1964). Continuity in delinquency area research: A comparison of studies for Baltimore, Detroit, and Indianapolis. *American Sociological Review, 29*(1), 71–83.

Clarke, R. V. (1980). "Situational" crime prevention: Theory and practice. *British Journal of Criminology, 20*(2), 136–47.

Clarke, R. V. (1983). Situational crime prevention: Its theoretical basis and practical scope. In M. Tonry & N. Morris (eds.), *Crime and Justice: A Review of Research*, vol. 14 (pp. 225–56). Chicago: University of Chicago Press.

Clarke, R. V. (1992). *Situational crime prevention: Successful case studies.* 2nd ed. Albany, NY: Harrow & Heston Publishers.

Clarke, R. V. (1995). Situational crime prevention. In M. Tonry & D. P. Farrington (eds.), *Building a safer society: Strategic approaches to crime prevention. Crime and Justice: A Review of Research*, vol. 19 (pp. 91–150). Chicago: University of Chicago Press.

Clarke, R. V., & Cornish, D. B. (1985). Modeling offender's decisions: A framework for research and policy. In M. Tonry & N. Morris (eds.), *Crime and Justice: A Review of Research*, vol. 6 (pp. 147–86). Chicago: University of Chicago Press.

Clarke, R. V., & Felson, M. (1993). Introduction: Criminology, routine activity, and rational choice. In R. V. Clarke & M. Felson (eds.), *Routine activity and rational choice. Advances in Criminological Theory*, vol. 5 (pp. 1–14). New Brunswick, NJ: Transaction Publishers.

Clarke, R. V., & Weisburd, D. (1994). Diffusion of crime control benefits: Observations on the reverse of displacement. In R. V. Clarke (ed.), *Crime Prevention Studies*, vol. 2 (pp. 165–84). Monsey, NY: Criminal Justice Press.

Clarke, R. V., & Cornish, D. B. (2001). Rational choice. In R. Paternoster & R. Bachman (eds.), *Explaining criminals and crime* (pp. 23–42). Los Angeles: Roxbury Publishing.

Clear, T. R. (2008). The effects of high imprisonment rates on communities. In M. Tonry (ed.), *Crime and Justice: A Review of Research*, vol. 37 (pp. 97–132). Chicago: University of Chicago Press.

Clear, T. R., Rose, D. R., Waring, E., & Scully, K. (2003). Coercive mobility and crime: A preliminary examination of concentrated incarceration and social disorganization. *Justice Quarterly, 20*(1), 33–64.

Cloward, R. A. (1959). Illegitimate means, anomie, and deviant behavior. *American Sociological Review, 24*(2), 164–76.

Cloward, R. A., & Ohlin, L. E. (1960). *Delinquency and opportunity: A theory of delinquent gangs.* Glencoe, IL: Free Press of Glencoe.

Cohen, L. E. (1981). Modeling crime trends: A crime opportunity perspective. *Journal of Research in Crime & Delinquency, 18*(1), 138–64.

Cohen, L. E., & Felson, M. (1979). Social change and crime rate trends: A routine activity approach. *American Sociological Review, 44*(4), 588–608.

Cohen, J., & Tita, G. (1999). Diffusion in homicide: Exploring a general method for detecting spatial diffusion processes. *Journal of Quantitative Criminology, 15*(4), 451–93.

Cohn, E. G., & Rotton, J. (2000). Weather, seasonal trends and property crime in Minneapolis, 1987–1988: A moderator-variable time-series analysis of routine activities. *Journal of Environmental Psychology, 20*(3), 257–72.

Coleman, A. (1989). Disposition and situation: Two sides of the same crime. In D. J. Evans & D. Herbert (eds.), *The geography of crime* (pp. 109–34). London: Routledge.

Coleman, J. S. (1990). *Foundations of social theory.* Cambridge, MA: Harvard University Press.

Coleman, J. S. (1993). The rational reconstruction of society: 1992 presidential address. *American Sociological Review, 58*(1), 1–15.

Coleman, S. (2002). A test for the effect of conformity on crime rate using voter turnout. *The Sociological Quarterly, 43*(2), 257–76.

Connolly, S., O'Reilly, D., & Rosato, M. (2010). House value as an indicator of cumulative wealth is strongly related to morbidity and mortality risk in older people: A census-based cross-sectional and longitudinal study. *Journal of Epidemiology, 39*(2), 383–91.

Cook, T. D., & Campbell, D. (1979). *Quasi-experimentation: Design and analysis issues for field settings.* Chicago: Rand McNally.

Cook, P. J., & Laub, J. H. (1998). The unprecedented epidemic of youth violence. In M. Tonry & M. H. Moore (eds.), *Youth violence. Crime and Justice: A Review of Research*, vol. 24 (pp. 27–64). Chicago: University of Chicago Press.

Cook, P. J., & Laub, J. H. (2002). After the epidemic: Recent trends in youth violence in the United States. In M. Tonry (ed.), *Crime and Justice: A Review of Research*, vol. 29 (pp. 1–17). Chicago: University of Chicago Press.

Cork, D. (1999). Examining space-time interaction in city-level homicide data: Crack markets and the diffusion of guns among youth. *Journal of Quantitative Criminology, 15*(4), 379–406.

Corman, H., & Mocan, H. N. (2005). Carrots, sticks and broken windows. *Journal of Law and Economics, 48*(1), 235–66.

Cornish, D. (1993). Theories of action in criminology. Learning theory and rational choice approaches. In R. V. Clarke & M. Felson (eds.), *Routine activity and rational choice. Advances in Criminological Theory*, vol. 5 (pp. 351–82). New Brunswick, NJ: Transaction Publishers.

Cornish, D., & Clarke, R. V. (eds.). (1986). *The reasoning criminal: Rational choice perspectives on offending*. New York: Springer-Verlag.

Cox, D. R., & Snell, E. J. (1989). *The analysis of binary data.* 2nd ed. London: Chapman & Hall.

Crewe, K. (2001). Linear parks and urban neighborhoods: A case study of the crime impact of the Boston South-west corridor. *Journal of Urban Design, 6*(3), 245–64.

Cromwell, P, Alexander, G., & Dotson, P. (2008). Crime and incivilities in libraries: Situational crime prevention strategies for thwarting biblio-bandits and problem patrons. *Security Journal, 21,* 147–58.

Crow, W., & Bull, J. (1975). *Robbery deterrence: An applied behavioral science demonstration— Final report*. La Jolla, CA: Western Behavioral Science Institute.

Crowley, W. (1999). Pike Place Market. *HistoryLink.org Online Encyclopedia of Washington State History*. Accessed November 6, 2011, at: http://www.historylink.org/index.cfm?DisplayPage=output.cfm&file_id=3392.

Crowley, W. (2001). Seattle neighborhoods: Pioneer Square. *HistoryLink.org Online Encyclopedia of Washington State History*. Accessed November 6, 2011, at: http://www.historylink.org/index.cfm?DisplayPage=output.cfm&file_id=3392.

Crowley, W. (2006). Seattle—thumbnail history. *HistoryLink.org Online Encyclopedia of Washington State History*. Accessed November 6, 2011, at: http://www.historylink.org/index.cfm?DisplayPage=output.cfm&file_id=7934.

Cullen. F. T. (1988). Were Cloward and Ohlin strain theorists? Delinquency and opportunity revisited. *Journal of Research in Crime and Delinquency, 25*(3), 214–41.

Cullen, F. T. (2010). Cloward, Richard A.: The theory of illegitimate means. In F. T. Cullen & P. Wilcox (eds.), *Encyclopedia of criminological theory* (pp. 167–70). Thousand Oaks, CA: Sage Publications.

Curtis, L. A. (1974). *Criminal violence: National patterns and behavior.* Lexington, MA: Lexington Books.

Decker, D., Shichor, D., & O'Brien, R. (1982). *Urban structure and victimization*. Lexington, MA: D. C. Heath.

Dryfoos, J. G. (1990). *Adolescents at risk: Prevalence and prevention*. New York: Oxford University Press.

Duffala, D. C. (1976). Convenience stores, armed robbery, and physical environmental features. *American Behavioral Scientist, 20*(2), 227–46.

D'Unger, A. V., Land, K. C., McCall, P. L., & Nagin, D. S. (1998). How many latent classes of delinquent/criminal careers? Results from mixed Poisson regression analysis. *American Journal of Sociology, 103*(6), 1593–630.

Durlauf, S., & Nagin, D. S. (2011). Imprisonment and crime: Can both be reduced? *Criminology and Public Policy, 10*(1), 13–54.

Durkheim, E. (1893 [1964]). *The division of labour in society*. New York: Free Press.

Durkheim, E. (1895 [1964]). *The rules of sociological method*. Edited by G. E. G. Catlin. Translated by S. A. Solovay and J. H. Mueller. New York: Free Press.

Earls, F. (1991). Not fear, nor quarantine, but science: Preparation for a decade of research to advance knowledge about causes and control of violence in youths. *Journal of Adolescent Health, 12*(8), 619–29.

Eck, J. E. (1993). The threat of crime displacement. *Criminal Justice Abstracts, 25*, 527–46.

Eck, J. E. (1995a). Examining routine activity theory: A review of two books. *Justice Quarterly, 12*(4), 783–97.

Eck, J. E. (1995b). A general model of the geography of illicit retail marketplaces. In J. E. Eck & D. Weisburd (eds.), *Crime and place. Crime Prevention Studies*, vol. 4 (pp. 67–93). Monsey, NY: Willow Tree Press.

Eck, J. E. (2002). Preventing crime at places. In L.W. Sherman, D. P. Farrington, B. C. Welsh, & D. L. MacKenzie (eds.), *Evidence-based crime prevention* (pp. 241–94). New York: Routledge.

Eck, J. E., & Weisburd, D. (1995). Crime places in crime theory. In J. E. Eck & D. Weisburd (eds.), *Crime and place. Crime Prevention Studies*, vol. 4 (pp. 1–33). Monsey, NY: Willow Tree Press.

Eck, J. E., & Madensen, T. (2009). Using signatures of opportunity structures to examine mechanisms in crime prevention evaluations. In J. Knutsson & N. Tilley (eds.), *Evaluating crime reduction initiatives. Crime Prevention Studies*, vol. 24 (pp. 59–84). Monsey, NY: Criminal Justice Press.

Eck, J. E., & Eck, E. B. (2012). Crime place and pollution: Expanding crime reduction options through a regulatory approach. *Criminology and Public Policy, 11*(2), 281–316.

Eck, J. E., Gersh, J. S., & Taylor, C. (2000). Finding crime hot spots through repeat address mapping. In V. Goldsmith, P. McGuir, J. H. Mollenkopf, & T. A. Ross (eds.), *Analyzing crime patterns: Frontiers of practice* (pp. 49–64). Thousand Oaks, CA: Sage Publications.

Eck, J. E., Clarke, R. V., & Guerette, R. T. (2007). Risky facilities: Crime concentration in homogenous sets of establishments and facilities. In G. Farrell, K. J. Bowers, S. D. Johnson, & M. Townsley (eds.), *Imagination in crime prevention. Crime Prevention Studies*, vol. 21 (pp. 225–64).

Eck, J. E., Chainey, S., Cameron, J. G., Leitner, M., & Wilson, R. E. (2005). *Mapping crime: Understanding hot spots*. Washington, DC: National Institute of Justice, U.S. Department of Justice.

Eggleston, E. P., Laub, J. H., & Sampson, R. J. (2004). Methodological sensitivities to latent class analysis of long-term criminal trajectories. *Journal of Quantitative Criminology, 20*(1), 1–26.

Elliott, D. S. (1985). The assumption that theories can be combined with increased explanatory power. In R. F. Meier (ed.), *Theoretical methods in criminology* (pp. 123–49). Beverly Hills, CA: Sage Publications.

Elliott, D. S., Huizinga, D., & Ageton, S. S. (1985). *Explaining delinquency and drug use.* Beverly Hills, CA: Sage Publications.

Elliott, D. S., Dunford, F. W., &, Huizinga, D. (1987). Identification and prediction of career offenders utilizing self-reported and official data. In J. D. Burchard & S. N. Burchard (eds.), *Prevention of delinquent behavior.* Newbury Park, CA: Sage Publications.

Elmer, M. C. (1933). Century-old ecological studies in France. *American Journal of Sociology, 39*(1), 63–70.

Erikson, K. T. (1966). *Wayward puritans: A study in the sociology of deviance.* New York: Wiley.

Estrict, S., Moore, M. H., McGillis, D., & Spelman, W. (1983). *Dealing with dangerous offenders— Executive summary.* Rockville, MD: National Criminal Justice Reference Service (NCJRS).

Evans, D. J., & Oulds, G. (1984). Geographical aspects of the incidence of residential burglary in Newcastle-Under-Lyme, U.K. *Tijdschrift voor Economische Sociale Geografie, 75*(5), 344–55.

Ezell, M. E., & Cohen, L. E. (2005). *Desisting from crime: Continuity and change in long-term crime patterns of serious chronic offenders.* New York: Oxford University Press.

Faris, R. E. L. (1967). *Chicago sociology, 1920–1932.* San Francisco: Chandler.

Farrell, G., & Pease, K. (1993). *One bitten, twice bitten: Repeat victimization and its implications for crime prevention.* Police Research Group, Crime Prevention Unit Paper 46. London: Home Office.

Farrell, G., & Pease, K. (1994). Crime seasonality: Domestic disputes and residential burglary in Merseyside, 1988–90. *British Journal of Criminology, 34*(4), 487–98.

Farrington, D. P. (1997). Early prediction of violent and non-violent youthful offending. *European Journal on Criminal Policy and Research, 5*(2), 51–66.

Farrington, D. P. (2003). Methodological quality standards for evaluation research. *Annals of the American Academy of Political and Social Sciences, 587*, 49–68.

Farrington, D. P., & West, D. J. (1993). Criminal, penal and life histories of chronic offenders: Risk and protective factors and early identification. *Criminal Behaviour and Mental Health, 3*(4), 492–523.

Farrington, D. P., & Welsh, B. C. (2002). Improved street lighting and crime prevention. *Justice Quarterly, 19*(2), 313–42.

Farrington, D. P., Ohlin, L., & Wilson, J. Q. (1986). *Understanding and controlling crime.* New York: Springer-Verlag.

Felson, M. (1986). Predicting crime potential at any point on the city map. In R. M. Figlio, S. Hakim, & G. F. Rengert (eds.), *Metropolitan crime patterns* (pp. 127–36). Monsey, NY: Criminal Justice Press.

Felson, M. (1987). Routine activities and crime prevention in the developing metropolis. *Criminology, 25*(4), 911–31.

Felson, M. (1994). *Crime and everyday life: Insight and implications for society.* Thousand Oaks, CA: Pine Forge Press.

Felson, M. (2001). The routine activity approach: A very versatile theory of crime. In R. Paternoster & R. Bachman (eds.), *Explaining criminals and crime* (pp. 43–46). Los Angeles: Roxbury Publishing.

Felson, M. (2006). *Crime and nature.* Thousand Oaks, CA: Sage Publications.

Felson, M., & Clarke, R. V. (1998). *Opportunity makes the thief: Practical theory for crime prevention.* Police Research Series Paper 98. London: Policing and Reducing Crime Unit; Research, Development and Statistics Directorate, Home Office.

Felson, M., & Poulsen, E. (2003). Simple indicators of crime by time of day. *International Journal of Forecasting, 19*(4), 595–601.

Felson, M., & Boba, R. (2010). *Crime and everyday life.* 4th ed. Thousand Oaks, CA: Sage Publications.

Fitzpatrick, K., & LaGory, M. (2010). *Unhealthy cities: Poverty, race, and place in America.* New York: Routledge.

Fletcher, J. (1850). *Summary of the moral statistics of England and Wales.* London: Private distribution of the author.

Fotheringham, A. S., Brundson, C., & Charlton, M. (2000). *Quantitative geography.* London: Sage Publications.

Frisbie, D. W., Fishbine, G., Hintz, R., Joelson, M., & Nutter, J. B. (1978). *Crime in Minneapolis: Proposals for prevention.* Minneapolis: Minnesota Crime Prevention Center.

Galton, F. (1886). Regression towards mediocrity in hereditary stature. *Journal of the Anthropological Institute, 15*, 246–63.

Geller, A. (2007). Neighborhood disorder and crime: An analysis of *broken windows* in New York City. Unpublished Ph.D. dissertation. New York: Columbia University.

Glyde, J. (1856). Localities of crime in Suffolk. *Journal of the Statistical Society of London, 19*, 102–106.

Goldstein, H. (1995). *Multilevel statistical models.* London: Edward Arnold.

Gordon, R. A. (1967). Issues in the ecological study of delinquency. *American Sociological Review, 32*(6), 927–44.

Gorman, D. M., Speer, P. W., Gruenefeld, P. J., & Labouvie, E. W. (2001). Spatial dynamics of alcohol availability, neighborhood structure, and violent crime. *Journal of Studies on Alcohol and Drugs, 62*(5), 628–36.

Gottfredson, M., & Hirschi, T. (1990). *A general theory of crime.* Stanford, CA: Stanford University Press.

Gottfredson, S., & Gottfredson, D. (1992). *Classification, prediction, and the criminal justice system.* Rockville, MD: National Criminal Justice Reference Service.

Gottfredson, D. C., Gottfredson, G. D., & Weisman, S. A. (2001). The timing of delinquent behavior and its implications for after-school programs. *Criminology and Public Policy, 1*(1), 61–86.

Grannis, R. (1998). The importance of trivial streets: Residential streets and residential segregation. *American Journal of Sociology, 103*(6), 1530–64.

Green, L. (1996). *Policing places with drug problems.* Thousand Oaks, CA: Sage Publications.

Green, A. E., Gesten, E. L., Greenwald, M. A., & Salcedo, O. (2008). Predicting delinquency in adolescence and young adulthood. A longitudinal study of early risk factors. *Youth Violence and Juvenile Justice, 6*(4), 323–42.

Greenberg, S. W., Rohe, W. M., & Williams, J. R. (1982). Safety in urban neighborhoods: A comparison of physical characteristics and informal territorial control in high and low crime neighborhoods. *Population and Environment, 5*(3), 141–65.

Greenland, S., Robins, J. M., & Pearl, J. (1999). Confounding and collapsibility in causal inference. *Statistical Science, 14*(1), 29–46.

Greg, W. R. (1839). *Social statistics of the Netherlands.* London: Ridgway, Harrison & Crosfield.

Griffiths, E., & Chavez, J. M. (2004). Communities, street guns, and homicide trajectories in Chicago, 1980–1995: Merging methods for examining homicide trends across space and time. *Criminology, 42*(4), 941–78.

Groff, E. R. (2011). Exploring "near": Characterizing the spatial extent of drinking place influence on crime. *Australian and New Zealand Journal of Criminology, 44*(2), 156–79.

Groff, E. R., & LaVigne, N. G. (2001). Mapping an opportunity surface of residential burglary. *Journal of Research in Crime and Delinquency, 38*(3), 257–78.

Groff, E. R., Weisburd, D., & Morris, N. (2009). Where the action is at places: Examining spatio-temporal patterns of juvenile crime at places using trajectory analysis and GIS. In D. Weisburd, W. Bernasco, & G. J. N. Bruinsma (eds.), *Putting crime in its place: Units of analysis in spatial crime research* (pp. 61–86). New York: Springer.

Groff, E. R., Weisburd, D., & Yang, S.-M. (2010). Is it important to examine crime trends at a local "micro" level? A longitudinal analysis of street to street variability in crime trajectories. *Journal of Quantitative Criminology, 26*(1), 7–32.

Groff, E. R., & McCord, E. S. (2012). The role of neighborhood parks as crime generators. *Security Journal, 25*(1), 1–25.

Guerette, R. T., & Bowers, K. J. (2009). Assessing the extent of crime displacement and diffusion of benefits: A review of situational crime prevention evaluations. *Criminology, 47*(4), 1331–68.

Guerry, A-M. (1833). *Essai sur la statistique morale de la France.* Paris: Crochard.

Hagan, J., Hewitt, J. D., & Alwin, D. F. (1979). Ceremonial justice: Crime and punishment in a loosely coupled system. *Social Forces, 58*(2), 506–27.

Hakim, S., Rengert, G. F., & Shachamurove, Y. (2000). *Knowing your odds: Home burglary and the odds ratio.* (Working paper #00-14). Philadelphia: Center for Analytic Research in Economics and the Social Sciences, University of Pennsylvania.

Harcourt, B. E., & Ludwig, L. (2006). Broken windows: New evidence from New York City and a five-city social experiment. *University of Chicago Law Review, 73, 271*–320.

Harries, K. D. (1999). *Mapping crime: Principle and practice.* Washington, DC: National Institute of Justice, U. S. Department of Justice.

Harvey, L. (1987). *Myths of the Chicago School of sociology*, Aldershot, UK: Avebury.

Hawkins, J. D., Herrenkohl, T. L., Farrington, D. P., Brewer, D., Catalano, R. F., & Harachi, T. W. (1998). A review of predictors of youth violence. In R. Loeber & D. P. Farrington (eds.), *Serious and violent juvenile offenders: Risk factors and successful interventions* (pp. 106–46). Thousand Oaks, CA: Sage Publications.

Hawley, A. H. (1950). *Human ecology.* New York: Ronald Press Company.

Herbert, D. (1982). *The geography of urban crime.* London: Longman Group.

Hesseling, R. B. P. (1994). Displacement: A review of the empirical literature. In R. V. Clarke (ed.), *Crime Prevention Studies*, vol. 3 (pp. 197–230). Monsey, NY: Criminal Justice Press.

Hill, L. G., Maucione, K., & Hood, B. K. (2007). A focused approach to assessing program fidelity. *Prevention Science, 8*(1), 25–34.

Hillier, B. (1999). The common language of space: A way of looking at the social, economic and environmental functioning of cities on a common basis. Accessed November 7, 2011, at: http://www.spacesyntax.org/publications/commonlang.html.

Hillier, B. (2004). Can streets be made safe? *Urban Design International, 9*(1), 31–45.

Hillier, B., & Shu, S. C. F. (2000). Crime and urban layout: The need for evidence. In S. Ballintyne, K. Pease, & V. McLaren (eds.), *Secure foundations: Key issues in crime prevention, crime reduction and community safety* (pp. 224–48). London: Institute for Public Policy Research.

Hillier, B., & Sahbaz, O. (2005). High resolution analysis of crime patterns in urban street networks: An initial statistical sketch from an ongoing study of a London borough. Proceedings of the 5th International Space Syntax Symposium, University of Delft, Delft, The Netherlands.

Hillier, B., Leaman, A., Stansall, P., & Bedford, M. (1976). Space syntax. *Environment and Planning B, 3*(2), 147–85.

Hindelang, M. J. (1976). With a little help from their friends: Group participation in reported offending behaviour. *British Journal of Criminology, 16*(2), 109–25.

Hinkle, J. C., & Weisburd, D. (2008). The irony of broken windows: A micro-place study of the relationship between disorder, focused police crackdowns, and fear of crime. *Journal of Criminal Justice, 36*(6), 503–12.

Hipp, J. R. (2007). Block, tract, and level of aggregation: Neighborhood structure and crime and disorder as a case in point. *American Sociological Review, 72*(5), 659–80.

Hipp, J. R. (2010) Micro-structure in micro-neighborhoods: A new social distance measure, and its effect on individual and aggregated perceptions of crime and disorder. *Social Networks, 32*(2), 148–59.

Hipp, J. R., Bauer, D. J., Curran, P. J., & Bollen, K. A. (2004). Crimes of opportunity or crimes of emotion? Two explanations of seasonal change in crime. *Social Forces, 82*(4), 1333–72.

Hirschi, T. (1969). *Causes of delinquency*. Berkeley: University of California Press.

Hirschi, T. (1979). Separate but unequal is better. *Journal of Research in Crime and Delinquency, 16*(1), 34–38.

Hirschi, T. (1989). Exploring alternatives to integrated theory. In S. F. Messner, M. D. Krohn, & A. E. Liska (eds.), *Theoretical integration in the study of deviance and crime* (pp. 37–49). Albany: State University of New York Press.

Hollinger, R. C., & Dabney, D. A. (1999). Motor vehicle theft in at the shopping centre: An application of the routine activities approach. *Security Journal, 12*, 63–78.

Hunter, R. D. (1988). Environmental characteristics of convenience store robberies in the state of Florida. Paper presented at the meeting of the American Society of Criminology, Chicago.

Jacobs, J. (1961). *The death and life of great American cities.* New York: Vintage Books.

Jefferis, E. (2004). *Criminal places: A micro-level study of residential theft.* Unpublished Ph.D. dissertation. Cincinnati, OH: University of Cincinnati.

Jeffery, C. R. (1971). *Crime prevention through environmental design.* Beverly Hills, CA: Sage Publications.

Johnson, E., & Payne, J. (1986). The decision to commit a crime: An information-processing analysis. In D. B. Cornish & R. V. Clarke (eds.), *The reasoning criminal: Rational choice perspectives on offending* (pp. 170–85). New York: Springer-Verlag.

Johnson, S. D., & Bowers, K. J. (2004). The burglary as clue to the future. *European Journal of Criminology, 1*(2), 237–55.

Johnson, S., & Bowers, K. J. (2010). Permeability and burglary risk: Are cul-de-sacs safer? *Journal of Quantitative Criminology, 26*(1), 89–111.

Johnson, S. D., Bowers, K. J., & Hirschfield, A. (1997). New insights into the spatial and temporal distribution of repeat victimization. *British Journal of Criminology, 37*(2), 224–41.

Johnson, S. D., Lab, S. P., & Bowers, K. J. (2008). Stable and fluid hotspots of crime: Differentiation and identification. *Built Environment, 34*(1), 32–45.

Joiner, T. M., & Mansourian, J. A. (2009). Integrating social disorganization and routine activity theories: A look at urban crime in Morristown, New Jersey. Unpublished report, presented to the Morristown Police Department (NJ); Boston, MA: Northeastern University.

Juran, J. M. (1951). *Quality control handbook*. New York: McGraw-Hill.

Kaluzny, S. P., Vega, S. C., Cardoso, T. P., & Shelly, A. A. (1997). *S+ SpatialStats. User's manual for Windows and UNIX*. New York: Springer.

Kaufman, R. L. (1996). Comparing effects in dichotomous logistic regression: A variety of standardized coefficients. *Social Science Quarterly, 77*(1), 90–109.

Kelling, G. L., & Coles, C. M. (1996). *Fixing broken windows: Restoring order and reducing crime in our communities*. New York: Touchstone.

King County Budget Office. (2004). 2004 *King County annual growth report*. Seattle, WA: King County Government.

Klinger, D., & Bridges, G. (1997). Measurement error in calls-for-service as an indicator of crime. *Criminology, 35*(4), 705–26.

Knutsson, J. (1997). Restoring public order in a city park. In R. Homel (ed.), *Policing for prevention: Reducing crime, public intoxication and injury. Crime Prevention Studies*, vol. 7 (pp. 133–51). Monsey, NY: Criminal Justice Press.

Kobrin, S., & Schuerman, L. A. (1981). Ecological processes in the creation of delinquency areas: An update. Paper presented at the meeting of the American Sociological Association, Toronto, ON.

Koch, R. (1999). *The 80/20 principle: The secret of achieving more with less*. Naperville, IL: Nicholas Brealey Publishing.

Kornhauser, R. (1978). *Social sources of delinquency*. Chicago: University of Chicago Press.

Kubrin, C. E., & Weitzer, R. (2003). New directions in social disorganization theory. *Journal of Research in Crime and Delinquency, 40*(4), 374–402.

Kurtz, E. M., Koons, B. A., & Taylor, R. B. (1998). Land use, physical deterioration, resident-based control, and calls for service on urban streetblocks. *Justice Quarterly, 15*(1), 121–49.

Kvålseth, T. O. (1985). Cautionary note about R^2. *The American Statistician, 39*(4), 279–85.

Lab, S. P. (2007). *Crime prevention: Approaches, practices, evaluations*. Cincinnati, OH: Anderson.

LaGrange, T. C. (1999). The impact of neighborhoods, schools, and malls on the spatial distribution of property damage. *Journal of Research in Crime and Delinquency, 36*(4), 393–422.

Landau, D., & Lazarsfeld, P. F. (1968). Quetelet, Adolphe. *International Encyclopedia of the Social Sciences, 13*, 247–57.

Lander, B. (1954). *Towards an understanding of juvenile delinquency*. New York: Columbia University Press.

Lange, G. (1999). Seattle's great fire. *HistoryLink.org Online Encyclopedia of Washington State History*. Accessed November 6, 2011, at: http://www.historylink.org/index.cfm?DisplayPage=output.cfm&File_Id=715.

Laub, J. H. (2006). Edwin H. Sutherland and the Michael-Adler Report: Searching for the soul of criminology seventy years later. *Criminology, 44*(2), 235–57.

Laub, J. H., & Sampson, R. J. (2003). *Shared beginnings, divergent lives: Delinquent boys to age 70*. Cambridge, MA: Harvard University Press.

Lauritsen, J. L., Sampson, R. J., & Laub, J. H. (1991). The link between offending and victimization among adolescents. *Criminology, 29*(2), 265–91.

LaVigne, N. G. (1994). Gasoline drive-offs: Designing a less convenient environment. In R. V. Clarke (ed.), *Crime Prevention Studies*, vol. 2 (pp. 91–114). Monsey, NY: Criminal Justice Press.

LeBeau, J. L. (1987). The methods and measures of centrography and the spatial dynamics of rape. *Journal of Quantitative Criminology, 3*(2), 125–41.

Levine, N. (2005). *CrimeStat: A spatial statistics program for the analysis of crime incident locations (v. 3.0)*. Washington, DC: Ned Levine & Associates, Houston, TX, and the National Institute of Justice, U.S. Department of Justice.

Levine, N., & Wachs, M. (1986). Bus crime in Los Angeles I: Measuring the incidence. *Transportation Research, 20A*(4), 273–84.

Levitt, S. (2004). Understanding why crime fell in the 1990s: Four factors that explain the decline and six that do not. *Journal of Economic Perspectives, 18*(1), 163–90.

Lipovetsky, S. (2009). Pareto 80/20 law: Derivation via random partitioning. *International Journal of Mathematical Education in Science and Technology, 40*(2), 271–77.

Lipsey, M., Petrie, C., Weisburd, D., & Gottfredson, D. (2006). Improving evaluation of anti-crime programs: Summary of a National Research Council report. *Journal of Experimental Criminology, 2*(3), 271–307.

Lipton, D., Martinson, R., & Wilks, J. (1975). *The effectiveness of correctional treatment*. New York: Praeger.

Loeber, R., & Farrington, D. P. (eds.). (1998). *Serious and violent juvenile offenders: Risk factors and successful interventions*. Thousand Oaks, CA: Sage Publications.

Loeber, R., Farrington, D. P., Stouthamer-Loeber, M., Moffitt, T. E., Caspi, A., & Lynam, D. (2001). Male mental health problems, psychopathy, and personality traits: Key findings from the first 14 years of the Pittsburgh Youth Study. *Clinical Child and Family Psychology Review, 4*(4), 273–97.

Loftin, C., & Hill, R. H. (1974). Regional subculture and homicide: An examination of the Gastil-Hackney thesis. *American Sociological Review, 39*(5), 714–24.

Long, J. S. (1997). *Regression models for categorical and limited dependent variables*. Thousand Oaks, CA: Sage Publications.

Loukaitou-Sideris, A. (1999). Hot spots of bus stop crime: The importance of environmental attributes. *Journal of the American Planning Association, 65*(4), 395–411.

Lum, C. (2003). *The spatial relationship between street-level drug activity and violence*. Unpublished Ph.D. dissertation. College Park: University of Maryland.

Macionis, J. J., & Plummer, K. (2005). *Sociology: A global introduction*. Upper Saddle River, NJ: Pearson Prentice Hall.

MacKenzie, D. (2006). *What works in corrections? Reducing the criminal activities of offenders and delinquents*. New York: Cambridge University Press.

Madensen, T. D., & Eck, J. E. (2008). Violence in bars: Exploring the impact of place manager decision-making. *Crime Prevention and Community Safety, 10*, 111–25.

Madensen, T. D., & Eck, J. E. (2012). Crime places and place management. In F. T. Cullen & P. Wilcox (eds.), *The Oxford handbook of criminological theory*. New York: Oxford University Press.

Maguire, M. (1982). *Burglary in a dwelling.* London: Heinemann.

Maguire, E. R., & Katz, C. M. (2002). Community policing, loose coupling, and sensemaking in American police agencies. *Justice Quarterly, 19*(3), 503–36.

Maimon, D., & Browning, C. R. (2010). Unstructured socializing, collective efficacy, and violent behavior among urban youth. *Criminology, 48*(2), 443–74.

Maltz, M. D., Gordon, A. C., & Friedman, W. (1990 [2000]). *Mapping crime in its community setting: Event geography analysis.* Originally published, New York: Springer-Verlag.

Manning, P. K. (1982). Producing drama: Symbolic communication and the police. *Symbolic Interaction, 5*(2), 223–42.

Martinson, R. (1974). What works? Questions and answers about prison reform. *Public Interest, 35*, 22–54.

Matthews, R. (1990). Developing more effective strategies for curbing prostitution. *Security Journal, 1*, 182–87.

Mayhew, H. (1851 [1950]). *London's underworld. Being selections from "Those that will not work," the 4th vol. of "London labour and the London poor."* Edited by P. Quennell. London: Spring Books.

Mayhew, P., Clarke, R. V., Sturman, A., & Hough, M. (1976). *Crime as opportunity*. Home Office Research Study, vol. 34. London: Home Office, H.M. Stationary Office.

McArdle, J. J., & Epstein, D. (1987). Latent growth curves within developmental structural equation models. *Child Development, 58*(1), 110–33.

McNulty, T. L., & Holloway, S. R. (2000). Race, crime, and public housing in Atlanta: Testing a conditional effect hypothesis. *Social Forces, 79*(2), 707–29.

Meinert, C. L. (1986). *Clinical trials: Design, conduct, and analysis.* New York: Oxford University Press.

Meredith, W., & Tisak, J. (1990). Latent curve analysis. *Psychometrika, 55*(1), 107–22.

Merton, R. K. (1938). Social structure and anomie. *American Sociological Review, 3*(5), 672–82.

Merton, R. K. (1968). *Social theory and social structure.* New York: Free Press.

Messner, S. F. (1983). Regional and racial effects on the urban homicide rate: The subculture of violence revisited. *American Journal of Sociology 88*(5), 997–1007.

Messner, S. F., & Anselin, L. (2004). Spatial analysis of homicide with areal data. In M. F. Goodchild & D. G. Janelle (eds.), *Spatially integrated social science* (pp. 127–44). New York: Oxford University Press.

Metropolitan Police Department. (2010). Citywide crime statistics, annual totals 1993–2009. Accessed November 6, 2011 at: http://mpdc.dc.gov/mpdc/cwp/view,a,1239,q,547256,mpdcNav_GID,1556.asp.

Mitchell, O., Wilson, D. B., & MacKenzie, D. L. (2007). Does incarceration-based drug treatment reduce recidivism? A meta-analytic synthesis of the research. *Journal of Experimental Criminology, 3*(4), 353–75.

Moffitt, T. E. (1993). Adolescence-limited and life-course persistent antisocial behavior: A developmental taxonomy. *Psychological Review, 100*(4), 674–701.

Moffitt, T. E. (2006). A review of research on the taxonomy of life-course persistent versus adolescence-limited antisocial behavior. In F. T Cullen, J.P. Wright, & M. Coleman (eds.), *Taking stock: The status of criminological theory. Advances in Criminological Theory*, vol. 15 (pp. 277–312). New Brunswick, NJ: Transaction Publishers.

Moffitt, T. E., Lynam, D. R., & Silva, P. A. (1994). Neuropsychological tests predicting persistent male delinquency. *Criminology, 32*(2), 277–300.

Morenoff, J. D., & Sampson, R. J. (1997). Violent crime and the spatial dynamics of neighborhood transition: Chicago, 1970–1990. *Social Forces, 76*(1), 31–64.

Morenoff, J. D., Sampson, R. J., & Raudenbush, S. W. (2001). Neighborhood inequality, collective efficacy, and the spatial dynamics of urban violence. *Criminology, 39*(3), 517–60.

Morgan, F. (2001). Repeat burglary in a Perth suburb: Indicator of short-term or long-term risk. In G. Farrell & K. Pease (eds.), *Repeat victimisation. Crime Prevention Studies*, vol. 12 (pp. 83–118). Monsey, NY: Criminal Justice Press.

Morris, T. (1957). *The criminal area. A study in social ecology*. London: Routledge & Kegan Paul.

Muthén, B. (1989). Latent variable modeling in heterogeneous populations. *Psychometrika, 54*(4), 557–85.

Muthén, B. (2001). Second general structural equation modeling with a combination of categorical and continuous latent variables: New opportunities for latent class-latent growth modeling. In L. M. Collins & A. G. Sayers (eds.), *New methods for the analysis of change* (pp. 291–322). Washington, DC: American Psychological Association.

Nagelkerke, N. J. D. (1991). A note on the general definition of the coefficient of determination. *Biometrika, 78*(3), 791–92.

Nagin, D. S. (1999). Analyzing developmental trajectories: A semiparametric group-based approach. *Psychological Methods, 4*(2), 139–57.

Nagin, D. (2005). *Group-based modeling of development over the life course*. Cambridge, MA: Harvard University Press.

Nagin, D. S., & Land, K. C. (1993). Age, criminal careers, and population heterogeneity: Specification and estimation of a nonparametric, mixed Poisson model. *Criminology, 31*(3), 327–62.

Nagin, D. S., & Tremblay, R. E. (1999). Trajectories of boys' physical aggression, opposition, and hyperactivity on the path to physically violent and nonviolent juvenile delinquency. *Child Development, 70*(5), 1181–96.

Nagin, D. S., & Tremblay, R. E. (2001). Parental and early childhood predictors of persistent physical aggression in boys from kindergarten to high school. *Archives of General Psychiatry, 58*(4), 389–94.

Nagin, D. S., Farrington D. P., & Moffitt, T. E. (1995). Life-course trajectories of different types of offenders. *Criminology, 33*(1), 111–39.

Nagin, D. S., Cullen, F. T., & Jonson, C. L. (2009). Imprisonment and reoffending. In M. Tonry (ed.), *Crime and Justice: A Review of Research*, vol. 38. (pp. 115–200). Chicago: University of Chicago Press.

National Research Council. (2004). *Fairness and effectiveness in policing: The evidence*. Committee to Review Research on Police Policy and Practices. Edited by W. Skogan & K. Frydl. Committee on Law and Justice, Division of Behavioral and Social Sciences and Education. Washington, DC: National Academies Press.

Nettler, G. (1978). *Explaining crime*. 2nd ed. Montreal: McGraw-Hill.

Newell, G. (1956). *Totem tales of old Seattle*. Seattle: Superior Publishing Company.

Newman, O. (1972). *Defensible space: Crime prevention through environmental design*. New York: Macmillan.

New York Police Department (2010). Compstat report. Accessed November 6, 2011 at: http://www.nyc.gov/html/nypd/downloads/pdf/crime_statistics/cscity.pdf.

Oberwittler, D., & Wikström, P.-O. H. (2009). Why small is better: Advancing the study of the role of behavioral contexts in crime causation. In D. Weisburd, W. Bernasco, & G. J. N. Bruinsma (eds.), *Putting crime in its place: Units of analysis in geographic criminology* (pp. 35–60). New York: Springer.

Office of Financial Management. (2008). April 1 population of cities, towns, and counties used for allocation of selected state revenues, state of Washington. Olympia, WA: Office of Financial Management.

Office of Intergovernmental Relations. (2008). The greater Seattle datasheet. Accessed November 6, 2011, at: http://www.cityofseattle.net/oir/datasheet/Datasheet2008.pdf.

Orton, J. D., & Weick, K. E. (1990). Loosely coupled systems: A reconceptualization. *Academy of Management Review, 15*(2), 203–23.

Osgood, D. W., Wilson, J. K., O'Malley, P. M., Bachman, J. G., Johnston, L. D. (1996). Routine activities and individual deviant behavior. *American Sociological Review, 61*(4), 635–55.

Painter, K. A., & Farrington, D. P. (1997). The crime reducing effect of improved street lighting: The Dudley project. In R. V. Clarke (ed.), *Situational crime prevention: Successful case studies*, 2nd ed. (pp. 209–26). Albany, NY: Harrow & Heston Publishers.

Painter, K. A., & Farrington, D. P. (1999). Street lighting and crime: Diffusion of benefits in the Stoke-On-Trent project. In K. Painter & N. Tilley (eds.), *Surveillance of public space: CCTV, street lighting, and crime prevention. Crime Prevention Studies*, vol. 10 (pp. 77–122). Monsey, NY: Willow Tree Press.

Parent-Duchâtelet, A. J. B. (1837). *Prostitution dans la ville de Paris*. Paris: J.B. Baillière.

Pareto, V. (1909). *Manuel d'économie politique*. Vol. 7 of *Oeuvres complètes*. Geneva: Droz.

Park, R. E. (1925 [1967]). The city: Suggestions for the investigation of human behaviour in the urban environment. In R. E. Park & E. W. Burgess (eds.), *The city: Suggestions for the investigation of human behaviour in the urban environment* (pp. 1–46). Chicago: University of Chicago Press.

Pease, K. (1998). *Repeat victimization: Taking stock*. London: Home Office.

Pease, K. (1999). A review of street lighting evaluations: Crime reduction effects. In K. Painter & N. Tilley (eds.), *Surveillance of public space: CCTV, street lighting and crime prevention. Crime Prevention Studies*, vol. 10 (pp. 47–76). Monsey, NY: Willow Tree Press.

Peng, C.-Y. J., & Nichols, R. N. (2003). Using multinomial logistic regression to predict adolescent behavioral risk. *Journal of Modern Applied Statistical Methods, 2*(1), 177–88.

Perkins, D., Wandersman, A., Rich, R., & Taylor, R. B. (1993). The physical environment of street crime: Defensible space, territoriality and incivilities. *Journal of Environmental Psychology, 13*(1), 29–49.

Perkins, D. D., Florin, P., Rich, R. C., Wandersman, A., & Chavis, D. M. (1990). Participation and the social and physical environment of residential blocks: Crime and community context. *American Journal of Community Psychology, 18*(1), 83–115.

Pierce, G., Spaar, S., & Briggs, L. R. (1988). *The character of police work: Strategic and tactical implications.* Boston, MA: Center for Applied Social Research, Northeastern University.

Poyner, B., & Webb, B. (1987). *Successful crime prevention: Case studies.* London: Tavistock Institute of Human Relations.

Poyner, B., Warne, C., Webb, B., Woodall, R., & Meakin, R. (1988). *Preventing violence to staff.* London: H.M. Stationery Office.

Putnam, R. D. (2001). *Bowling alone: The collapse and revival of American community.* New York: Simon & Schuster.

Pyle, G. F. (1976). Spatial and temporal aspects of crime in Cleveland, Ohio. *American Behavioral Scientist, 20*(2), 175–98.

Quetelet, A. J. (1831 [1984]). *Research on the propensity for crime at different ages.* Translated by S. F. Test Sylvester. Cincinnati, OH: Anderson Publishing Co.

Raine, A. (1993). Features of borderline personality and violence. *Journal of Clinical Psychology, 49*(2), 277–81.

Ratcliffe, J. H. (2004). Geocoding crime and a first estimate of a minimum acceptable hit rate. *International Journal of Geographical Information Science, 18*(1), 61–72.

Ratcliffe, J. H. (2005). Detecting spatial movement of intra-region crime patterns over time. *Journal of Quantitative Criminology, 21*(1), 103–23.

Ratcliffe, J. H., & Rengert, G. F. (2008). Near-repeat patterns in Philadelphia shootings. *Security Journal, 21*, 58–76.

Ratcliffe, J. H., Taniguchi, T., Groff, E. R., & Wood, J. D. (2011). The Philadelphia Foot Patrol Experiment: A randomized controlled trial of police patrol effectiveness in violent crime hotspots. *Criminology, 49*(3), 795–831.

Raudenbush, S. (2001). Toward a coherent framework for comparing trajectories of individual change. In L. M. Collins & A. G. Sayers (eds.), *New methods for the analysis of change* (pp. 35–63). Washington, DC: American Psychological Association.

Rawson, R.W. (1839). An inquiry into the statistics of crime in England and Wales. *Journal of the Statistical Society of London, 2*, 316–44.

Reiss, A. J., Jr. (1986). Why are communities important in understanding crime? In M. Tonry & N. Morris (eds.), *Communities and crime. Crime and Justice: A Review of Research*, vol. 8 (pp. 1–33). Chicago: University of Chicago Press.

Reiss, A. J., Jr. (1988). Co-offending and criminal careers. In M. Tonry & N. Morris (eds.), *Crime and Justice: A Review of Research*, vol. 10. (pp. 117–70). Chicago: University of Chicago Press.

Reiss, A. J., Jr., & Tonry, M. (1986). Preface. In A. J. Reiss Jr. & M. Tonry (eds.), *Communities and crime. Crime and Justice: A Review of Research*, vol. 8 (pp. vii–viii). Chicago: University of Chicago Press.

Reiss, A. J., Jr., & Farrington, D. P. (1991). Advancing knowledge about co-offending: Results from a prospective longitudinal survey of London males. *Journal of Criminal Law and Criminology, 82*(2), 360–95.

Reiss, A. J., Jr., & Roth, J. A. (eds.). (1993). *Understanding and preventing violence.* Panel on the Understanding and Control of Violent Behavior, Committee on Law and Justice,

Commission on Behavioral and Social Sciences and Education, National Research Council. Washington, DC: National Academy Press.

Rengert, G. F. (1980). Spatial aspects of criminal behavior. In D. E. Georges-Abeyie & K. D. Harries (eds.), *Crime: A spatial perspective* (pp. 47–57). New York: Columbia University Press.

Rengert, G. F. (1981). Burglary in Philadelphia: A critique of an opportunity structure model. In P. Brantingham & P. Brantingham (eds.), *Environmental criminology* (pp. 189–201). Beverly Hills, CA: Sage Publications.

Rengert, G., & Wasilchick, J. (2000). *Suburban burglary*. Springfield, IL: Charles C. Thomas Publisher.

Rengert, G. F., & Lockwood, B. (2009). Geographical units of analysis and the analysis of crime. In D. Weisburd, W. Bernasco, & G. J. N. Bruinsma (eds.), *Putting crime in its place: Units of analysis in spatial crime research* (pp. 109–22). New York: Springer.

Reppetto, T. (1976). Crime prevention and the displacement phenomenon. *Crime & Delinquency, 22*(2), 166–77.

Reynald, D., Averdijk, M., Elffers, H., & Bernasco, W. (2008). Do social barriers affect urban crime trips? The effects of ethnic and economic neighbourhood compositions on the flow of crime in The Hague, The Netherlands. *Built Environment, 34*(1), 21–31.

Reynolds, H. T. (1977). *Analysis of nominal data.* 2nd ed. Beverly Hills, CA: Sage Publications.

Rice, K. J., & Smith, W. R. (2002). Sociological models of automotive theft: Integrating routine activity and social disorganization approaches. *Journal of Research in Crime and Delinquency, 39*(3), 304–36.

Robins, L. N. (1966). *Deviant children grown up: A sociological and psychiatric study of sociopathic personality.* Oxford: Williams & Wilkins.

Robins, J. M. (1989). The control of confounding by intermediate variables. *Statistics in Medicine, 8,* 679–701.

Robins, L. N., & Ratcliff, K. S. (1978). *Long-range outcomes associated with school truancy.* Washington, DC: Public Health Service.

Robinson, W. S. (1950). Ecological correlations and the behavior of individuals. *American Sociological Review, 15*(3), 351–57.

Roeder, K., Lynch, K. G., & Nagin, D. S. (1999). Modeling uncertainty in latent class membership: A case study in criminology. *Journal of the American Statistical Association, 94*(447), 766–76.

Roman, C. G. (2002). *Schools as generators of crime: Routine activities and the sociology of place.* Unpublished Ph.D. dissertation. Washington, DC: American University.

Roman, C. G. (2005). Routine activities of youth and neighborhood violence: Spatial modeling of place, time, and crime. In F. Wang (ed.), *Geographic information systems and crime analysis* (pp. 293–310). Hershey, PA: Idea Group.

Roncek, D. W. (2000). Schools and crime. In V. Goldsmith, P. G. McGuire, J. H. Mollenkopf, & T. A. Ross (eds.), *Analyzing crime patterns: Frontiers of practice* (pp. 153–65). Thousand Oaks, CA: Sage Publications.

Roncek, D. W., & Bell, R. (1981). Bars, blocks, and crimes. *Journal of Environmental Systems, 11*(1), 35–47.

Roncek, D. W., & Maier, P. A. (1991). Bars, blocks, and crime revisited: Linking the theory of routine activities to the empiricism of "hot spots." *Criminology, 29*(4), 725–53.

Rosenfeld, R., Fornango, R., & Rengifo, A. (2007). The impact of order-maintenance policing on New York City robbery and homicide rates: 1988–2001. *Criminology, 45*(2), 355–84.

Roseth, R. (2007). University of Washington achieves $1 billion research milestone. University of Washington news. Accessed November 6, 2011, at: http://www.washington.edu/news/archive/id/35716.

Rowlingson, B. S., & Diggle, P. J. (1993). Splancs: Spatial point pattern analysis code in S-Plus. *Computers and Geosciences, 19*(5), 627–55.

Sampson, R. J. (1985). Neighborhood and crime: The structural determinants of personal victimization. *Journal of Research in Crime and Delinquency, 22*(1), 7–40.

Sampson, R. J. (1993). Linking time and place: Dynamic contextualism and the future of criminological inquiry. *Journal of Research in Crime and Delinquency, 30*(4), 426–44.

Sampson, R. J. (2004). Neighborhood and community: Collective efficacy and community safety. *New Economy, 11*, 106–13.

Sampson, R. J. (2009). Racial stratification and durable tangle of neighborhood inequality. *Annals of the American Academy of Political and Social Sciences, 621*, 260–80.

Sampson, R. J., & Groves, W. B. (1989). Community structure and crime: Testing social-disorganization theory. *American Journal of Sociology, 94*(4), 774–802.

Sampson, R. J., & Laub, J. (1993). *Crime in the making: Pathways and turning points through life*. Cambridge, MA: Harvard University Press.

Sampson, R. J., & Wilson, W. J. (1995). Toward a theory of race, crime, and urban inequality. In J. Hagan & R. D. Peterson (eds.), *Crime and inequality* (pp. 37–54). Stanford, CA: Stanford University Press.

Sampson, R. J., & Morenoff, J. D. (1997). Ecological perspectives on the neighborhood context of urban poverty: Past and present. In J. Brooks-Gunn, G. J. Duncan, & J. L. Aber (eds.), *Neighborhood poverty: Policy implications in studying poverty* (pp. 1–22). New York: Russell Sage Foundation.

Sampson, R. J., & Raudenbush, S. W. (1999). Systematic social observation of public spaces: A new look at disorder in urban neighborhoods. *American Journal of Sociology, 105*(3), 603–51.

Sampson, R. J., & Laub, J. H. (2003). Life-course desisters? Trajectories of crime among delinquent boys followed to age 70. *Criminology, 41*(3), 301–40.

Sampson, R. J., & Lauritsen, J. L. (2004). Violent victimization and offending: Individual-, situational-, and community-level risk factors. In A. J. Reiss Jr. & J. A. Roth (eds.), *Understanding and preventing violence*, vol. 3 (pp. 1–114). Panel on the Understanding and Control of Violent Behavior, Committee on Law and Justice, Commission on Behavioral and Social Sciences and Education, National Research Council. Washington, DC: National Academy Press.

Sampson, R. J., & Raudenbush, S. W. (2004). Seeing disorder: Neighborhood stigma and the construction of "broken windows." *Social Science Quarterly, 67*(4), 319–42.

Sampson, R. J., & Morenoff, J. D. (2004). Spatial (dis)advantage and homicide in Chicago neighborhoods. In M. F. Goodchild & D. G. Janelle (eds.), *Spatially integrated social science* (pp. 145–70). Oxford: Oxford University Press.

Sampson, R. J., & Laub, J. H. (2005). A life-course view of the development of crime. *Annals of the American Academy of Political and Social Sciences, 602*, 12–45.

Sampson, R. J., Raudenbush, S. W., & Earls, F. (1997). Neighborhoods and violent crime: A multilevel study of collective efficacy. *Science, 277*(5328), 918–24.

Sampson, R. J., Morenoff, J. D., & Gannon-Rowley, J. (2002). Assessing "neighborhood effects": Social processes and new directions in research. *Annual Review of Sociology, 28,* 443–78.

Sampson, R. J., Laub, J. H., & Eggleston, E. P. (2004). On the robustness and validity or groups. *Journal of Quantitative Criminology, 20*(1), 37–42.

Schmid, C. F. (1960a). Urban crime areas: Part I. *American Sociological Review, 25*(4), 527–42.

Schmid, C. F. (1960b). Urban crime areas: Part II. *American Sociological Review, 25*(5), 655–78.

Schmitt, R. C. (1957). Density, delinquency and crime in Honolulu. *Sociology and Social Research, 41,* 274–76.

Schneider, V. W., & Wiersema, B. (1990). Limits and use of the UCR. In D. L. MacKenzie, P. J. Baunach, & R. R. Roberg (eds.), *Measuring crime: Large-scale, long range efforts* (pp. 21–48). Albany: State University of New York Press.

Schneider, R. H., & Kitchen, T. (2007). *Crime prevention and the built environment.* New York: Routledge.

Schuerman, L., & Kobrin, S. (1986). Community careers in crime. In A. J. Reiss Jr. & M. Tonry (eds.), *Communities and crime. Crime and Justice: A Review of Research*, vol. 8 (pp. 67–100). Chicago: University of Chicago Press.

Seattle City Government (2009). Quick information: Area of the city [Electronic Version]. Accessed November 6, 2011, at: http://www.cityofseattle.net/CityArchives/Facts/info.htm.

Seattle Post-Intelligencer. (2005). Redmond council OKs Microsoft expansion. *Seattle Post-Intelligencer*, May 5.

Sechrest, L., White, S. O., & Brown, E. D. (1979). *The rehabilitation of criminal offenders: Problems and prospects.* Washington, DC: National Academies Press.

Shadish, W. R., Cook, T. D., & Campbell, D. T. (2002). *Experimental and quasi-experimental designs for generalized causal inference.* Boston: Houghton Mifflin Company.

Shaw, C. R. (with F. M. Zorbaugh, H. D. McKay, & L. S. Cottrell). (1929). *Delinquency areas: A study of the geographical distribution of school truants, juvenile delinquents, and adult offenders in Chicago.* Chicago: University of Chicago Press.

Shaw, C. R., & McKay, H. D. (1942 [1969]). *Juvenile delinquency and urban areas. A study of rates of delinquency in relation to differential characteristics of local communities in American cities.* Rev. ed. Chicago: University of Chicago Press.

Sherman, L. W. (1995). Hot spots of crime and criminal careers of places. In J. Eck & D. Weisburd (eds.), *Crime and place. Crime Prevention Studies*, vol. 4 (pp. 35–52). Monsey, NY: Willow Tree Press.

Sherman, L. W. (2007). The power few: Experimental criminology and the reduction of harm *Journal of Experimental Criminology, 3*(4), 299–321.

Sherman, L. W., & Weisburd, D. (1995). General deterrent effects of police patrol in crime "hot spots": A randomized, controlled trial. *Justice Quarterly, 12*(4), 625–48.

Sherman, L. W., Gartin, P., & Buerger, M. E. (1989). Hot spots of predatory crime: Routine activities and the criminology of place. *Criminology, 27*(1), 27–55.

Skardhamar, T. (2010). Distinguishing facts and artifacts in group-based modeling. *Criminology, 48*(1), 295–320.

Skogan, W. G. (1986). Fear of crime and neighborhood change. In A. J. Reiss Jr. & M. Tonry (eds.), *Communities and crime. Crime and Justice: A Review of Research*, vol. 8 (pp. 203–29). Chicago: University of Chicago Press.

Skogan, W. G. (1987). *Disorder and community decline.* Final report. Washington, DC: National Institute of Justice, U.S. Department of Justice.

Skogan, W. G. (1990). *Disorder and decline: Crime and the spiral of decay in American cities.* New York: Free Press.

Skogan, W. G., & Annan, S. (1994). Drugs and public housing: Toward an effective police response. In D. MacKenzie & C. D. Uchida (eds.), *Drugs and crime: Evaluating public policy initiatives* (pp. 129–48). Thousand Oaks, CA: Sage Publications.

Smargiassi, A., Berrada, K., Fortier, I., & Kosatsky, T. (2006). Traffic intensity, dwelling value, and hospital admissions for respiratory disease among the elderly in Montreal (Canada): A case-control analysis. *Journal of Epidemiology and Community Health, 60*(6), 507–12.

Smith, D. A. (1986). The neighborhood context of police behavior. In A. J. Reiss Jr. & M. Tonry (eds.), *Communities and crime. Crime and Justice: A Review of Research*, vol. 8 (pp. 313–41). Chicago: University of Chicago Press.

Smith, D. A., & Jarjoura, G. R. (1988). Social structure and criminal victimization. *Journal of Research in Crime and Delinquency, 25*(1), 27–52.

Smith, W. R., Frazee, S. G., & Davison, E. L. (2000). Furthering the integration of routine activity and social disorganization theories: Small units of analysis and the study of street robbery as a diffusion process. *Criminology, 38*(2), 489–523.

Snodgrass, J. (1976). Clifford R. Shaw and Henry D. McKay: Chicago criminologists. *British Journal of Criminology, 16*(1), 1–19.

Snyder, H. N., & Sickmund, M. (2006). *Juvenile offenders and victims:* 2006 *national report.* Washington, DC: Office of Juvenile Justice and Crime Prevention, U.S. Department of Justice.

Spelman, W. (1995). Criminal careers of public places. In J. E. Eck & D. Weisburd (eds.), *Crime and place. Crime Prevention Studies*, vol. 4 (pp. 115–44). Monsey, NY: Willow Tree Press.

Stark, R. (1987). Deviant places: A theory of the ecology of crime. *Criminology, 25*(4), 893–909.

Stephenson, L. K. (1974). Spatial dispersion of intra-urban juvenile delinquency. *Journal of Geography, 73*(3), 20–26.

St. Jean, P. K. B. (2007). *Pockets of crime: Broken windows, collective efficacy, and the criminal point of view.* Chicago: University of Chicago Press.

Stoks, F. G. (1981). *Assessing urban public space environments for danger of violent crime.* Unpublished Ph.D. dissertation. Seattle: University of Washington.

Sutherland, E. H. (1947). *Principles of criminology: A sociological theory of criminal behavior.* New York: J.B. Lippincott Company.

Sykes, G. M., & Matza, D. (1957). Techniques of neutralization: A theory of delinquency. *American Sociological Review, 22*(6), 664–70.

Tabachnick, B. G., & Fidell, L. S. (2001). *Using multivariate statistics.* 4th ed. Boston: Allyn & Bacon.

Taylor, R. B. (1988). *Human territorial functioning: An empirical, evolutional perspective on individual and small group territorial cognitions, behaviors and consequences.* Cambridge: Cambridge University Press.

Taylor, R. B. (1996). Neighborhood responses to disorder and local attachments: The systemic model of attachment, social disorganization, and neighborhood use value. *Sociological Forum, 11*(1), 41–74.

Taylor, R. B. (1997). Social order and disorder of street blocks and neighborhoods: Ecology, microecology, and the systemic model of social disorganization. *Journal of Research in Crime and Delinquency, 34*(1), 113–55.

Taylor, R. B. (1998). Crime and small-scale places: What we know, what we can prevent, and what else we need to know. In R. B. Taylor, G. Bazemore, B. Boland, T. R. Clear, R. P. J. Corbett, J. Feinblatt, G. Berman, M. Sviridoff, & C. Stone (eds.), *Crime and place: Plenary papers of the* 1997 *Conference on Criminal Justice Research and Evaluation* (pp. 1–22). Washington, DC: National Institute of Justice, U.S. Department of Justice.

Taylor, R. B. (1999). *Crime, grime, fear, and decline: A longitudinal look*. Research in Brief. Washington, DC: National Institute of Justice, U.S. Department of Justice.

Taylor, R. B. (2001). *Breaking away from broken windows: Baltimore neighborhoods and the nationwide fight against crime, grime, fear and decline*. Boulder, CO: Westview Press.

Taylor, R. B. (In press). *A general metatheory of crime and communities*. New York: New York University Press.

Taylor, R. B., Gottfredson, S. D., & Brower, S. (1984). Block crime and fear: Defensible space, local social ties, and territorial functioning. *Journal of Research in Crime and Delinquency, 21*(4), 303–31.

Taylor, R. B., Kelly, C. E., & Salvatore, C. (2010). Where concerned citizens perceive police as more responsive to troublesome teen groups: Theoretical implications for political economy, incivilities and policing. *Policing & Society, 20*(2), 143–71.

Taylor, R. B., Koons, B. A., Kurtz, E. M., Greene, J. R., & Perkins, D. D. (1995). Street blocks with more nonresidential land use have more physical deterioration: Evidence from Baltimore and Philadelphia. *Urban Affairs Review, 31*(1), 120–36.

Thomas, W. I. (1966). *On social organization and social personality. Selected papers*. Edited by M. Janovitz. Chicago: University of Chicago Press.

Thomas, J. (1984). Some aspects of negotiated order, loose coupling, and mesostructure in maximum security prisons. *Symbolic Interaction, 7*(2), 213–31.

Thrasher, F.M. (1927 [1963]). *The gang: A study of* 1,313 *gangs in Chicago*. Chicago: Phoenix Books.

Tilley, N. (2009). *Crime prevention*. Devon: Willan Publishing.

Tita, G. E., & Radil, S. M. (2010). Making space for theory: The challenges of theorizing space and place for spatial analysis in criminology. *Journal of Quantitative Criminology, 26*(4), 467–79.

Tonry, M., & Farrington, D. P. (1995). Strategic approaches to crime prevention. In M. Tonry & D. P. Farrington (eds.), Building a safer society: Strategic approaches to crime prevention. *Crime and Justice: A Review of Research*, vol. 19 (pp. 1–20). Chicago: Chicago University Press.

Townsley, M., Homel, R., & Chaseling, J. (2003). Infectious burglaries: A test of the near repeat hypothesis. *British Journal of Criminology, 43*(3), 615–33.

Trasler, G. (1993). Conscience, opportunity, rational choice, and crime. In R. V. Clarke & M. Felson (eds.), *Routine activity and rational choice. Advances in Criminological Theory*, vol. 5 (pp. 305–22). New Brunswick, NJ: Transaction Publishers.

Travis, J., & Waul, M. (2002). *Reflections on the crime decline: Lessons for the future?* Proceedings from the Urban Institute Crime Decline Forum. Washington, DC: The Urban Institute.

Tremblay, P. (1986). The stability of punishment: A follow-up of Blumstein's hypothesis. *Journal of Quantitative Criminology, 2*(2), 157–80.

Turner, S. (1969) The ecology of delinquency. In T. Sellin & E. M. Wolfgang (eds.), *Delinquency: Selected studies* (pp. 27–60). New York: John Wiley & Sons.

Turner, W. (1986). A clash over aid effort on the first "skid row." *New York Times*, December 2, p. A20.

Unger, D., & Wandersman, A. (1983). Neighboring and its role in block organizations: An exploratory report. *American Journal of Community Psychology, 11*(3), 291–300.

Uniform Crime Report. (2005). *Crime in the United States, 2004.* Washington, DC: Federal Bureau of Investigation, U.S. Department of Justice.

U.S. Census Bureau (Cartographer). (1990). *Census 1900: Summary Tape File 1 (SF1).* Washington, DC: Author.

U.S. Census Bureau (1994). *Geographic areas reference manual.* Washington, DC: U.S. Department of Commerce.

U.S. Census Bureau (Cartographer). (2000). *Census 2000: Summary Tape File 1 (SF1).* Washington, DC: Author.

U.S. Census Bureau. (2005). *American Community Survey.* Washington, DC: Author.

U.S. Department of Housing and Urban Development website. http://portal.hud.gov/ portal/page/portal/HUD/topics/rental_assistance/phprog.

van Wilselm, J. (2009). Urban streets as micro contexts to commit violence. In D. Weisburd, W. Bernasco, & G. J. N. Bruinsma (eds.), *Putting crime in its place: Units of analysis in spatial crime research* (pp. 199–216). New York: Springer.

Veysey, B. M., & Messner, S. F. (1999). Further testing of social disorganization theory: An elaboration of Sampson and Groves's "community structure and crime." *Journal of Research in Crime and Delinquency, 36*(2), 156–74.

Vold, G. B., Bernard, T. J., & Snipes, J. B. (2002). *Theoretical criminology.* 5th ed. New York: Oxford University Press.

Warner, B. D., & Pierce, G. L. (1993). Rexamining social disorganization theory using calls to the police as a measure of crime. *Criminology, 31*(4), 493–518.

Webb, B., & Laycock, G. (1992). *Tackling car crime: The nature and extent of the problem.* Police Research Group, Crime Prevention Unit Paper 32. London: Home Office.

Weisburd, D. (2002). From criminals to criminal contexts: Reorienting criminal justice research and policy. In E. Waring & D. Weisburd (eds.), *Crime and social organization. Advances in Criminological Theory*, vol. 10 (pp. 197–216). New Brunswick, NJ: Transaction Publishers.

Weisburd, D. (2003). Ethical practice and evaluation of interventions in crime and justice: The moral imperative for randomized trials. *Evaluation Review, 27*(3), 336–54.

Weisburd, D. (2008). Place-based policing. *Ideas in American Policing*. Washington, DC: Police Foundation.

Weisburd, D., & Green, L. (1994). Defining the drug market: The case of the Jersey City DMA system. In D. L. MacKenzie & C. D. Uchida (eds.), *Drugs and crime: Evaluating public policy initiatives* (pp. 61–76). Thousand Oaks, CA: Sage Publications.

Weisburd, D., & Green, L. (1995). Policing drug hot spots: The Jersey City drug market analysis experiment. *Justice Quarterly, 12*(4), 711–35.

Weisburd, D., & McEwen, T. (1997). Introduction: Crime mapping and crime prevention. In D. Weisburd & T. McEwen (eds.), *Crime mapping and crime prevention. Crime Prevention Studies*, vol. 8 (pp. 1–23). Monsey, NY: Criminal Justice Press.

Weisburd, D., & Mazerolle, L. G. (2000). Crime and disorder in drug hot spots: Implications for theory and practice in policing. *Police Quarterly, 3*(3), 331–49.

Weisburd, D., & Eck, J. E. (2004). What can the police do to reduce crime, disorder, and fear? *Annals of the American Academy of Political and Social Science, 593*, 42–65.

Weisburd, D., & Braga, A. A. (2006). Hot spots policing as a model for police innovation. In D. Weisburd & A. A. Braga (eds.), *Police innovation: Contrasting perspectives* (pp. 225–44). New York: Cambridge University Press.

Weisburd, D., & Britt, C. (2007). *Statistics in criminal justice*. 3rd ed. New York: Springer.

Weisburd, D., & Piquero, A. R. (2008). How well do criminologists explain crime? Statistical modeling in published studies. In M. Tonry (ed.), *Crime and Justice: A Review of Research*, vol. 37 (pp. 453–502). Chicago: University of Chicago Press.

Weisburd, D., & Telep, C. W. (2010). The efficiency of place-based policing. *Journal of Police Studies, 17*, 247–62.

Weisburd, D., & Hinkle, J. (2012). The importance of randomized experiments in evaluating crime prevention. In B. C. Welsh & D. P. Farrington (eds.), *The Oxford handbook on crime prevention* (pp. 445–464). New York: Oxford University Press.

Weisburd, D., & Telep, C. W. (2012). Spatial displacement and diffusion of crime control benefits revisited: New evidence on why crime doesn't just move around the corner. In N. Tilley & G. Farrell (eds.), *The reasoning criminologist: Essays in honour of Ronald V. Clarke*, (pp. 142–159). New York: Routledge.

Weisburd, D., & Amram, S. (Forthcoming). The law of concentrations of crime at place: The case of Tel Aviv. *Police Practice and Research.*

Weisburd, D., Maher, L. & Sherman, L. (1992). Contrasting crime general and crime specific theory: The case of hot spots of crime. In F. Adler & W. S. Laufer (eds.), *Advances in Criminological Theory*, vol. 4 (pp. 45–70). New Brunswick, NJ: Transaction Publishers.

Weisburd, D., Waring, E., & Chayet, E. (1995). Specific deterrence in a sample of offenders convicted of white collar crimes. *Criminology, 33*, 587–607.

Weisburd, D. L., Lum, C., & Yang, S.-M. (2004). *The criminal careers of places: A longitudinal study*. Washington, DC: National Institute of Justice, U.S. Department of Justice.

Weisburd, D., Morris, N.A., & Ready, J. (2008). Risk-focused policing at places: An experimental evaluation. *Justice Quarterly, 25*(1), 163–99.

Weisburd, D., Bernasco, W., & Bruinsma, G. J. N. (eds.). (2009). *Putting crime in its place: Units of analysis in spatial crime research*. New York: Springer-Verlag.

Weisburd, D., Bruinsma, G. J. N., & Bernasco, W. (2009). Units of analysis in geographic criminology: Historical development, critical issues, and open questions. In D. Weisburd, W. Bernasco, & G. J. N. Bruinsma (eds.), *Putting crime in its place: Units of analysis in spatial crime research* (pp. 3–31). New York: Springer-Verlag.

Weisburd, D., Morris, N. A., & Groff, E. R. (2009). Hot spots of juvenile crime: A longitudinal study of street segments in Seattle, Washington. *Journal of Quantitative Criminology, 25*(4), 443–67.

Weisburd, D., Groff, E. R., & Yang, S.-M. (2010). *Understanding developmental crime trajectories at places: Social disorganization and opportunity perspectives at micro units of geography.* Washington, DC: National Institute of Justice, U.S. Department of Justice.

Weisburd, D., Lawton, B., & Ready, J. (2012). Staking out the next generation of studies of the criminology of place: Collecting prospective longitudinal data at crime hot spots. In R. Loeber & B. Welsh (eds.), *The future of criminology.* New York: Oxford University Press.

Weisburd, D., Bushway, S., Lum, C., & Yang, S.-M. (2004). Trajectories of crime at places: A longitudinal study of street segments in the city of Seattle. *Criminology, 42*(2), 283–321.

Weisburd, D., Wyckoff, L. A., Ready, J., Eck, J. E., Hinkle, J. C., & Gajewski, F. (2006). Does crime just move around the corner? A controlled study of spatial displacement and diffusion of crime control benefits. *Criminology, 44*(3), 549–92.

Welsh, B. P., & Farrington, D. P. (2008). *Effects of improved street lighting on crime.* Campbell Collaboration systematic review. Accessed November 6, 2011, at: http:// campbellcollaboration.org/lib/download/223/.

Welsh, B. P., Sullivan, C. J., & Olds, D. L. (2010). When early crime prevention goes to scale: A new look at the evidence. *Prevention Science, 11*(2), 115–25.

White, G. F. (1990). Neighborhood permeability and burglary rates. *Justice Quarterly, 7*(1), 57–67.

Whitehead, J. T., & Lab, S. P. (1989). A meta-analysis of juvenile correctional treatment. *Journal of Research in Crime and Delinquency, 26*(3), 276–95.

Wicker, A. W. (1987). Behavior settings reconsidered: Temporal stages, resources, internal dynamics, context. In D. Stokels & I. Altman (eds.), *Handbook of environmental psychology* (pp. 613–53). New York: Wiley-Interscience.

Wikström, P.-O. H. (2004). Crime as alternative: Towards a cross-level situational action theory of crime causation. In J. McCord (ed.), *Beyond empiricism: Institutions and intentions in the study of crime* (pp. 1–37). New Brunswick, NJ: Transaction Publishers.

Wikström, P.-O. H., & Loeber, R. (2000). Do disadvantaged neighborhoods cause well-adjusted children to become adolescent delinquents? A study of male juvenile serious offending, individual risk and protective factors, and neighborhood context. *Criminology, 38*(4), 1109–42.

Wikström, P.-O. H., Ceccato, V., Hardie, B., & Treiber, K. (2010). Activity fields and the dynamics of crime: Advancing knowledge about the role of the environment in crime causation. *Journal of Quantitative Criminology, 26*(1), 55–87.

Wilcox, P., & Eck, J. E. (2011). Criminology of the unpopular: Implications for policy aimed at payday lending facilities. *Criminology and Public Policy, 10*(2), 473–82.

Wilcox, P., Land, K. C., & Hunt, S. C. (2003). *Criminal circumstance: A dynamic multicontextual criminal opportunity theory.* New York: Walter de Gruyter.

Wilcox, P., Quisenberry, N., Cabrera, D. T., & Jones, S. (2004). Busy places and broken windows? Toward defining the role of physical structure and process in community crime models. *Sociological Quarterly, 45*(2), 185–207.

Wilcox, P., Madensen, T. D., & Tillyer, M. S. (2007). Guardianship in context: Implications for burglary victimization risk and prevention. *Criminology, 45*(4), 775–803.

Willet, J. B., & Sayer, A. G. (1994). Using covariance structure analysis to detect correlates and predictors of individual change over time. *Psychological Bulletin, 116*(2), 363–81.

Williams, K. (1984). Economic sources of homicide: Reestimating the effects of poverty and inequality. *American Sociological Review, 49*(2), 283–89.

Wilma, D. (2000). Starbucks Coffee opens its first store in Pike Place Market in April 1971. *HistoryLink.org Online Encyclopedia of Washington State History*. Accessed November 6, 2011, at: http://www.historylink.org/index.cfm?DisplayPage=output.cfm&file_id=2075.

Wilson, W. J. (1987). *The truly disadvantaged: The inner city, the underclass, and public policy*. Chicago: University of Chicago Press.

Wilson, J. W., & Kelling, G. (1982). The police and neighborhood safety: Broken windows. *Atlantic Monthly, 127,* 29–38.

Wolfgang M .E., & Ferracuti, F. (1967). *The subculture of violence: Towards an integrated theory in criminology*. London: Tavistock.

Wolfgang, M. E., Figlio, R. M., & Sellin, T. (1972). *Delinquency in a birth cohort*. Chicago: University of Chicago Press.

Wolfgang, M., Thornberry, T. P., & Figlio, R. M. (1987). *From boy to man, from delinquency to crime*. Chicago: University of Chicago Press.

Worden, R., Bynum, T., & Frank, J. (1994). Police crackdowns on drug abuse and trafficking. In D. MacKenzie & C. D. Uchida (eds.), *Drugs and crime: Evaluating public policy initiatives* (pp. 95–113). Thousand Oaks, CA: Sage Publications.

Wright, R. T., & Decker, S. H. (1997). *Armed robbers in action: Stickups and street culture*. Boston: Northeastern University Press.

Xu, Y., Fiedler, M., & Flaming, K. H. (2005). Discovering the impact of community policing, the broken windows thesis, collective efficacy, and citizens' judgment. *Journal of Research in Crime and Delinquency, 42* (2), 147–86.

Yang, S.-M. (2010). Assessing the spatial-temporal relationship between disorder and violence. *Journal of Quantitative Criminology, 26*(1), 139–63.

Zorbaugh, H. W. (1929). *The gold coast and the slum: A sociological study of Chicago's near north side*. Chicago: University of Chicago Press.

{PROPER NAME INDEX}

{INDEX}